LIFE, DEATH
AND CONSCIOUSNESS

Experiences Near and After Death

FILIPPO LIVERZIANI

PRISM · UNITY

Published in Great Britain 1991 by

PRISM PRESS
2 South Street
Bridport
Dorset DT6 3NQ

Distributed in the USA by
AVERY PUBLISHING GROUP
120 Old Broadway
Garden City Park
NY 11040

Published in Australia by
UNITY PRESS
Lindfield
NSW 2070

ISBN 1 85327 067 9

© Original edition Edizioni Mediterranee, Roma SRL
    Represented by The Cathy Miller Foreign Rights Agency,
    London
© English language edition Prism Press 1991

Typeset by Prism Press, Bridport, Dorset.
Printed by The Guernsey Press Ltd, The Channel Islands.

Contents

Biographical Details

Dr Filippo Liverziani was born in Florence, Italy, on 28th December 1926. In 1951 he took a degree in Philosophy (*Laurea in Filosofia*) in the Università degli Studi 'La Sapienza', Rome, and thereafter held the following posts: from 1958 to 1961, Assistant of the Chair of Pedagogy, and from 1962 to 1966, Assistant of the Chair of Philosophy, in the same University; from 1973 to 1975, Professor of Theoretical Philosophy in the Pontifical Theological Faculty 'Marianum' in Rome; from 1974 to 1977, Assistant in the Pontifical Gregorian University in Rome; from 1966 to 1977, Secretary of the Group of Study and Research of the Institute of Religious Sciences of the same University. In 1966 and 1967, Dr Liverziani was Director of the Course of Philosophy and Sociology of Religion in the Fourth and Fifth Seminaries 'Culture and Society' in Rome; since 1980 he has been Director of The Convivium (Study of Philosophy and Sciences of Man) in Rome; and since 1989, Vice-President of the Associazione Italiana per gli Studi Psichici (Italian Association for Psychic Studies), also in Rome, where he now lives.

Introduction

This book is dedicated to the question of survival or living-on after death, and sets out to treat the matter not in the abstract manner of a certain tradition of Western philosophy but rather in the concrete terms of lived experience.

Experiencing survival: strictly speaking, only the disincarnate, only the 'dead', could do this, always provided they effectively succeed in surviving the disintegration of their material shell. This would undoubtedly succeed. Nevertheless, one can qualify this by pointing out that there are separation experiences that living men can have even while fully and perfectly alive, just as they can return to full life after coming close to death. Here I am referring, respectively, to people who have had 'out-of-the-body experiences' and others who have had 'near-death' experiences. Men and women who have passed through such separation experiences can provide evidence for us. As we shall see, their testimonies assume additional value because they tend to confirm each other.

We also have at our disposal an extensive literature regarding mediumistic communications. After many years of studying this entire phenomenology I deduce that, while there are numerous pseudo-communications that can be more readily and properly attributed to the unconscious psyche of the medium, there are also many communications that seem to justify more or less strong suspicions; yet there still remains a hard core that resists all attempts at reduction. I am quite convinced that any unprejudiced, painstaking and thorough examination of the communications in this third category will only serve to make them seem more and more reliable. Indeed, these 'serious' mediumistic communications seem not only to be substantially consistent with each other, but also with the testimonies of people who have undergone separation experiences.

We thus come face to face with testimony, given by either the living or the dead, that is truly impressive. The laws obeyed by these phenomena are obviously different from those of the phenomena of nature. All the same, the laws underlying the phenomena of nature, and especially those underlying the phenomena of life, seem to come closer and closer to the laws of the spiritual world as one gets away from the mechanistic model and approaches the finalistic one of spontaneity, liberty and creativity, as one passes from the physical sciences to those of organic and living matter, to the sciences of man, to the psychology of the profound, to parapsychology. The spiritual world thus reveals a logic of its own, a logic that is different from that of the world of life, even though not radically different at its roots: it is a logic that has to be discovered, a logic into which one has to feel one's way. We, too, shall try to feel our way into it little by little, following a guiding thread that, starting from out-of-the-body experiences and passing through those of the near-death type, will eventually lead us resolutely into experience of the crisis of death and into what seem to be the subsequent experiences of the new dimension.

No matter what general considerations we may subsequently make, no matter what conclusions we may subsequently seek to formulate in more general terms, these will always be based on an analysis of the available testimony. Since the author is alive, he necessarily has to limit himself to a comparative analysis of the testimony provided by others. Although he endeavours to immerse himself in their experiences, as it were, and thus to relive the spirit of these experiences to the extent to which this may be possible, he clearly could not do more.

Now, each individual testimony is always wholly

personal. One has to accept it just as the person concerned offers it. But if this person were to be in bad faith?
If he were to tell falsehoods or, more simply, something
that is not exactly 'the whole truth and nothing but the
truth'? If he were to have hallucinations or indulged in
judgement errors that had a distorting effect on his
manner of recounting the experiences, thus making them
seem something other than what they really are? Can we
be sure that such accounts are always scrupulously
exact? Can memory always be relied upon? All these
doubts, each of which is wholly legitimate, ought to
induce extreme prudence in anyone who presumes to
attribute absolute importance to any individual case.

On the other hand, even though one person could be
mistaken, another could forget or distort, a third could
wittingly deceive and a fourth indulge in over-hasty
approximation, can one really believe that all these
witnesses are either deceiving themselves or are bent on
deceiving us, seeing that there are many thousands of
subjects all over the world who offer testimony to the
same type of experience and, what is more, do so in
equivalent terms? It is precisely for this reason that, no
matter how great our doubts regarding an individual
case, the totality of such a large number of analogous
cases, after all the necessary pruning and weeding,
becomes worthy of attention.

Nor can one protest at this point that the totality is
nothing other than the sum of the individual cases, so
that the reasonable doubt attaching to individual cases is
just as relevant as far as the totality is concerned. We
know only too well that whenever an analysis is absolut-
ized, it ends up by dominating the synthesis and does so
with negative and disintegrating consequences. Once we
keep our analysis logic within its proper limits, however,
we cannot fail to note how greatly these individual
testimonies become strengthened by the fact that others
agree with them. After all, common-sense tells us that the
testimony of a single person must be taken with a pinch
of salt, and also that, when faced with the concordant

testimony of so many subjects of a certain type, all reporting equivalent experiences, it becomes extremely improbable that all of them aim to deceive us or are deceiving themselves.

It is precisely here that lies the basis of the interest these spontaneous cases have for parapsychology: an individual case, which may be related by very simple people or by those one may not consider to be particularly intelligent, can never be fully guaranteed, but such a phenomenon will be taken into serious consideration when it emerges from a plurality of cases, especially when these are numerous and distributed all over the world.

For the same reason, the testimony I here offer — be it given by the living or the deceased (or supposedly such) — is not intended to be of value as an individual case, but is related solely and exclusively as an example: each of these testimonies is but an example of an entire class of analogous or equivalent phenomena. The individual cases I shall mention, even when there are two or three of the same type, have no function other than to give a concrete idea of the type of phenomenon that I affirm to be real. The example may be one, sometimes two or three, or four at the very most: a hundred clearly cannot be quoted for lack of space. Right from the beginning, however, let me emphasise that each of the quoted cases could be supplemented by many others. The reader must take my word for this, place a little trust in me.

I quote testimony by the deceased side by side with that of the living, but not because I want to sow the tares with the wheat. Nobody is more conscious than I of the fact that, passing from the living to the dead, the entire matter becomes decidedly more 'phantomatic', as one is tempted to say. The living are closer at hand: they exist and act beside us, we can readily form a concrete idea about them, not least by listening to what other living people have to say about them. When it comes to the deceased, however, anybody familiar with mediumistic experiences will know just how difficult it is to obtain a true and complete identification in individual cases. There can be no doubt that testimony by the deceased always contains something that escapes us, and this even when it is presented *en bloc*, as a consistent and organic whole.

The familiar 'animist' objection is also lying in wait: the content of these mediumistic communications is claimed to be wholly attributable to motives operating in the unconscious of the medium in particular, but also and more generally of those who participate in the experiment. It is not my intention here to deal with the animist objection in the various forms in which it is usually put forward. Since the question goes beyond the topic of the book, I shall limit myself to saying that to all intents and purposes I share and accept the classical replies given by Ernesto Bozzano.[1]

Here I shall do no more than ask why it is that these mediumistic communications, taken as a whole, should convey to us a representation of an ultra-terrestrial world with such particular characteristics. No matter how many-splendoured may seem to us the description of a beyond with 'many rooms', no matter how different may seem the condition of the souls at the various levels, there can be no doubt that the descriptions of life after death found in the more reliable mediumistic literature, vast as it is, are characterised (as we shall see) by more than considerable analogies and seem to derive quite readily from a common pattern.

What is suggested to us by these mediumistic communications is not mere survival in the most general sense, but rather a life-after-death with characteristics that point in a precise direction, even though it is articulated into a wide variety of conditions of existence and different itineraries of spiritual development.

In animist terms, or in terms of reductive parapsychology, one can also object that the representation of a beyond where we survive is consolatory for the human psyche: and therefore it is claimed that our unconscious operates in such a manner as to offer us a representation of 'after death' that will comfort us, banishing all fear and anguish. Let us even admit that factors of this type operate in the human psyche, as the psychology of the profound tends to teach us: but can everything really be reduced to these factors? How is it that in these medium-istic communications there recurs a representation of the beyond so precise and so frequently interwoven with anthropomorphic elements that our habitual manner of conceiving disincarnate finds so repugnant? As we shall see, these anthropomorphisms derive their justification from the fact that disincarnate life is primarily of an oneiric character: in certain respects, it has to be consid-ered as a great collective dream. Is there somebody who, dreaming, has not at a certain moment become aware of having a quasi-corporeal form, finding himself in an anthropomorphic environment similar to the earth? The dream analogy may well eventually provide an explana-tion of the many anthropomorphisms that we so often find in many of these mediumistic communications; what is certain is that the spiritist representation of the beyond, at least on first impact, is such as to cause perplexity in many subjects, notwithstanding the fact that these people — by simple virtue of participating in these sessions or acting as mediums on these occasions — were themselves the vehicles of the communications from which these descriptions emerge. If the human psyche is constituted so as to justify and console our subjects with a certain representation of life after death, how can one explain the fact that this representation is so full of elements that the mentality of these self-same subjects find repugnant?

This simple observation, surely, lends considerable force of conviction to the very opposite assumption. In other words, representations of the beyond that are so closely analogous to each other and yet so indigestible have to be attributed to common experiences of an ambit that transcends the human psyche, and are therefore experiences of a reality that can in some way be defined as objective and independent of the many subjectivisms with which they are coloured.

Introduction

If the reality of life-after-death to which these testimonies jointly refer can in some way be defined as objective, in the sense just mentioned, it is nevertheless true that it can be grasped only via interior and subjective experiences. There is no objective yardstick that could be used to value it, at least in a direct manner.

Parapsychology, which uses more objective methods of verification, could provide indirect confirmation, while separation experiences and *post mortem* experiences can provide more direct evidence, though only through the personal testimony of the subject, i.e. the person, living or deceased, who tells us what he has personally lived and experienced.

The only criterion that we can therefore use is that of considering these testimonies as a whole, comparing them to bring out their constant features and their variants, the possible agreement between them. As already suggested, we could also compare these findings with the data obtained by the more objective methods of parapsychology: but the primary, essential and direct comparison remains that of seeing these testimonies together.

We therefore have to embrace the whole in the unity of a single look. This means that we must know how to 'look' in order to 'see'. There are people who are very good at analysing individual trees, lots of them, but somehow fail to see the forest; such people possess highly refined instruments of analysis, but lack the eye that sees the essence. The whole escapes them, so that they never succeed in seeing the whole or in grasping in that whole the indefinable something that is more substantial (and therefore also less readily perceived) and, when applied to individuals, applied to details, would enable them to see even these particulars in a new and different light, to understand them more thoroughly.

One therefore has to exercise one's eyes, train them to see the whole: one has to develop one's peculiar and personal faculty of overall, summary consideration. In this matter each one of us is responsible for himself. Each one of us has to work and mature on his own, must educate himself and attempt what, in the wider sense of the term, could also be called a mystical experience.

Here nobody can do the work of another. Nevertheless, it is possible to stimulate the personal maturing that this other has to attempt on his own. This is precisely what the present book sets out to do, proposing the various phenomena as a whole, though in a gradual succession and in such a manner as to permit the sense and meaning of their interconnections to be acquired little by little. The answer at the end of the road can only be given by the individual reader who has let himself be guided a little in this ultramundane trip of a new kind, keeping his critical spirit alive and alert at every step along the way, but without falling prey to the temptation of being excessively critical. The author will be grateful to any reader who will collaborate with him in this sense.

And while on the subject of gratitude, the author feels that he must acknowledge the debt that he owes to his wife, Elisabetta Pozzan, whose collaboration proved as precious as it was solicitous and discreet (though she is here mentioned 'by treason' and against her express desire, confident of her forgiveness); also to Silvio Ravaldini, editor-in-chief of the review *Luce e ombra*, who is currently reorganising that incomparable research tool, the Bozzano-De Boni Library at Bologna; also to Miss Eleanor O'Keeffe, Secretary of the Society for Psychical Research, and to the society's librarian, Mr D.N. Clark-Lowes. Before concluding, moreover, I am particularly anxious to acknowledge that from the work of Ernesto Bozzano has been drawn not only a large number of indications and suggestions (without always stating their source in the text), but also and above all his basic and essential inspiration.

Chapter 1
Discovery of the Soul and its Autonomy from the Body

Do we survive the death of our body? That is the great and basic question to which, boldly but without presumption, I propose to dedicate this study. I shall face up to the problem of survival not in the customary abstract terms, but rather in the light of what appears to be a very concrete, precise and consistent phenomenology.

A new possibility is beginning to take shape today: a new approach is becoming possible to the old problem of the psyche and its autonomy from the physical body, and therefore also to the problem of the survival of the psyche when the body dies. This new approach can be defined as experimental.

Our Western philosophy has always tried to 'demonstrate' the immortality of the soul, but has limited itself to arguing the matter with pure and simple reasonings and without making any reference to concrete phenomena. We shall not here concern ourselves with the question of immortality understood as perennial survival, as surviving forever; rather, we shall limit ourselves to examining the possibility of simply surviving the death of the body. In this more limited forum and for reasons based on concrete phenomena, I deem myself to have good grounds for affirming that such a survival can not only be argued, but can actually be experienced.

I have in mind the so-called 'ecsomatic experiences', or if you prefer a less aridly technical term, we may call them 'out-of-the-body experiences' (now often abbreviated to OBEs), sometimes known as 'astral projections'.

Our psyche normally works and manifests itself via the body in which it is immersed. The stimuli received by our sense organs reach it via the brain, the psyche then orders the various body movements by pulses that travel along nerves in an outward, opposite, direction and thus reach the muscles.

If this ordinary situation of the psyche were the only possible one, if the psyche were necessarily conditioned to live and act within these limits, we would have to infer that the psyche can do nothing without the mediation of the brain, could not even exist without it. We would therefore be authorised to conclude that when the body dies, and with it the brain that forms a part of it, the psyche would also come to an end. It is a fact, however, that the aforementioned out-of-the-body experiences suggest exactly the opposite conclusion.

For the great majority of human beings an out-of-the-body experience constitutes an altogether exceptional event. Only a very few men and women experience them repeatedly, and there are some extremely rare cases where such experiences become ordinary, almost everyday events.

Let us now try to define these experiences in some way. The subject feels himself to be projected outside his body. In this situation he is led to identify the centre of his personality no longer with the brain, no longer with his physical body, but with some immaterial *quid*, with some fluid reality that seems to be located elsewhere. From this new and different location the subject then looks at his own body, almost as if it had become an object estranged from him; at that time the body may lie there insensate, or it may continue to move and even to act.

Reference to Celia Green's book *Out-of-the-Body Experiences* is very useful to get a first concrete idea of what these experiences are like.[2] The author relates that a newspaper advertisement published in Great Britain in 1966, accompanied by similar announcements on the wireless, invited testimonies and first-hand accounts of experiences in which the subject had the feeling of observing things from a vantage point outside his physical body. Some four-hundred replies were received, and each of the people involved was then asked to answer a series of very precise and detailed questions. The resulting data were analyzed, selected and electronically processed, thus ascertaining the presence and frequency of certain factors and obtaining a set of comparative statistics.

Celia Green notes that out-of-the-body experiences can be subdivided into two groups, 'parasomatic' and 'asomatic'. In the first group the subject feels detached from his physical body, which he contemplates from a certain distance, and yet has the sensation that the true centre of his personality consists — as it were — of a second body: what we are here concerned with is a kind of 'ethereal double', something that has the same form and size as the physical body, but is perceived as impalpable and fluid. In 'asomatic' experiences, on the other hand, the subject feels himself to be out of his body and also detached from any specific form whatsoever.

And what does the physical body do while all this is going on? This can vary widely from one case to another. Thus, the physical body may find itself lying in bed, in hospital or elsewhere,[3] or in the process of falling freely from a certain height;[4] but it may also find itself engaged in office work,[5] walking or running,[6] going for a ride in a bus,[7] or it may be sleeping[8] or lying down either in expectation of sleep[9] or wide awake,[10] just as it may be listening to music[11] or watching a film;[12] it may be engaged in some relaxation exercise[13] or, more actively, in conversation,[14]. in preaching a sermon (with great success),[15] in a driving test (with less positive results),[16] in driving a car (this time impeccably and with great skill),[17] or in playing a piece of music on the piano.[18] But at the opposite end of the scale, it can also become rigid and remain for some time as if paralysed.[19]

At what distance from the body does the psyche find

itself during these OBEs? This, too, can vary a great deal. The psyche may feel itself lifted out of the body for a yard or two, or for a considerable distance. It may feel located just below the ceiling, but at times also above the roof of the building. It may be worthwhile at this point to make specific mention of the testimony of a subject who felt himself projected out of his body, in parasomatic form, while watching an opera performance:

> 'I listened with great enjoyment to the overture before the curtain rose, and suddenly found myself floating above the great dome of the theatre and thought how dirty it looked in the misty night air ... I thought how the whole roof structure needed a good clean ... My emotion was wonder at how I came to be up there in my own body and clothes.'[20]

Another subject, describing an experience of the same type, notes that no solid obstacle seemed capable of limiting his field of view, as would have happened if he had been looking with the eye of his physical body:

> 'I saw my entire school from above with the roof off, seeing forbidden parts clearly. Later I found excuses to go to these parts (or stole in to see) and found it just so.'[21]

As is becoming apparent, in certain special conditions the psyche is capable of seeing and more generally perceiving things without having to rely on the mediation of the eyes, the other sense organs, or even the brain. And here we may recall the testimony of another subject, who was in hospital at the time she had the experience:

> 'I wondered as I saw my physical body in the bed "Is my hearing acute, without ears?" and I approached a patient who was asleep, and listened to her breathing. I could hear it extremely clearly. I thought "My sight is acutely clear too".'[22]

The physical bodies are perceived in an almost physical manner, but this cannot be said for the psyche. In parasomatic experiences the psyche sees itself in human form and, most of the time, dressed. But in one of the quoted cases there is no reflection in the looking glass: 'I found I was standing in front of the dressing-table mirror'; or as another woman recalls:

> 'I looked into it, there was no reflection of me. I touched the mirror to make sure it was there. It was, but I was not, but I could see across the room in the mirror.'[2 3]

However, there are other subjects who see themselves as centred in a psyche that assumes corporeal form. There is also a small number of the subjects studied by Celia Green who talk about seeing other souls (for want of a better term), for we are told that they 'report "meetings" with deceased relatives or other ostensibly discarnate entities'.[2 4] I shall leave this passing mention without any comment, for it seems premature to do so at this stage.

Colours appear 'normal' as a general rule, albeit a little more 'brilliant', 'clear' and 'bright'. There is a heightened sensitivity, a kind of hypersensitivity:

> 'Everything was quite logical, except for the way in which they affected me; for example a table looked quite normal and if I touched the wood the sensation of smoothness or roughness would be ridiculously exaggerated.'[2 5]

Certain subjects note that, unlike their experiences when they look at things in the normal way with their bodily eyes, they perceive the various objects directly — let us use the term — with 'the eyes of the soul'; indeed, they succeed in seeing things quite distinctly even in the dark. It is as if the objects and the environments were brightly lit, or at least made visible, by some mysterious light.[2 6]

Subjects suffering from some specific sensorial defect, once their sensitivity can exercise itself by a more immediate contact with the surrounding objects and is no longer dependent on a defective and inadequate sense organ, suddenly find that they can see, hear, taste and smell in an unexpectedly normal and perfect manner. As one woman put it:

> 'I "drifted" or "floated" through the door of my room, up the stairs, and into the dimly-lighted room of my young

niece ... By her bedside was an open book, and I found no
difficulty in reading the two open pages (which would
have been impossible in my physical body, without my
glasses) ...'[27]

Another subject, who had lost his sense of taste and of
smell following a skull fracture, expressed himself as
follows:

'I have just begun to get back faint traces of smell, but in
this experience ... I could smell quite normally, and I
believe I could have tasted too, if food had been part of
the experience. I was smelling everything in the room.
The sensation was of ordinary smell, but when I returned
to my normal self, I was, and still am, in the same
condition as previously — that is, with very poor taste
and smell.'[28]

In ecsomatic experiences the senses not only reacquire
their normal potential or become more vivid and acute,
but also lose some of their limitations: for example, sight
is no longer subject to the limit encountered when we
look with our bodily eyes, which inevitably have a limited
field of view. In certain cases, as Celia Green notes, the
subject tells us that during an out-of-the-body experience
'he had a more comprehensive field of vision than
normal', or he may even describe himself as being able 'to
see all around me at once'.[29] Here is another report:

'I now possessed a super-sense whose functioning was
immensely superior to that of my former five. Employing
it I found that without turning I was aware of everything
around me in a full circle of 360 degrees to the distance
of the horizon.'[30]

And another put it as follows:

'They looked different in that you could see the whole
thing in a glance, for instance you saw the ceiling, walls,
whole room at once.'[31]

Subjects of this kind, moreover, may be able to see things
they simply could not perceive in normal conditions:
some report seeing straight through solid bodies ('things
looked normal but with some transparency'), while at
other times some obstacle that could have obstructed

their line of sight, a wall for example, seems to disappear.[3] [2]

In the ecsomatic condition, however, it is not only the senses that function well (and, in certain cases, even much better than usual), but also the intellective processes. Far from suffering any reduction, the intellective processes occur just as well, indeed with a rapidity, lucidity and efficiency far greater than when expressed via the mediation of the brain. Some subjects report: 'Thoughts follow normal sequence as they would at any other time'; or, 'I could think and remember normally'; 'My reasoning power was quite normal', said a third, while yet another put it as follows: 'I was as clear-thinking as at any time in my life.'[3] [3] But in other subjects one can also grasp a rather more positive appreciation of the manner in which their mental faculties were working at the time: 'The mind is clear as a bell'; 'Thoughts come to one in a flash'; '... my mind was clearer and more active than ever before'; 'I felt as I do when I'm concentrating — *intelligent*'. Yet another spoke of 'a disembodied but very acute consciousness', and another described himself as 'vividly awake, observant and clear-headed'. Others remember themselves as 'more alive', 'more conscious', or 'more awake and receptive' than normal. Lastly, there is one who tells us, 'I have never been so wide awake or experienced such a wonderful sense of freedom ever before.'[3] [4]

Celia Green provides a great deal of statistical data about these cases. Here, however, I must limit myself to a summary, mentioning only such data as may prove useful in support of a particular thesis. And the thesis is this. In normal conditions the soul lives incarnate in a body and its sensitive and intellective functions are performed through the sense organs, the nervous system, the brain. This, of course, is a traditionally affirmed fact. No matter how true it may be, however, there is yet another truth that is brought out by a comparative analysis of the aforementioned ecsomatic experiences: albeit in very special, abnormal, exceptional and temporary conditions, the psyche on its own shows itself to possess full self-sufficiency: it can stay by itself, it can of itself exercise all its spiritual functions, it can live the whole of its intellective, volitive, emotive and sensitive life.

To find oneself outside one's body, and acting independently of it, is an altogether exceptional fact in the course of an incarnate life. Face to face with this new and absolutely unexpected fact, the subject may find himself taken by a sense of preoccupation and even fear. Psychologically, this would be quite normal and is readily explained. But this does not mean that, thinking about the phenomenon more serenely, the subject must necessarily be induced to consider it as a situation that is of itself abnormal, a situation of crisis and unbalance of his being. The testimonies, rather, seem to suggest the very opposite. Some recollections were as follows: 'It seemed very normal for me to be like this'; 'At the time of happening it seemed very usual, not even surprising'; 'The experience seemed perfectly natural to me at the time'; 'The part of me that was out of my body was the real me, as I knew it, the part that sees, thinks and feels emotionally'; 'My identity and consciousness were exactly the same as usual'; 'I felt like a real solid person watching myself', 'I felt completely me'.[3 5]

These testimonies also dwell at some length on the sensation of well-being, of lightness and freedom that can be felt in these discarnate situations. Here, therefore, the subject lives the situation not only with a sense of self-sufficiency, but, as many of them actually put it, 'feeling superior' or even 'feeling very superior'.[3 6]

Celia Green's book examines many other aspects of out-of-the-body experiences, but we shall concentrate on the one essential point that represents the conclusion of our present analysis: in the normal condition of our human life on earth the psyche lives incarnate in a physical body and exercises its functions through the mediation of the nervous system; yet it can also live a full and autonomous life independently of the body. This phenomenon is extremely rare and normally of very brief duration, but it has considerable implications from the philosophical point of view. To speak of 'demonstrations' of the immortality of the soul would be going a little too far; however, I see no reason why we should not use the data relating to ecsomatic experiences for a new approach to this classical and 'eternal' problem — a problem of such great interest to mankind, if we really want to give a significance to our life that is somewhat more than just precarious.

Chapter 2
A New Approach to the Problem of Survival

Immortality or, more simply, survival after death, does indeed constitute a big problem. Once we really come to grips with it, at a certain point a life that proceeds towards no goal other than full and total death seems inconceivable. How can we attribute true significance to a life at the end of which, together with the dissolution of our physical body, we know ourselves to be condemned to die in all and everything?

That death as the total dissolution of my individuality should cause me personal concern may seem no more than an egoistical motive; but the fact is that, in such a perspective, it is not only I who am condemned to come to a complete end, but also humanity as a whole with all its achievements, projects and hopes. All humanism is rendered vain, as also any other reality that has some sense or value. Everything comes to an end: in the last resort, therefore, all is vain. The whole universe is nothing other than a kind of immense death cell, in that each and every one of us shares the condition of being condemned to death.

If I may transform this condition into an image, it is as if we were all embarked on a train that is running towards nothingness in the dead of night. The train is brightly lit: the passengers live an intense and passionate life there, but also an ephemeral one, a reflection of the train's fatuous light destined to go out before long. Every now and again a door opens and one of the passengers is sucked out of the train to disappear in the night.

Such a thought can become intolerable, and many people therefore 'remove' it from their mind. Death is always the death of somebody else, it is never my own death. As we look at the paper in the morning, it may well be that our eyes happen to fall on the obituary column: 'Oh, so and so died the other day. What a pity, just think that I saw him a month ago and he seemed so full of life.' And with that we immediately turn to another page, our thoughts run to other things, problems, concerns of everyday life. Life goes on, *primum vivere* — life comes first; and then perhaps, *mors tua vita mea* — your death is my life. I remember that in a television debate on death one of the participants, a professor, said that in the last resort dying meant leaving one's place to others: could it be that he was giving vent to another and more occult thought, less philosophical and also less confessable?

On the subject of room and the place we occupy, in this long train travelling through the night of nothingness it is always better to have a comfortable seat than to be standing in the corridor; it is better to be in a first-class compartment than in a second-class one, better still to be in the sleeping car or to have the entire car to yourself. Everybody tries to improve his position, making it more comfortable; everybody gets busy with initiatives of his own. But then there are the mass movements of those who travel 'standing room only' and, becoming aware of the injustice that is being perpetrated at their expense, start a revolution to occupy the cars where a few privileged passengers had previously assumed the right to stretch their legs in a compartment all of their own — luxury cars where good food is served, where one can nourish the spirit too with films, television, books, culture and art, where the 'quality of life' is better, but where the passengers still travel through nothingness to death, just like the others in the more plebeian cars.

It is fine and noble to dedicate the whole of one's existence to organizing the masses of those standing passengers, helping them to conquer a seat, a 'place in the sun' that is materially and culturally as comfortable as possible. Anyone who dedicates himself to such an apostolate has undoubtedly chosen a pastime far less trite and banal than someone who does no more than kill time, day-in day-out, reading detective stories, solving charades and crossword puzzles, flirting, or playing chequers. Yet what good is he doing other than helping himself and others to kill time, to while away the hours of a voyage that has no goal?

Given a situation of this kind, one can delude oneself into believing one has given meaning and purpose to one's life; one can close one's eyes or turn one's head in order not to see our common destiny of death and the situation that we all share of being passengers on a train that is nothing other than a long death cell; one can touch wood or speak of 'birds of ill omen' when reminded of this situation; but when one looks with a cold and clinical eye at all that a situation of this kind implies, one cannot but agree that, all things considered, there is really very little to be happy about.

Martin Heidegger notes that the average man does not have the courage to look death in the face, that he always thinks of death in connection with other people, and never of his own death.[3][7]

For Jean-Paul Sartre death is the destruction of all our projects and, consequently, death is something that deprives our life of all meaning. One of Sartre's characters, the hero of the short story *Le Mur* (*The Wall*, from the book of the same name), is a Spanish Republican called Pablo Ibbieta who, on being captured by Franco's men, is summarily tried and condemned to death. At that moment Pablo's life loses all significance. He asks himself how he could possibly have taken seriously so many things in the course of his past existence, before the moment of the illuminating crisis that showed him the nonsense, the inconsistency, the vacuity of it all.

Meursault, protagonist of Albert Camus' *L'Étranger* (*The Stranger*), is another to have been condemned to death, in this case by an assize court in French Algeria for the killing of an Arab. When asked to sign a petition for mercy, he refuses, preferring death. The experience he has gone through has led him to a new awareness: once you fully realize that you have to die, it no longer matters whether you die a little earlier or a little later, or even twenty years earlier or later, it makes no difference at all.

If we really go into this problem, we cannot but come to the eventual conclusion that only immortality can confer true and full significance on our life as men, and on all its positive instances. Kant, indeed, says that the immortality of the soul is a basic 'postulate' of 'practical pure reason'. As far as Kant is concerned, the perfect conformity of human will to moral law is the ultimate goal of an infinite progress, and this progress is made possible only by virtue of the immortality of the soul.[38] Kant arrived at this conclusion having excluded all possibility of demonstrating the immortality of the soul in rational terms, and in a manner that can be considered fully valid from a theoretical and speculative point of view.[39]

Many attempts in this direction had been made even before Kant — indeed, they have been made throughout the history of human thought. Many philosophers had previously tried their hand at 'demonstrating the immortality of the soul' at a purely theoretical level. The oldest and best known of these attempts is to be found in Plato's *Phaedo*. Socrates, the time-honoured protagonist of the Platonian dialogues, infers the immortality of the soul by using the following three arguments:

1. All things come into being from their opposites: death from life, life from death. Nobody could therefore come to live unless the souls of the deceased continued to exist in a beyond.[40]

2. If knowing is equivalent to remembering, the soul must already have existed before it became incarnate in this earthly life.[41]

3. Only compound things can decompose: while the body decomposes, being made up of different elements, the soul survives because it represents something far more similar to the elementary beings or substances that, precisely on

account of their absolutely simple nature, always remain identical to themselves. [4] [2]

Towards the end of the dialogue these three essential arguments are supplemented by yet another: the soul never gives anything but life, it cannot therefore accommodate or receive death within itself. [4] [3]

Plato's arguments in favour of the soul's immortality merit every possible consideration. Nevertheless, they suffer from a grave defect or limit: though based on a generic and summary consideration of the things of the world, Plato's arguments derive primarily from logic definitions and are essentially of a rational character.

Plato's line of argument seeks to affirm a factual reality, but it does so in a far too intellectualistic manner. The reference Plato makes to facts is not specific, it is not sufficient to justify him in affirming something (in this case, the immortality of the soul) as a fact, as something that constitutes a fact. A judgement regarding the reality of a fact cannot but refer to and derive from concrete facts, it cannot but be justified by a consideration of specific, clear and precise facts.

Kant, on the other hand, bases himself on facts that can be ascertained by the experience of our senses. However, the 'five senses' of our physical body do not in any way perceive the soul: consequently, they cannot tell us anything about the soul or its possible immortality.

If we really base ourselves on the assumption that sensorial perception is the only possible form of experience, we must necessarily conclude, as the dictates of logic demand, that we cannot perceive or infer anything outside the experience of our bodily senses. Kant quite rightly concludes that we cannot affirm anything about the immortality of the soul if our basis is constituted by nothing other than sensorial experience conceived as the only possible form of experience: indeed, if we accept his premises, we cannot in any way criticize Kant for this conclusion, a perfectly correct consequence of the premises as far as logic is concerned.

It is quite true that Plato himself never even dreamed of limiting the whole of possible experience to what the five senses of our body can convey to us. Indeed, in the *Republic* he speaks of the 'eye of the soul' as an 'organ' of 'perception' that enables us 'to contemplate being' and 'to see the truth'.[4 4]

In any case, if we consider Plato's arguments as purely rational ones and devoid of any reference to interior experience, the undoubted value of his approach cannot but be diminished as a result. Vice versa, the value of Plato's approach could not but be enhanced every time we reinterpret his arguments by attributing a more existential and experiential character to them, and ultimately deriving them from a basic human, interior and metaphysico-religious experience.

At this point, however, one can readily raise an objection: existential knowledge conceived in this manner is nothing other than a subjective and private experience; it is valid for those who feel it but not for others, since it cannot be communicated to others and therefore remains devoid of sense as far as they are concerned. This, to all intents and purposes, is the great objection raised by Neopositivism and all the currents of thought that derive from it. In this connection one may recall Moritz Schlick, Rudolf Carnap and Alfred Ayer, amongst others.[4 5]

One could reply to a critical objection of this kind by saying that existential knowledge is subjective only in the sense that it is a subjective manner of grasping something that is very real: it is a manner in which several subjects, albeit from different points of view, can obtain knowledge of one and the same reality, a reality that has a consistency of its own, is independent of the subjects, and forms part of a sphere that transcends them.

Undoubtedly, the truth to which we accede in this manner cannot be defined as *objective* in the scientific sense; it will nevertheless be a truth *in se*, a truth that transcends the subject, even though the subject can only grasp it by living it within himself and filtering it through his own personality. It is a truth that each one of us must achieve as best he can, in his own personal manner. It is a truth that each one of us must seek within himself, in his own interiority. In this connection one may recall the famous maxim of the Delphian oracle, 'Know thyself', as also the words of St Augustine, 'Do not go out of yourself, but turn within, for truth dwells in the intimacy of man.'[4][6]

Let us make it clear, however, that even though we are far removed from science we are nevertheless within philosophy, for we are concerned with philosophical truths in the sense of an existential philosophy. These truths, clearly, are far removed from satisfying the needs of science, but they are more than sufficient for satisfying the vital needs of our human existence. So much so that when we have to take some vital decision, we very often make this decision on the basis of existential knowledge rather than on the basis of scientific knowledge, often to our great advantage. It is true that the information on the basis of which we make our decision tends to be formulated to an ever greater extent in scientific terms; it is true that the execution of our decisions is being entrusted to technology to an ever greater extent; but the decisions themselves, as an expression of our specific and peculiar will, are made more than anything else on the basis of the knowledge that we have of our existential situation.

But let us now come back to astral projections, to out-of-the-body experiences, and note right away that the people who have such experiences generally consider them — and, even more so, feel them — as something that does not seem to be altogether different from death, as something that will continue in death, as the beginning of a process that will find its completion and perfection in death. One can readily understand, therefore, that people who have passed through an out-of-the-body experience do not, as a general rule, fear death.

A well-known English parapsychologist, Susan Blackmore, endeavours to provide an extremely reductive interpretation of these ecsomatic experiences in her book *Beyond the Body*.[4][7] And yet, at the very beginning of the book, where she recalls that she herself had such an experience just once in her life, she tells us that the following thought came immediately and spontaneously to her: 'This shows that "I" can function without my physical body and see without my eyes. surely then I can survive the death of that body. I have another immortal body; there is no death.'[48] It is quite true that she later came to define these conclusions as 'hasty' and 'based more on emotion than reasoning';[49] all the same, it is highly significant that her immediate reaction to that experience was to 'jump' to these conclusions on the spur of the moment.

On the other hand, Sylvan Muldoon, a subject who frequently went through experiences of this kind, tells us that astral projections and death are not dissimilar events, and that 'exteriorization of the astral body is, in fact, the first step into that mysterious realm called "death", which sooner or later all of us must enter.'[50]

In his introduction to the book *Journeys Out of the Body* (in which another famous subject, Robert Monroe, recounts his experiences), the American psychologist and parapsychologist Charles Tart bluntly states: 'This book is going to make you think about death.'[51] What, then does Monroe himself have to say? He not only confirms the reality of the 'second body', but tells us about his discovery of what he considers to be a new kingdom of existence: he calls it 'Locale II', attributing characteristics to it that are specifically different from those of the physical world in which we live as incarnate men (Locale I). As far as Monroe is concerned, Locale II is not a 'hypothesis' but a true 'discovery', and his 'experience' of it is such that he feels himself authorised to infer that 'the human person survives the transition of death and continues in Locale II'.[52]

Robert Crookall, another well-known and greatly esteemed author of several books dedicated to a far-reaching comparative analysis of out-of-the-body and other related experiences, feels that he can conclude as follows:

'Astral projection assures us of survival and indicates the mechanism involved in the process. It also provides definite information, though of a general nature, as to the conditions and environments of the successive after-death states. It points to still "higher" experiences, those called "spiritual".'[5 3]

As far as our immediate purposes are concerned, I think we can conclude that, even though these out-of-the-body experiences are not such as to *demonstrate* survival, they do at least *suggest* it. Consequently, living one or more such ecsomatic experiences — or at least carefully examining the relevant testimonies given by other subjects — can undoubtedly be considered a good (and possibly even the best) approach to the long-standing problem of the immortality of the soul, or, more simply and as a step on the way, its survival after death. By virtue of this new approach, survival of the psyche need no longer be seen as something that is merely *inferred* or even simply *postulated*, for here survival is something that is really *experienced*: in its own way, it here becomes the reality of experience, the focus of vital knowledge.

Whilst discussing here the philosophical aspect of the question of survival, mention should be made of a book by Curt John Ducasse entitled *The Belief in a Life after Death*.[5 4] Here the problem of survival is not treated in an abstract manner, but rather by very clear and precise reference to empirical facts, both those that seem to exclude any possibility of survival (at least if considered in the more limited perspective of a reductivist-scientistic mentality) and those other facts that, already on first sight, suggest this possibility. The latter are the phenomena studied by parapsychology. They include apparitions, materialisations, 'possessions', mediumistic communications, xenoglossia, cross correspondences and many other facts, including the out-of-the-body experiences here considered. Ducasse's analysis clarifies the key concepts of what can be defined as 'material', 'living', 'mental', and so on, subsequently examining the relationship between mind and body and all the various theories that either see mental phenomena as determined by the brain, or alternatively consider the living body as an effect or product of the mind that organises it; lastly, it passes on to consider the facts that suggest the reality of a disincarnate mental life.

This last part of Ducasse's book is to a very large extent dedicated to reincarnation, an aspect I have treated in detail in another book,[55] to which I would refer readers for any questions arising in this connection.

Ducasse's conclusion is closely analogous to that reached by many valid parapsychologists, including such illustrious ones as Lodge, Hyslop and Hodgson, and also by many people who, while possessing the gift of paranormal sensitivity, are also experts in this field and very balanced in their judgements: taken on the whole, the testimonies and the ascertained facts speak in favour of the reality of survival and, in the best cases, not only of mere survival of memories of life on earth, but also of survival of the more significant capacities of the human mind and their continued exercise.[56]

It is true that this extremely comforting conclusion is suggested by the facts rather than being demonstrable in objective and definitive scientific terms. There can be no doubt, however, as to its validity for us in existential terms. And, as we have seen here, a decisive contribution to the construction of this existential certainty is made by the out-of-the-body experiences here considered.

Chapter 3
Out-Of-The-Body
Experiences

In Chapter 1, to give a first general idea of this phenomenon, I quoted a few out-of-the-body experiences. I then asked myself in the second chapter whether and how such ecsomatic experiences could provide a new approach to the old problem of survival (as a first step on the way to the wider one of immortality): such an approach would seem incomparably more in keeping with concrete experience than any of the 'demonstrations' or 'postulates' of our old Western philosophy.

At this point it would therefore be appropriate to consider the data resulting from these experiences in a more ample and systematic manner.[5][7] In subsequent chapters I propose to examine analogous data emerging from near-death experiences, and from testimonies relating to the crisis of death and to subsequent existence (i.e. to 'life after death') that are provided by mediumistic communications (limiting myself to the more credible ones, all of which seem to confirm each other in many essential respects). Following a detailed comparison with the phenomena of parapsychology, we shall then examine this wealth of data from different sources, noting any specific aspects in which they coincide.

In this general perspective, I shall dedicate the present chapter to a more detailed analysis of out-of-the-body experiences, examining their principal features one by one. Let us begin by considering the subject of the phenomenon, commonly known as the projector, and ask ourselves two essential questions: (1) How does the projector see and, more generally, how does he perceive? (2) How does he act?

The first question can be answered fairly quickly, but the second will call for a somewhat lengthier treatment. As far as the visual and perceptive capacities of the projector are concerned, particular significance attaches to an aspect that is well put by Robert Monroe. The subject, as Monroe writes, may have the impression that he continues to see the things around him in exactly the same manner as he sees them with his physical eyes. But this is because, as human beings, we are accustomed to perceiving things through our sensorial perception; even realities that we perceive without any mediation of the bodily senses are 'translated at first into terms and meanings appreciated by the five physical senses.'[58]

No matter how much the subject may see things in physical terms, the substantial fact remains this: the projector grasps the essence of these things at a psychic level; and this may explain the fact that the projector's manner of knowing is essentially telepathic. Indeed, it is well known that it is not unusual for out-of-the-body experiences to be associated with the phenomena of clairvoyance, which may be in the present (telesthesia), in the past (psychometry), or in the future (precognition or foreknowledge).[59]

Another characteristic feature of ecsomatic experiences is, to quote Monroe once again, that 'you learn that you can see in all directions at once, without turning the head.'[60] Studying a number of such subjects, Karlis Osis noted that, even though the majority continued to see things in a normal perspective, about 40 percent sometimes achieved a vision different from normal, in many cases even 360-degree vision. Furthermore, 52 percent of his projectors saw objects in a brilliant and transparent fashion, each surrounded by a kind of halo.[61]

Let us now try to answer, albeit at much greater length, the question regarding the projector's manner of acting. It is to be defined as a creative action: a creation that expresses itself first and foremost in the ambit of mental reality.

Following a description of things seen during one of his experiences, Monroe wonders whether the 'entities' he sees around him have to be considered as existing or as mere mental products of the subject. In the latter case they could be defined as dissociated parts of the subject: that is to say, as thought entities or thought forms that the subject has created in keeping with his customary mental models.[6 2]

Also basing himself on data and concepts proposed by other authors, Scott Rogo suggests the idea that ecsomatic experiences may take place in a non-physical duplicate of our world that appears as real to a projector, or even to several projectors at one and the same time, as our own world appears to us.[6 3]

Talking about one of his own experiments, Yram mentions the fact that he once found himself sitting and chatting with some friends in a kind of astral drawing-room: in the image of a drawing-room that they had created for the occasion.[6 4]

For Mrs Blackmore, however, 'the idea of a shared thought-world, attractive as it is ... makes no sense'.[6 5] I would argue that, on the contrary, the idea should make a great deal of sense to anybody who considers thought to be something creative: any creation of thought, consisting of mental substance, must surely have some consistency of its own, at the mental level if not the physical one.

Indeed, what is telepathy if not the capacity of perceiving something that is solely of a mental nature? Telepathy is a fact. It really grasps the thought of other subjects, in some elements and within certain limits. This is confirmed not only in subjective fashion by the interested parties themselves, but also by statistical calculations applied to a large number of experiments carried out in laboratory conditions: Joseph Banks Rhine, pioneer of quantitative parapsychology, was the first to point out that random probability is far exceeded by the effective percentage of successful experiments; the more this is repeated, the more it confirms that telepathy really exists.

At a certain point one can even say that thoughts can be photographed.[66] Particularly interesting in this connection are the experiments carried out by Jule Eisenbud with the telepathic medium Ted Serios, in the course of which he obtained photographs of images on which his subject was concentrating at the time.[67]

If, therefore, a thought can have a consistency of its own, why should it not be able to persist, have a duration, at least for a certain period of time? Why should it have to vanish, dissolve as it were, a bare instant after it has been thought, at the very moment in which a human being stops thinking it? Nothing, surely, prevents us from conceiving thought, once it has been generated, as being capable of persisting, as being capable of continuing and having a concrete and real existence. I am not saying that this must necessarily happen forever, but at least for as long as the effect of the mental act that has called the thought into being is maintained by the mental activity of other subjects who continue to think this thought, even after the subject that called it into being no longer thinks it.

In a perspective of this type we shall be more ready to accept a testimony of Oliver Fox, seeing it as part of a more plausible pattern. This famous English projector, a true pioneer of these experiences, tells us that on one occasion he saw a palace, or a temple, he could not really be sure, with windows of stained glass and people who kept climbing up and down the stairs. Fox remembers that in the end he understood that this building was of an exclusively mental nature: it came and kept coming, called into being by the joint or associated memory of many human beings who had exercised there for a long period of time.[68]

Muldoon and Carrington express the conviction that in astral voyages 'much that one apparently perceives represents merely mental constructs': this happens by virtue of 'the very great influence of the mind in shaping and moulding one's environment.'[6] [9]

One may therefore wonder where such mental constructs might be located in terms of our space. Benjamin Walker compares these experiences to dreams. A long and complex dream can take place within a fraction of a second of our time. To give but one of many possible examples: a baldachin pole falling on the neck of a person sleeping in the bed, caused him to dream that he was going through a whole series of events at the time of the French Revolution, ending with his being guillotined. Walker observes that 'time' — as we know and conceive it — does not exist in dreams, 'neither do dreams exist in a measurable space', because 'they have a dimension of their own'.[7] [0] Consequently, in the words of Henry Price, there is no point in asking oneself whether an image seen in a dream is situated at more or less than two and a half inches to the northeast of the dreamer's left ear. Such an image 'belongs to a different place',[7] [1] and I am certain that the same is true for out-of-the-body experiences (and also near-death experiences, which we shall consider in the next chapter), because these experiences seem to be emancipated from material space, and to form part of a space of their own that is of a purely mental nature.

This does not mean that at the boundary between the two spaces (the material and the mental) it is not possible for 'thought forms' to assume concrete shapes that are located in the immediate vicinity of the physical body of the subject who brings them into being with his mental activity. Theosophers, clairvoyants, projectors and communicating deceased often agree in speaking of an 'aura' of ovoid shape, which seems to be made of an energetic substance lighter than that of our physical body, which surrounds it rather in the manner of a halo. This halo can be perceived by those who have developed a particular form of extrasensorial perception. The thought-forms involved are said to correspond to the subject's feelings and thoughts, and to have a certain reality that, even though not physical in the proper sense, can yet be defined in terms of a subtler capacity. Even though the thoughts and feelings of a given subject assume consistency only in a mental dimension peculiar to that subject, they may nevertheless seem to be located within the aura as if they were expressed by that selfsame aura. It is here, as it were, that the physical dimension of a given subject is said to meet and to become merged with his mental dimension, with his interior world.[7] [2]

However, once the projector has emerged from his physical body, the first thing to which he gives shape is his own astral body; and he does this by simply thinking it. Such creative thought may consist either of an act, which by definition is voluntary and conscious, or of a spontaneous and unconscious movement. The projector may thus become aware of having the form of a small cloud, a wad of cotton or a luminous ball floating in space, just as he may see himself as possessing a very clearly defined human form that closely resembles that of his physical body (so much so that the astral body is often referred to as the 'double').

The astral body may be either 'naked' or 'dressed'. At times the subject may discover himself to be naked, but he hardly has time to feel embarrassed by this situation before he finds himself — in a flash as it were — to be dressed again. The form of the astral dress may vary according to the dress effectively worn by the physical body. The astral dress may also correspond to the subject's idea of how he is effectively dressed, or how he would like to be dressed.

In general, therefore, a projector may give his body such form as he likes. A reflection by Monroe is particularly interesting in this connection:

'If you have been conditioned to acute awareness of nakedness, you will automatically think you are clothed — and so you are. The form of your physical body is carried over in replica down to the last hair follicle and scar, unless you deliberately think otherwise.

Conversely, if your thought habits have been in other directions, you may take whatever form is most convenient, deliberately or otherwise. I suspect that one may modify the Second Body into whatever form is desired. Once the thought is discarded, the Second Body will drop back into its habitual humanoid shape. This opens up some interesting speculations into man's mythology. If one wished to experience the existence of a quadruped, the Second Body might be transformed temporarily into a large dog, and someone with Second State vision (there probably are many such people) might encounter a werewolf. Or the fables of half man, half goat/horse could be the result. One might "think" wings and fly, and be transformed momentarily into a vampire bat. It seems less impossible when one experiments with the power of thought in the Second State.'[7 3]

Indeed, a conclusion of this general character can be drawn from experience, as can readily be seen from the following example. Monroe, speaking about one of his many ecsomatic projections, at a certain moment concentrates his attention on his astral arms and goes on to tell us: 'I looked upward to where I felt them, and I saw the shimmering outlines of my arms and hands in exactly the place they felt they were!'[7 4] The fact is that Monroe could see at one and the same time, both his extended astral arms and his physical arms folded (as they effectively were). As regards his astral arms, every time he decided — for example — to move his fingers, he *saw* them move and at the same time *felt* them move. Again 'I put my hands together, and the glowing hands came together, and I felt my hands clasp each other. They felt just like ordinary hands, no different.'[7 5]

Muldoon notes in this connection that 'the astral counterpart is the *exact duplicate* of the physical body, in every center and cell.'[7 6] The entire context of Muldoon's book makes it very clear that this exactly determined form springs from the creativity of mental activity, be it conscious or unconscious, voluntary or involuntary. Muldoon testifies that a projector can even find his sexual organs in his astral duplicate, but again the entire context makes it clear that he finds himself in possession of the astral counterpart of these organs, only to the extent to which he succeeds in concentrating his attention, however momentarily, on this particular part of his astral body.

Herbert Greenhouse writes that 'the second body may be altered to fit the desires of the projector.'[7 7] For example, as Greenhouse himself notes, the subject may often see his astral body as younger than his physical body, especially in the mirror. There are also subjects whose astral double at times seems taller or bigger than their actual physical bodies.[7 8]

We have already seen that the creative energy of thought causes the astral clothes to assume a form in keeping with what the subject is actually wearing or would like to wear. Indeed, Muldoon remarks in this connection that 'thought *creates* in the astral, and one will appear to others as he *is* in mind'; rather, one can say quite generally that 'the whole astral world is governed by thought.'[7 9]

A detailed and accurate description of a particular experience lived by Muldoon is of special interest here:

> 'On one occasion, I noticed the clothing forming itself out of the emanation surrounding my astral body, when only a few feet out of coincidence, and the clothing was exactly like that covering my physical body. On another occasion I awakened and found myself moving along at the intermediate speed. A very dense aura surrounded me — so dense, in fact, that I could scarcely see my own body. It remained so until the phantom came to a stop, when it was dressed in the typical ghost-like garb!'[8 0]

Muldoon adds that the mind that creates these forms is not necessarily the conscious mind. This creation is a spontaneous process that in the great majority of cases is as sudden and unexpected as it is unconscious. Muldoon recalls that at times his double was seen by his mother, always dressed in pyjamas exactly like the ones his physical body was wearing at that moment.

However strange this may seem (even though it can be explained on the basis of the principle of mental creation as influenced by the mental habits of the subject), we find it fully confirmed by the extensive documentation collected by Robert Crookall in his book *The Next World*

— and the Next.[8][1] In the first part of this book, entitled 'The Clothes of Ghosts', the author relates a wide range of different experiences: there are astral projectors who describe the clothes of their astral doubles, outside observers who describe the doubles (and dress) of astral projectors, there is one observer who describes the fully dressed double of a dying person becoming detached from his physical body, there are descriptions of the (dressed) doubles of deceased as observed by living people, and there are even descriptions of the particular doubles that are known as 'materialisations'.

As you can see, since astral projection is the first step of a detachment that becomes total and definitive on the occasion of death, and because the astral reproduction of the body and its dress takes place by virtue of one of those processes of mental creation that the deceased can continue to call into being just like living people, it is readily possible to see the creation of the body and its dress by living projectors in close continuity with the corresponding mental creations brought about by the deceased. Indeed, it is without any solution of continuity that Crookall passes on to considering mediumistic communications from this particular point of view. Faced with such a massive concordance of testimony, the fact itself — no matter how one may eventually interpret it — can hardly be denied, nor can it be considered as a strictly personal illusion: that, in fact, is exactly the conclusion reached by Crookall.

Greenhouse, in turn, recalls that at times an astral double not only appears dressed, but even carrying some object not necessarily always small (some jewel or a brooch, for example), but sometimes as large as a candlestick, an electric iron, a walking stick, a fishing net, and so on.[8][2]

Though something of this kind may be very difficult to believe for people not yet familiar with the entire range of this phenomenology, there are cases where the objects carried by the astral double become materialized and are left behind. To give just one example, one may here recall the case of Lucian Landau, who in September 1955 was lying sick at his home in Kent. His girlfriend Eileen, whom he was later to marry, was at that time staying in the guest-room on the opposite side of the hall and told him that every night she came to him, though only with her astral body, to check his pulse and respiration. He was wondering whether this was really possible and therefore asked Eileen that her double should try to take his diary, which was lying on a table in her room, and bring it to him during one of these astral visits. The next night Lucian really saw Eileen's astral image and something was effectively brought from her room into his: however, it was not the diary but rather a small rubber dog that was found to weigh 107 grams, while the diary weighed only 37 grams — far less. The girl later told him that she had brought the rubber dog because she had not succeeded in lifting the little book even though it was much lighter. She tried to explain this by remembering that as a child she had always been told not to touch other people's letters or diaries.[8 3]

Clearly, we are here concerned with one of the two phenomena that parapsychologists refer to as *apports*. One may speak of an apport when a given object is dematerialized in the place where it is situated, and then rematerializes in some other place. But it is well known that in certain ecsomatic experiences it can happen that the projector, having moved astrally to some different place, will materialize there for a few instants. In that case one has the phenomenon known as bilocation.

In this connection Greenhouse recalls the case of Mark Macdonnell, a Member of Parliament in Britain. Although seriously ill and in bed, Macdonnell succeeded in making an appearance in the House of Commons and voting in one of the divisions, as is readily borne out by *the report in Hansard*.[8 4]

Charles Good, another politician though this time Canadian and a member of the Legislative Council of British Columbia, was likewise ill in bed; nevertheless, a photograph published by a local newspaper shows Good together with his colleagues, although his face seems somewhat transparent.[8][5]

A third projection of the same type is attested as having taken place in 1909, and is attributed to another member of the British House of Commons. Sir Carne Raschse wanted to take part in an important debate, but illness obliged him to remain in bed and made this impossible. Nevertheless, three fellow members testified that they saw him sitting in his usual place in the House. The only thing that had seemed strange at the time was the fact that he had not answered a question put to him by one of them.[8][6]

One of the most famous cases of the materialization of an astral double is that of Emilie Sagée, a French teacher who lived in the nineteenth century. Although she was very capable and conscientious in her work, she would invariably be dismissed within a relatively short time of commencing work at a new school or girls' college. The fact was that it frequently happened for her to double during a lesson: the double, perfectly identical to the real Emilie, would appear, for example, while she was writing at the blackboard and would then repeat all her movements in perfect synchrony, the only difference being that it did not actually hold a piece of chalk in its hand. Since many girls took fright and their parents protested and threatened to take them away from school, Emilie would invariably end up by being dismissed, though the school also gave her excellent references so that she had little or no difficulty in finding work at some other school — only for the same thing to happen all over again.

She thus moved from school to school, and eventually took service at a college for the daughters of the nobility in Livonia. One day she was picking flowers in the school garden during one of the hours she was free of class duties when, looking through one of the large windows on the ground-floor she realized that the forty-two girls assembled there for their sewing exercises, sitting around a long table, had been left without supervision. In the circumstances Emilie could not but be concerned that some of the livelier spirits among the girls might get up to some mischief: but in the vacant teacher's chair there suddenly appeared a second Mademoiselle Sagée, in every respect identical to the real one in the garden. All the time her double assumed and maintained material consistency in the teacher's chair, the girls could see the original through the window, still picking flowers, though her movements seemed to have become far slower, as if she somehow lacked power and energy. Her movements resumed their erstwhile vivacity at the very moment when the image projected in the classroom chair began to dissolve again, giving the impression that her body had suddenly recovered its energy. However, before the double disappeared two of the more enterprising girls went up to it and one of them even had the audacity to pass her hand through it: she had the impression of passing through some thick muslin veil or something similar.[8][7]

This is a particularly well known and significant case. But literature offers us a wide and conspicuous variety of cases of astral projections (or 'ESP projections') brought about either by hypnosis or by simple concentration, as also by more complex methods, and even cases that occurred quite spontaneously. The latter often take the form of dreams or visions experienced by a projector, while many others involve the phantasm of the projector being seen by other people in a place to which he, too, had perceived himself to have become transferred. Hornell Hart, for example, provides a classification of as many as ninety-nine such cases.[8][8]

So far we have considered the phenomenon of the materialization of an astral body primarily and essentially from an external viewpoint. But if we want to get some idea of how this phenomenon can be lived from within, we have to do no more than read the testimony of a projector. Sylvan Muldoon, for instance, wonders in what way the projector's psychic force can acquire the characteristic of 'solidity'. He tries to provide an answer by saying this may well be due to the crypto-conscious mind, even though the subject retains no more than marginal control over it. Muldoon recalls that on several occasions he tried to shift the physical objects, though without success. He ascribed these failures to the fact that in all these cases he had acted by relying on a conscious act of the will. In actual practice he has succeeded in shifting even rather heavy objects, but only when relying on his crypto-conscious mind in a wholly spontaneous manner and without ever formulating what we might call a conscious act, i.e. an act of his will in the strict sense of the term.

Muldoon gives us a very interesting example of this. One night in 1928 he was lying in bed in his own room on the ground floor of the house, while his mother and baby brother shared a bed on the first floor. A little before midnight Sylvan suddenly felt a terrible pain in his stomach. He called his mother at the top of his voice, but she was so fast asleep she did not hear his desperate appeals. And so, without any conscious effort and guided solely by his unconscious will, Sylvan Muldoon's astral double got up from the bed, went up the stairs to the first floor, crossed his mother's bedroom and arrived next to the bed in which she slept with his little brother. At that point Sylvan lost consciousness for a few moments; when he came to again, he saw his mother on her feet and his baby brother half in and half out of the bed, both of them frightened and wondering what had happened. An invisible force had evidently raised the mattress and thrown them both onto the floor. Sylvan's astral double had then quickly returned to his physical body, so that he began to shout for help again and eventually succeeded in getting his mother to hear him. Still gasping for breath, she came into his room to tell him that 'the spirits' had thrown her down from her bed. [8] [9]

Another case is that of Vincent Turvey: though physically a rather weak person, he relates having lifted a bed with two people in it during one of his astral voyages. He gained the clear impression that this displacement of physical bodies had been made possible by the fact that his projected double used a kind of viscous substance that issued from the wrist or the knees of a medium, and which, as far as he could tell, seemed to be identifiable with a part of his 'energy' or 'vitality' body.[90] This is another example among the many that could be quoted, to show that at times the astral double possesses (or succeeds in drawing upon) far more energy than the subject's physical body is known to have.

Robert Monroe, in turn, speaks of a 'terrible pinch' that his astral double gave to a woman in order to demonstrate to her in a very tangible manner that he was present in that place, even though she could not see him.[91] On another occasion he recalls pinching a second woman for the same reason, though in a rather more gentle manner.[92] Greenhouse reports a number of examples of a presumed astral double said to have rung the bell or to have knocked at a door.[93]

We may well wonder how it is that one and the same double can prove so ethereal at one moment as to be able to pass through a wall, and yet a few moments later to be so dense and solid as to have to open a door, being unable to pass through it when closed. We may also wonder why a double should be able to pass through the body of another person, and then a moment or two later pinch or hit that person, or exert some other form of physical action on it.

I think that a subject who projects himself out of his physical body and into his pure and simple astral body can confer upon the latter any kind of density he desires, in exactly the same manner and by virtue of the same principle that enables him to confer upon the double any form that he may desire. But one must remember that the will that acts in the most effective manner to this end is not the conscious will at all, but rather what Muldoon calls the crypto-conscious will.

Subject to the same reservation, one may also add that the double can move through space and transfer from one place to another just as the subject desires. Thus, the astral body may walk in the same way as the physical body, or in a manner very similar to it, but it can also move at an intermediate velocity (as Muldoon puts it). This speed is far greater than walking pace and enables the double to cover very considerable distances.

Lastly, the double can also move vast, sometimes continental distances, during which the subject may lose consciousness or at least have the impression of losing it for little more than an instant. Muldoon makes this distinction between the three possible speeds.[9][4] Why then does the subject lose consciousness at the very moment when such a long-distance movement is about to take place, as often seems to be the case? We have to see this phenomenon in relation to the fact that an effective intervention involving physical matter is brought about only by the crypto-conscious will: thus we can infer that these long-distance displacements call for the greater power that can be obtained only by immersion, if only for a moment, in a state of unconsciousness.

The selfsame projection process that brings the astral double to emerge from the physical body probably owes its success, first and foremost, to a factor that operates at the subliminal level. This may explain why on so many occasions the subject is not even conscious of the fact that the projection has already been achieved.

The physical action that an astral double may exert on an external body may also include healing, or at least cure and relief procured for the physical body of another subject afflicted by some illness. We could assume that we here have the direct action of a psychic agent (the astral double projecting itself) on the matter of the physical body of the other subject. But we can also formulate an alternative hypothesis: the psyche of the one subject can be conceived as acting on the psyche of the other, moulding it in some manner, so that the latter, having become rebalanced, harmonized (or healed if you prefer), can then heal and put to rights its own physical body by acting from within.

In the present century, the best-known reports of astral healing phenomena are those attributed to Father Pius of

Pietrelcina, of which we shall here recall two. The first concerns Father Placido Bux, who in 1957 was found to be suffering from cirrhosis of the liver and had been taken to hospital at San Severo in Apulia. His condition had become clinically desperate, but then Father Pius appeared to him one night, comforted him and assured him that he would get well again. Before leaving, the saintly Capucin placed his hand on the glass pane of one of the windows. This imprint, which reappeared every time the hospital staff tried to remove it, convinced Father Bux that his vision had been something more than a mere dream. The day after the apparition the patient already felt much better, and not much later was fit enough to be discharged from hospital. Another religious, Father Alberto D'Apolito, then went to pay a visit to Father Pius at San Giovanni Rotondo, who confirmed the facts, though asking him not to speak about them.[9] [5]

Ten years earlier in the small Calabrian township of Diamante on the Tyrrhenian seaboard, Mrs Ersilia Magurno was looking after her husband, gravely ill for the last two months suffering from cardiac insufficiency, made worse by a violent attack of influenza, which had sent his temperature up to 40°C. In constant danger of death, Ernesto Magurno had received the last sacraments when, during the night of 28th February 1947, he received a long astral visit from Father Pius, accompanied by another friar. Father Pius told him: 'This fever is going to disappear, tomorrow you will be well again and in four days' time you can get up.' The next day the fever had effectively gone. An intense odour of violets flooded the room, the characteristic perfume that revealed the astral presence of Father Pius in the course of his long-distance bilocations. Ernesto Magurno was soon completely fit again and five months later went to visit Father Pius at his convent in San Giovanni Rotondo. The monk, who had the same appearance as the astral visitor who had appeared to Magurno that night, showed himself to have full knowledge of the facts: he recognized Ernesto and confirmed that the apparition had been Father Pius in person, come as the bearer of divine grace to obtain for him such a rapid and wholly unexpected recovery.[9 6]

With this brief mention of the phenomenon of astral healing we can terminate this short and summary review of the essential features of out-of-the-body experiences. Having given a first general idea of these phenomena in the first chapter, we subsequently considered them as a possible starting point for a new approach to the old problem of survival, a first step to be taken on the way to a possible definition of the entire question of the immortality of the soul. In the present chapter we have just reviewed the characteristic features of these ecsomatic experiences, considering them one by one and in considerably more systematic fashion in order to obtain a more global view of the entire phenomenon. We are thus in a position to take a further step forward in the next chapter, where we shall complete the panorama by taking a look at near-death experiences, which mostly concern patients brought back to life in hospital resuscitation departments, or subjects who came close to death and then 'retraced their steps'. The picture will subsequently be completed by an examination and careful comparative analysis of mediumistic communications. Since the immense literature on these communications contains so many cases that inspire little or no confidence, we shall limit ourselves to those that provide adequate guarantees of credibility and reliability. In this way we shall see what we can learn about the crisis of death and the spiritual existence that follows it. Moreover, we shall be able to ascertain whether data and testimonies deriving from such widely differing sources do or do not suggest some significant concordance.

Chapter 4
Near-Death Experiences

Out-of-the-body experiences can be defined as the beginning of a process that attains its completion on the occasion of death. The second step in this direction, a further phase, is the one constituted by near-death experiences (NDEs).

These experiences concern people who, following some accident, a cardiac crisis or any similar reason, enter into a state of clinical death but somehow manage to return to life, either spontaneously or, as is more often the case, because they have been subjected to intensive therapies until they are 'resuscitated'. As soon as they are able to speak again, such people for the most part relate an experience characterized in the words of Raymond Moody, from his famous book *Life After Life*:

'A man is dying and, as he reaches the point of greatest physical distress, he hears himself pronounced dead by his doctor. He begins to hear an uncomfortable noise, a loud ringing or buzzing, and at the same time feels himself moving very rapidly through a long dark tunnel. After this, he suddenly finds himself outside of his own physical body, but still in the immediate physical environment, and he sees his own body from a distance, as though he is a spectator. He watches the resuscitation attempt from this unusual vantage point and is in a state of emotional upheaval.

'After a while, he collects himself and becomes more accustomed to his odd condition. He notices that he still has a "body", but one of a very different nature and with very different powers from the physical body he has left behind. Soon other things begin to happen. Others come to meet and to help him. He glimpses the spirits of relatives and friends who have already died, and a loving, warm spirit of a kind he has never encountered before — a being of light — appears before him. This being asks him a question, non verbally, to make him evaluate his life and helps him along by showing him a panoramic, instantaneous playback of the major events of his life. At some points he finds himself approaching some sort of barrier or border, apparently representing the limit between earthly life and the next life. Yet, he finds that he must go back to the earth, that the time for his death has not yet come. At this point he resists, for by now he is taken up with his experiences in the afterlife and does not want to return. He is overwhelmed by intense feelings of joy, love and peace. Despite his attitude, though, he somehow reunites with his physical body and lives.

'Later he tries to tell others, but he has trouble doing so. In the first place, he can find no human words adequate to describe these unearthly episodes. He also finds that others scoff, so he stops telling other people. Still the experience affects his life profoundly, especially his views about death and its relationship to life.'[9][7]

Moody notes that the accounts of such experiences resemble each other, even though one cannot find any elements of absolute identity in them. No subject has ever recounted all the individual experiences outlined above. Only a few elements recur always, or almost so; at least eight of them are normally present. The order or time succession may vary. There are subjects who remember nothing at all. In general one can say that 'persons who were "dead" seem to report more florid, complete experiences than those who only came close to death, and those who were "dead" for a longer period go deeper than those who were "dead" for a shorter time'.[9][8] It would therefore seem that near-death experiences can occur with different modalities and different degrees.

As in the case of out-of-the-body experiences, we have thus begun by giving an overall idea of near-death experiences. We can now pass on to considering the individual features of NDEs one by one. As a general rule, we shall look at them in the same order in which they are recounted by Moody, though we shall integrate his remarks with some particularly interesting aspects to be found in other authors, especially in Michael Sabom's *Recollections of Death*. The author of this book is a famous American cardiologist, who, after reading Raymond Moody's *Life After Life*, had the idea of comparing its findings with the testimonies of his own patients resuscitated after suffering clinical death due to a heart crisis.

First of all, however, it will be as well to give a precise definition of clinical death. A series of experiments were carried out on dogs, bringing them to the point of death by substantial, artificially induced hemorrhages. The results enabled Negovskij, a well-known Soviet scientist, to give the following definition:

> Clinical death is a state during which all external signs of life (consciousness, reflexes, respiration, cardiac activity) are absent, but the organism as a whole is not yet dead; the metabolic processes of its tissues proceed and under definite conditions it is possible to restore all its functions; i.e. this state is reversible under appropriate therapeutic intervention. If the organism in a state of clinical death is allowed to take the natural course of events, then the state of clinical death is followed by an irreversible state — biological death. The transition from the state of clinical death to biological death is both a break and a continuous process, because in its initial stages it is already impossible to restore the activity of the organism in all its functions, including those of the central nervous system, but it is still possible to restore the organism with altered functions of the brain cortex; i.e. an organism which cannot function under natural conditions of existence. Thereafter it becomes possible to restore under artificial conditions the activities only of certain organs, and further on, even this becomes no longer possible. During biological death, metabolic activity degradation, specific for a dead organism, sets in ... Considerable experimental material gathered by several authors indicates that 5-6 minutes is the maximum duration of the state of clinical death which the brain cortex of an adult organism can survive with subsequent recovery of all its functions.'[9] [9]

A first characteristic of near-death experiences is represented by the *difficulty in expressing them in human language*.[100] Here is how one patient put it: 'There is no feeling you experience in normal life that is anything like this.'[101]

A second characteristic is a special sensation that the subject feels, the *sense of being dead, though very much alive*. He hears other people all around him telling him that he is dead, and yet he feels fully and perfectly alive. Even though he may have been very badly wounded, he no longer feels any pain.[102]

Being alive, as a spirit, means above all to be in *full possession of one's mental faculties*. This, too, has been repeatedly testified. Moody comments as follows: 'Over and over, I have been told that once they became accustomed to their new situation, people undergoing this experience began to think more lucidly and rapidly than in physical existence.'[103]

A direct witness put it as follows: 'Your mind is so clear, it's so nice. My mind just took everything down and worked everything out for me the first time, without having to go through it more than once. After a while everything I was experiencing got to where it meant something to me in some way.'[104] A patient who had recovered from a severe thrombosis at the first-aid post of a New York hospital said afterwards: 'But I remember saying "I'm dying. I know I'm dying. Why are people so afraid of dying? Why? This is beautiful!".'[105] And here is how a former Air Force pilot put it after likewise recovering from a heart stoppage: 'It's like a dream. You're detached from the thing and watching it as a bystander.'[106]

What the subject feels is indeed a *sense of peace, wellbeing and felicity*.[107] The 'deceased' watches the grief of his relatives and friends, he would like to tell them that he is still very much alive, but he cannot. Feelings of sadness and melancholy, a sense of solitude, abandonment and even terror may become marginal, occasional and temporary elements mixed with what seems essentially an experience of wellbeing and peace. A man undergoing an open-heart operation without anesthetics lost consciousness due to shock, passing rapidly from an extremely painful experience to a sense of great wellbeing and happiness: 'That was the most beautiful instant in the whole world when I came out of that body! ... All I saw was extremely pleasant! I can't imagine anything in the world or out of the world that could anywhere compare. Even the most beautiful moments of life would not compare to what I was experiencing.'[108]

Brief mention should also be made of the *sound* that the subject sometimes perceives. Depending on the circumstances, it could be defined as jingling, humming or even a kind of music, a 'whistling sound, like the wind'.[109] One man resuscitated at the hospital remembered it in the following words: 'I would hear what seemed to be bells tinkling, a long way off, as if drifting through the wind. They sounded like Japanese wind bells.'[110]

At a certain point there then comes the *dark tunnel* experience. The subject has a very clear sensation of passing through a tunnel, a narrow tube, an underground channel, a deep and dark valley or a corridor, at the end of which he can glimpse a bright light.[111]

Abandonment of the physical body is associated with the strange sensation that the subject feels when he contemplates his physical body from outside it. The centre of his personality seems to have become projected outside the body, which the subject by then contemplates with a sense of estrangement and indifference, though occasionally also with acute concern. The subject feels himself to be devoid of solidity, ethereal, floating in the air, suspended above the body and below the ceiling of the room. He also feels the unaccustomed, strange sensation of passing through material things and the bodies of other people: (a) a wounded soldier during an operation in a field hospital in Vietnam vainly tried to touch the surgeon, and simply felt himself to be passing through him — his astral double lifted out of his physical body, lying inanimate on the operating table;[1][1][2] (b) a woman clearly heard the comments of the surgeon and his assistants, as well as the small talk that accompanied the operation;[1][1][3] (c) a colonel in the American Army had the impression of flying above the city, and with most acute eyesight saw right into the resuscitation department where lay his apparently lifeless body.[1][1][4]

Sabom uses the term *autoscopic experiences* to describe the situation in which the subject, having projected out of his body, considers this physical body and everything that is being done to it, to all intents and purposes watching the various resuscitation attempts, which he will afterwards describe very accurately. An objection to the presumed cognitive nature of these experiences can be raised by saying that the subject, already familiar with the situation, substantially knew beforehand what he later believed to be seeing. Sabom tested the validity of such an objection by taking twenty-five patients whom he had every reason to believe well informed about what normally happens in a resuscitation department, and subjecting them to a kind of examination or test. Twenty of these gave descriptions full of gross errors, and not more than three succeeded in giving a description of resuscitation procedures devoid of slight errors and with only a few inaccuracies.[1][1][5] This result adds further weight to the testimony of resuscitated subjects who claim to have effectively witnessed the attempts to resuscitate them and to have heard the words passing between the medical personnel, often giving accounts full of admirable detail.

So far we have considered how the subject of a near-death experience, projecting himself out of his body, subsequently sees his physical body and what happens to it or is being done to it. This leads one to wonder how the subject sees himself, how he sees and considers the *quid* with which he identifies himself at this stage and into which he seems to have displaced the centre of his personality. Let us say right away that in these experiences, which are in some ways similar to astral projections although constituting a further step, the astral body may once again appear to the subject as sometimes having a vaguely spherical or spherico-nebular form, or at other times it may assume a true human or parasomatic form corresponding exactly to that of the temporarily abandoned physical body. Centered in his astral body, the subject feels himself to have some density and consistency, though this is by no means similar to normal physical density or consistency. The subject therefore feels invisible, weightless, and extremely free in his movements (as we shall see a little further on).

Not only can the astral body assume the habitual form of the physical body, but once again it may appear dressed. Witness the testimony of a 43-year-old patient who used the following words to describe the appearance assumed by his astral body while, following a heart stoppage, it floated above his lifeless physical body: 'You feel like you're floating. I had a white robe on with a white belt which was interwoven and it had a tassel on both ends of it ... I had a white hood but I didn't have it up.'[116] This patient, too, thus saw himself in more or less ghost-like apparel, similar to Sylvan Muldoon's experience as reported in Chapter 3.

Further attention is also merited by the classical testimony of Dr Wiltse, whose case — which forms part of the history of psychic research — was investigated more than a century ago by Hodgson and Myers. Here we once again meet the phenomenon of a fully-shaped astral body, naked at first and then immediately dressed, as well as many other features that we have already considered in connection with these experiences. Himself a medical man, Dr Wiltse was able to analyze in great detail all aspects of the extraordinary experience he had when he suffered a heart stoppage for four hours, and was pronounced dead; indeed, he believed himself to be dead, even though he felt more alive than ever before. The feature that distinguishes his case from all those so far considered is that in all previous cases we saw only subjects who suddenly found themselves out of the body without in any way realizing how this had come about. It may be that the detachment process could take place so rapidly because it was occasioned by the crypto-conscious will, at a moment when the subject had fallen into a state of unconsciousness. However, this process can also take place more slowly and gradually. A contribution to this slowing down could be made by the fact that the subject remains conscious, for we have seen that certain phenomena are facilitated by being brought about at an unconscious level. However this may be, the Wiltse case is characteristic of a whole series of cases where the separation of the astral body from a physical body occurred more slowly, by stages, while the subject remained fully conscious and was therefore able to follow the process.

The accurate description Dr Wiltse has left us of his experience enables us to follow the various phases of a disincarnation process. As we shall see in the next chapter, the process is closely analogous to the one outlined in the testimony of psychic subjects, as also in that given through mediums by supposedly disincarnate people, who describe it in exactly the same terms.

'I watched,' says Dr Wiltse, 'the interesting process of the separation of soul and body. By some power, apparently not my own, the Ego was rocked to and fro, laterally, as a cradle is rocked, by which process its connection with the tissues of the body was broken up. After a little time the lateral motion ceased, and along the soles of the feet beginning at the toes, passing rapidly to the heels, I felt and heard, as it seemed, the snapping of innumerable small cords. When this was accomplished I began slowly to retreat from the feet, toward the head, as a rubber cord shortens. I remember reaching the hips and saying to myself, "Now there is no life below the hips". I can recall no memory of passing through the abdomen and chest, but recollect distinctly when my whole self was collected into the head, when I reflected thus: "I am all in the head now, and I shall soon be free". I passed around the brain as if I were hollow, compressing it and its membranes, slightly, on all sides, toward the centre and peeped out between the sutures of the skull, emerging like the flattened edges of a bag of membranes. I recollect distinctly how I appeared to myself something like a jellyfish as regards colour and form ... As I emerged from the head I floated up and down laterally like a soap-bubble attached to the bowl of a pipe until I at last broke loose from the body and fell lightly to the floor, where I slowly rose and expanded into the full stature of a man. I seemed to be translucent, of a bluish cast and perfectly naked. With a painful sense of embarrassment I fled towards the partially opened door to escape the eyes of the two ladies whom I was facing as well as others whom I knew were about me, but upon reaching the door I found myself clothed, and satisfied upon that point I turned and faced the company. As I turned, my left elbow came into contact with the arm of one of two gentlemen, who were standing in the door. To my surprise, his arm passed through mine without apparent resistance, the several parts closing again without pain, as air reunites. I looked quickly up at his face to see if he had noticed the contact, but he gave no sign — only stood and gazed toward the couch I had just left. I directed my gaze in the direction of his, and saw my own dead body. It was lying just as I had taken so much pains to place it, partially upon the right side, the feet close together and the hands clasped across the breast. I was surprised at the paleness of the face ...'.[117]

Dr Wiltse's account refers to *small movements* of the astral body within the limited physical space of a room. But the movements that seem far more characteristic of these near-death experiences, as also in the previously considered out-of-the-body experiences, are the *big displacements*, sometimes to very distant places, that occur in *instantaneous fashion* or, as one might say, with the speed of thought. When we try to think of a certain place that we know well and imagine we are there, in some particular position, it takes no more than that and we are there in thought, no matter how great the distance that separates us from the place we are thinking of. In the great instantaneous displacements that are sometimes made in NDEs the subject afterwards asserts that he suddenly found himself in the place of which he was thinking just a moment beforehand: and, what is more, having the experience of really being there. A few facts of this type should be quoted by way of example. A Vietnam veteran relates that, having been wounded in battle, he had been taken to the operating theatre of a small hospital, when suddenly he found himself (astrally) back on the battlefield where the dead and the wounded were being evacuated after the battle. Another instant later, he was back in the place where his physical body was undergoing an operation.[118]

Likewise a night-watchman, recounting his own experiences of being in a state of coma, remembered among other things that at a certain moment he had said to himself: 'Alright, let's go and see what is happening at the parking lot in the yard', and immediately 'a part of his mind' went there and then came back to 'tell him about the situation'. During a subsequent 'visit' to the wash-house he was struck by the great din the centrifuges were making. He next 'visited' the hospital's refreshment counter, to which he returned physically a few months later when visiting a friend at the hospital, and thus had occasion to verify that the place was exactly as he had seen it during his astral excursion. The following passage in this subject's account is particularly interesting: 'Are you familiar with a telephoto lens? I could adjust that at will. I could bring the subject closer to me or me closer to the subject. I could just think: Hey, it would be nice to be a little closer to the subject — I would just be there.'[119]

The subject may feel a sense of loneliness, although this tends to disappear as he becomes more accustomed to the new experience. Indeed, he will soon see people coming up to meet and receive him, to greet and instruct him and, more generally, guide his first steps in the new dimension he has just entered. These may be familiar faces, his own deceased relatives and friends, or unknown people. The subject may become aware of them in the same form they had during their earthly existence, but he can also perceive their presence in a different and less clearly definable manner.

Just two testimonies in this connection. The first comes from a patient, 43-years old, after recovering from a post-operatory thrombosis: 'I came to some place and there were all my relatives, my grandmother, my grandfather, my father, my uncle who had recently committed suicide. They all came towards me and greeted me ... My grandparents were dressed ... all in white and they had hoods over their heads ... It seems like I had just come upon them and they raised their heads up and they were all happy.'[120] The subject in question is the one who saw himself dressed in the same manner. The deceased, likewise, appeared to him in human form and in apparel associated with phantasms.

The second testimony is that of a soldier who had been seriously wounded in battle, and saw many of his comrades who had fallen the day before or earlier that month. Here is a part of his experience: 'All forty-two of those guys were there. They were not in the form we perceive the human body, and I can't tell you what form they were in because I don't know. But I know they were there.'[121] Nevertheless, their presence must have been sufficiently distinct and differentiated, seeing that the soldier, rather than saying that he met 'some' comrades, actually states their exact number: thirteen who had been killed the day before came up to him at once, to be followed little by little by another forty-two who had lost their lives during the course of the month.[122]

How do these deceased communicate with the subject? The civilian in the first of the two quoted cases says that at a certain point his grandmother shouted to him: 'We'll see you later, but not this time.'[123] But the soldier in the second example tells us: 'We communicated without talking with our voices.'[124] In 28 of the 116 cases studied by Sabom the subject had the sensation of being in contact with other personalities. Communications took place in 21 of these cases. The method of communication was verbal in twelve episodes ('I heard a clear, loud voice', 'a loud, thundering voice', 'words'), and involved gestures in another two ('outstretched arms', 'waving of the hand'); in a further three cases communication was both verbal and non-verbal, while in the remaining four cases we encounter true telepathic communication.[1 2 5]

At a certain moment the subject undergoing a near-death experience may have the feeling of *reading the thoughts* of the deceased people he meets and, indeed, even of living, incarnate people. A woman interviewed by Moody put it as follows: 'I could see people all around, and I could understand what they were saying. I didn't hear them, audibly, like I'm hearing you. It was more like knowing what they were thinking, exactly what they were thinking, but only in my mind, not in their actual vocabulary. I would catch it the second before they opened their mouths to speak.'[1 2 6]

Sabom's cases include some where the subject relates having met God or Christ. A Protestant shopkeeper noted the presence of Jesus and asked him to keep him in life a little longer to enable him to provide for his children: 'It was almost as if — and I'm not trying to dramatize and I hope it doesn't sound that way — I almost knew I was talking to God'.[1 2 7] Another Protestant woman met God in human form: 'Just as clear and plain the Lord came and stood and held his hands out for me ... He was tall with his hands out and he had all white on, like he had a white robe on ... It [the face] was more beautiful than anything you've ever seen.'[1 2 8] A mechanic spoke of a mysterious presence that he could not define more clearly, though he held it to be divine, or at least of a very high spiritual level: 'I was with an angel or God or somebody that I had total harmony with but with total communication without saying anything ... I was with somebody and I was moving out ... I was with a spirit or angel or I don't know. Somebody else will have to name my companion ... I was right with it.'[1 2 9]

This brings us to what Moody calls the *being of light*. 'What is perhaps the most incredible common element in the accounts I have studied,' writes Moody, 'and is certainly the element which has the most profound effect upon the individual, is the encounter with a very bright light.'[130] The light is at first uncertain, and then becomes stronger and stronger, until eventually it is indescribable in its brightness, though it neither hurts the eyes nor dazzles them, nor does it prevent the subject from seeing other things. The description of the being-of-light does not vary, even though its definition will vary from one case to another. The greater part of Christians identify it with Jesus Christ, but there are also Christians who are not at all inclined to do this.

A subject who has encountered the being-of-light will generally tell you that he had a kind of dialogue with him or it, but a dialogue not made of words and consisting rather of an exchange of thoughts. When the subject tries to translate into words the fundamental question asked by the being-of-light, he will normally say something like 'Are you prepared to die?', 'Are you ready to die?', 'What have you done with your life to show me?', or 'What have you done with your life that is sufficient?'.[131]

One man testified as follows: 'The voice asked me a question: "Is it worth it?". And what it meant was, did the kind of life I had been leading up to that point seem worthwhile to me then, knowing what I then knew.'[132]

Moody notes that all the subjects that spoke to him about the being-of-light underscored the fact that:

> '... this question, ultimate and profound as it may be in its emotional impact, is not at all asked in condemnation. The being, all seem to agree, does not direct the question to them to accuse or to threaten them, for they still feel the total love and acceptance coming from the light, no matter what their answer may be. Rather, the point of the question seems to be to make them think about their lives, to draw them out. It is, if you will, a Socratic question, one asked not to acquire information but to help the person who is being asked to proceed along the path to the truth by himself.'[133]

The subject receives an answer to the question about the significance and value of his entire earthly existence in the course of a strange experience, where he relives in the space of a few instants the whole of his past life in a kind of global overview. It is somewhat like an extremely rapid sequence of recollections: though the word 'recollection' may seem inadequate to express this experience, it is probably the one that comes closest to conveying the idea. Rather than *recollecting*, it consists of a kind of *reliving*, not least on account of the great vivacity of the images, their vibrant colours, and their occasionally three-dimensional character. Many subjects live the events in a succession, in a kind of film sequence that strangely runs its course within the space of a few instants. But others say that they had something like a simultaneous view: all seems to them to have happened at one and the same time and in such a manner as to be encompassed by a single mental look. However summary it may reveal itself to be, such an overview is never generic, never brings out only the general lines: quite the contrary, it is extremely rich in detail. The panoramic view of one's past life can also be had independently of the appearance of the being-of-light; but when it occurs in relation to this being, when it appears as an answer to a question asked by the being, the experience undoubtedly reveals itself to be of very profound significance.[134]

At a certain point the subject has the clear impression of reaching something that he feels spontaneously led to define as 'the boundary between life and death', the line of demarcation that divides this earthly existence of ours from the purely spiritual and mental existence of the beyond. Such an experience is lived as if in a dream, a dream where the images seem to have symbolic significance. One of Moody's subjects had the experience of finding himself in a field bounded at the far end by a hedge marking the confine between the two worlds.[135] Yet another subject, a woman, lived the experience of finding herself aboard a ship plying a vast expanse of water, approaching the far shore where her beloved dead were waiting for her.[136] Another man knows that there is a line to be crossed, even though he cannot see it.[137] Yet another sees a grey fog far ahead of her, glimpsing people behind it and even something like buildings, all enveloped in a bright golden splendour.[138] There was also a man who had the impression of running down a kind of narrow corridor, at the end of which he could see 'a beautiful, polished door, with no knob', but with very bright light issuing from its corners 'with rays just streaming like everybody was so happy in there'.[139] The person or persons on the other side of the symbolic boundary seem to be in anxious expectation of the subject, but suddenly tell him that he has to go back because his moment has not yet come, because the people he has left behind still need him badly.

Sabom reports similar experiences among his own subjects. To one of them there appeared the gates of heaven and also a staircase leading up to them; he had already begun to climb up when he was suddenly called back to a waking state.[140] Another found himself by a stream that had to be waded, a third saw a barbed wire enclosure in front of him, and a fourth had begun to climb towards the top of a mountain.[141] On the other side of this borderline there generally are, or are supposed to be, one or more people waiting for the new arrival. But at the very last moment some superior force obliges the subject to turn back, while somebody he sees in front of him and on the other side of the barrier, or in some cases a voice that he only hears, tells him that the time has not yet come to pass over the fatal threshold.

The various features just reviewed are also very extensively confirmed in the book *At the Hour of Death*, by Karlis Osis and Erlendur Haraldsson, which summarizes the results of two comparative surveys of more than a thousand death and near-death experiences in the United States and in India. A 50-year-old shopkeeper, dying of cancer, saw open gates and, beyond them, a marvellous garden.[142] A young Catholic missionary, in a violent access of fever, saw a boat coming to take her.[143] Four days before she died, an 80-year-old woman of excellent culture and with a fine sense of humour saw herself taken by taxi to a garden of beauty she had never seen. She did not really want to come back, but the driver proved impatient.[144] A woman, fifty years of age and suffering from a bad heart, saw a magnificent garden, and inside it there was God with an angel by his side.[145] A young nurse, suffering from malignant hypertension, set her eyes on gates leading into a vast country, into an enormous space,[146] while a 60-year-old woman saw gates formed by clouds.[147] An even older woman caught a glimpse of paradise and later commented on her experience with the following words: 'I don't think these are hallucinations, they are visions — very real.'[148] These are some of the things seen by people who either died a short time after or, having come close to death, succeeded in staging a 'comeback'. The 'paradise' they see is described in strangely material, sensible and mundane terms. Nobody, however, is surprised by this or even wonders why it should be so. Here is what the authors of the book have to say about this aspect: '"Seeing heaven" did not arouse such questions in any patient, regardless of education or occupation. Whether trees, buildings, or space rockets, the visions all used images of earthly things to fashion their heaven. Yet these experiences seemed to be very meaningful to the patients, often changing their outlook on life and death.'[149]

The corresponding testimonies of the Indian subjects are very similar. Dying of smallpox, a 20-year-old student saw buildings and gardens surrounded by hills, crowded with noble and cultured people, all seemingly happy and content.[150] A young nurse, a Christian converted to Islam by marriage, in the throes of a crisis caused by a grave hemorrhage following rupture of the uterus, saw all the comforts of future life, the interiors of houses magnificently furnished with divans, and so on. There was no sorrow there, no displeasure, everybody was gay and happy. Her visions were reported by a doctor, who then added dryly: 'She wanted to attain more worldly comfort there than a well-placed doctor can get in this world.'[151] A 40-year-old man suffering from a gastric infection told his nurse that he saw 'a temple with closed doors. Open the doors for me, I have to go to God.'[152] A cultured patient, about thirty years of age and suffering from a liver disease, saw himself in 'paradise', where 'there were magnificent gardens full of flowers' and where he saw the black messengers of death (the *Yamdot*) and also Yamaraj, king of death, tall and strong, and he too wholly black.[153] A policeman said, just two hours before he died, that he was in a garden of indescribable beauty.[154] A farmer who had suffered a heart stoppage but was resuscitated within a matter of minutes, said afterwards that he had been taken to a silver palace, where the furniture was likewise of silver and the cushions all silk. He had been so happy there, no least on account of a number of beautiful ladies with splendid ornaments, whom he found sitting in a circle as if they had been waiting for him, that he turned angrily to his doctor with the question 'Why have you saved me?'.[155] A young Hindu woman, who had been thought dead but had regained consciousness, recounted that two messengers had bound her with thongs to a stretcher and had carried her to God in a marvellous place, where there was a kind of court and people were cooking food that she was greatly tempted to eat. But a very important person sitting in a high place then asked, 'Why did you bring her?', as if she had been taken mistakenly in place of somebody else. And thus, unwillingly, she was carried back.[156] A Muslim housewife who had benefited from higher education was likewise taken to God, who was sitting in heaven in the midst of an open space of green, but she was then sent back to earth, much to her chagrin, as if a similar mistake had been made in her case.[157]

In striking contrast with this wealth of earth-like, anthropomorphic visions is the testimony — seemingly unique of its kind, certainly very rare — of a 40-year-old housewife who was also brought back to life: 'I was going in space. There was nothing but space.' Almost as if so abstract a vision had deluded her, the woman added that she had no wish to go back there at all.[158]

The further the subject proceeds in his near-death experience, the more he feels at ease and the more

reluctant he becomes to return to earth. If nevertheless at
a certain point he decides to turn back, it is because he
feels there are some people he cannot or must not leave,
small children for example, or because he feels there are
still some things to be done here on earth before he can
indulge in the luxury of a serene death. There are some
who say they were brought back by some irresistible
force, but also others who thought they could decide
whether to stay or turn back.[159] The return to earth can
be ordered or granted by God or the being-of-light.[160] At
a certain point, therefore, the subject finds himself
reintegrated into his physical body. As a general rule,
however, the subject has no idea at all how this return
came about; the very few accounts that contain some
detail concerning this aspect generally claim that re-entry
took place via the head.[161]

As a general rule, moreover, the subject is also
reluctant to relate his experience, especially when he
finds himself amongst unreceptive people and fears to be
taken for mad.[162] But they always concur that their
experiences were very real and far from being dreams or
hallucinations: one of Moody's subjects, for example, said
that he was astonished by what was happening to him
while he was out of the body, and yet it was all very real.
Another put it literally as follows: 'It was nothing like a
hallucination. I have had hallucinations once, when I was
given codeine in the hospital. But that happened long
before the accident which nearly killed me. And this
experience was nothing like the hallucinations, nothing
like them at all.'[163]

That we are here concerned with an experience that is
felt to be very real can also be deduced from the way such
subjects generally behave after a near-death experience.
'Many have told me,' says Moody, 'that they felt that their
lives were broadened and deepened by their experience,
that because of it they became more reflective and more
concerned with ultimate philosophical issues.'[164]
Subjects who have undergone so fundamental an
experience come out of it as from a kind of initiation.

Their sense of life, their attitude to life seems changed. They feel they are alive to absolve a task. The experience leaves them filled with a profound nostalgia. Nobody feels the temptation to commit suicide in order to repeat the experience, but all fear of death has left them. In fact, they feel that death does not exist: it is only a passage from one condition to another that is far better and happier.[165] Four testimonies given in Dr Sabom's book are particularly illuminating in this respect and merit being quoted at some length.

One 33-year-old man suffered a heart stoppage and afterwards said:

'It [the NDE] just changed my whole life like a flipflop ... I used to worry about life and living it and trying to get ahead, trying to make life easier by working harder to make more money to make life easier. I don't do that no more ... I just live from day to day. I used to live for what was ahead or behind me. You can't live a day in advance or a day behind. You can only live for the day that you're living ... Death is nothing to go through anymore. It's not that hard to die ... I know where I'm headed to and I've got my life to live.'[166]

A Vietnam veteran, mutilated in truly impressive fashion, put it as follows:

'[Following the NDE] I don't go to funerals. I don't send flowers. I don't tell people I'm sorry. Somebody tells me somebody died and I say we should be happy. Why don't we have parties at death? ... They left for a better life, a good feeling.'[167]

A woman patient became a voluntary hospital helper immediately after experiencing a near-death experience:

'One of the girls who was a psychologist and a social worker kind of knew how I felt about things and a lot of times they would call her if a doctor had to tell someone that he was going to die because they would like to have someone around afterwards. When she heard of someone who was upset, she would always call me and have me go in to talk to the people because if they were going to die, it didn't bother me. It was really easy for me to talk to the people about it.'[168]

An elderly man, fifty-four years of age, seemed to draw a very precise moral from all this: 'I feel that we are measured a great deal by what we do for others. That we're all put here to help one another ... the greatest law we have is love.'[169] This new existence inspired by love for one's neighbour receives food and sustenance from the fact that one really feels this love within one. A woman, 42-years old, put it as follows: 'When I look at people now, I feel that I really do love them, which is something I never felt before.'[170]

As far as a 35-year-old man was concerned, the experience had a very precise religious significance: 'I believed in Jesus Christ before, but I didn't actually live it. I live it today.'[171]

Dr Sabom dedicates the final part of his book to analyzing, one by one, the various hypotheses that try to explain these near-death phenomena in highly reductive terms; i.e. by reducing them to mere psychic phenomena. The factors capable of explaining these phenomena in such terms are very numerous indeed: state of semi-consciousness, conscious mental constructs and inventions, unconscious mental constructs and inventions, depersonalization (where the personality in crisis, seeking to defend itself against the fear of death, imagines surviving as a spectator and, dissociating itself from the body, sees what is happening to it as if it concerned somebody else), autoscopic hallucinations, dreams, *a priori* expectations, drug-induced visions and hallucinations, endorphin, spasms in the lobes of the brain, altered states of consciousness.[172]

Sabom bases his analysis on the hypothesis put forward by Sherrington and then further developed by Penfield. Sherrington distinguished the mind from the brain; the mind seems to be located in the diencephalon and not in the circumvolutions of the cerebral cortex. The mind can therefore detach itself from the brain, which is effectively what happens in out-of-the-body and near-death experiences. It can also perceive on its own, without standing in any need of mediation by the bodily senses.[173] This is corroborated by the exactness with which subjects relate down to the last detail what happened to them in the operating theatre, the resuscitation department or whatever other place might be involved.[174] Moody likewise confirms that, to the extent to which it proved possible to check and verify them, the autoscopic descriptions of facts and environments offered by his subjects were generally found to be exact and corresponding to truth. Even doctors are quite astonished when they hear untutored outsiders describe complex operations with such detail and accuracy.[175]

As a medical man and scientist, Sabom does not feel authorised to affirm that these near-death phenomena testify in a decisive and definitive manner in favour of survival. There remains the fact that these subjects have come close to death but have not died in the proper sense of the term — an important distinction. But Dr Sabom concludes that near-death experiences are caused by the separation of the soul from the body, a separation that in practice occurs at the threshold of death: and thus Sabom wonders whether the mind is not to be identified with the soul that most religions speak about.[176]

It is also interesting at this point to mention a number of considerations made by Osis and Haraldsson. Indeed, these two authors point out that, as their surveys have extensively shown, there is no reason whatsoever why one should conclude that the visions of the dying, or of subjects who have gone through a near-death experience, are brought about by their religious beliefs or have to be attributed to drug effects.[177] In Chapter VIII of their book, the authors re-emphasize the fact that these death-bed visions are relatively independent of medical conditions; i.e. cannot be correlated with such factors as administered drugs, high fevers, or brain disfunctions. Indeed, the more such factors were present, the more these visions tended to diminish.[178] Only in the case of brain disease can such visions be attributed to medical factors.[179]

As regards psychological factors capable of producing

hallucinations, there is no proof that such factors have caused even one of these visions of the beyond.[180] The apparitions seem to pursue ends of their own and tend to contradict the intentions of the patients.[181] These visions of the beyond are had also by patients who have no idea that they are about to die. All this seems to confirm the hypothesis that some of these apparitions are independent entities rather than simple projections of the patient's psyche.[182]

All things considered, Osis and Haraldsson deem that the facts presented by them sufficiently corroborate what they call their central hypothesis; namely that the dying become aware of existence after death by authentic extra-sensorial perception, by a form of clairvoyance. The message can be received and yet excluded from consciousness. In this way there is unconscious perception, which can be involuntarily expressed in a form of behaviour, in a certain emotional state, or in a change of mood. The authors therefore infer that 'the rise of mood at the time of death could also be based upon the patient's unconscious awareness of post-mortem survival.'[183]

Considering the results of the two surveys (from India and the United States) and comparing them with each other, Osis and Haraldsson even wondered whether the type of emotion present during the rise of mood could in some way be correlated with the mood of the patients on the day before. In this connection, however, they say that they were unable to discover any such relationship in either of the two countries. This leads them to conclude that 'the emotions present during the rise of mood were radically new and not simply a continuation of previous moods.'[184]

This is a further confirmation of the fact that the subject of near-death experiences finds himself for the first time face to face with a new reality. Whether he sees it clearly or merely derives a vague feeling, the coming into contact with this new reality is always and invariably an irreducible experience for him.

As regards the problem of whether such near-death experiences prove or at least suggest survival, the conclusions of the various researchers tend to differ. There are those who interpret NDEs as a mere emotional reaction to the prospect of imminent death, or as a defence mechanism that attenuates the subject's fear of death. There are also those who admit the possibility of individual consciousness persisting after death, but are adamant that however many well-documented near-death experiences are recorded, none can be proven. Even Moody himself is rather negative in this respect. On the other hand, Osis and Haraldsson conclude that their data tend to confirm survival. Nevertheless, it is a fact that the greater part of the researchers in this field seem to be studying near-death experiences without paying any attention to the implications for survival of the personality after physical death.[185]

Clearly this is a question of attitude. Scientific research *in se* never yields results that by themselves can demonstrate the validity or otherwise of a philosophical or speculative assumption. It is rather in the philosophical, existential ambit that there arises a problem if we deem it sufficiently important for our life. And it is always by assuming a certain type of philosophico-existential attitude that we decide whether certain scientific data are or are not relevant in confirming our basic existential choice, our philosophical interpretation of reality. The choice is certainly not an arbitrary one: one opts for a particular interpretation of reality because one sees, feels, perceives or experiences things to be that way, or at least one has some vague intuition to this effect. In this sense, therefore, anybody who makes a certain type of choice decides that he will consider all cognitive data, including scientific data, from a certain viewpoint, in a certain perspective.

Whether or not the data bear out our interpretation depends on the data themselves, on the (more objective) manner of being of things as brought out by those data; but it also depends on the fact that we have decided to formulate that interpretation, and to confront it with those data we have deemed relevant to the issue. It thus depends on us, depends on our philosophical option, which — always provided that it is a matter of existential and not abstract philosophy — is also a choice of life. And it is on the basis of an option of this kind that I hold and consider that near-death experiences, taken together with their out-of-the-body counterparts, strongly suggest survival: not just an isolated experience, of course, not just experiences of astral projection, not just near-death experiences by themselves, but all these experiences taken together and seen in conjunction with the other experiences (and the testimonies that bear witness to them) that I propose to examine in subsequent chapters.

Chapter 5
A Light Beyond
the Half-Open Door

Among all the cases reported in the twin surveys of India and the United States that we considered in the previous chapter, Osis and Haraldsson found only one in which the subject of such a near-death experience saw the 'inferno'. This subject was a housewife of Italian origin living in Rhode Island, and she had her vision immediately after a bladder operation. It was a kind of nightmare and it brought her to the verge of insanity. The authors attribute this experience, the only one of its kind, to the strong guilt feelings this woman harboured within her: she had married a man twenty-five years her senior, and maintained an extramarital relationship, bearing a son to her lover. She had also been overwhelmed by the death of her sister, and was quite convinced that God would punish her for her sins.[186]

Though other authors may record different views,[187] there remains the striking and significant fact that in as rigorous a study as that carried out by Osis and Haraldsson, based on statistical criteria, there should be only one experience capable of being defined as 'infernal'. This almost complete absence of negative experiences of 'hell', or 'purgatory', in these pre-death visions is a fact that merits special attention: let us therefore take a closer look at this phenomenon, in the hope of seeing it in a clearer perspective. At first sight it would seem to contrast not only with the most commonly held religious beliefs, be they Christian or otherwise, but also with a great deal of

the data of paranormal experience, when interpreted in
the light of the spiritist hypothesis they seem to suggest.
As we shall see later on, many medium-istic communications speak of spheres where the entities not yet freed of
the many forms of attachment to the earth lead an
existence enmeshed in a situation that, taken as a whole,
cannot but be considered negative and is often altogether
woeful. It is through suffering that many deceased
become purified, freeing themselves of the aftermath of
their earthly passions, before they succeed in rising to a
superior spiritual and clearly positive condition.

What, then, can we say about this aspect? Can it be
fitted into a wider pattern, and if so in what way? The
first thing to note is the very close analogy that seems to
exist between these pre-death experiences and the simple
astral projections (OBEs). In *What Happens When You
Die*[188] Robert Crookall concentrates his attention on
astral projections, including the ones that we have here
considered separately under the name of pre- or near-
death experiences. Crookall also gives a special name to
the out-of-the-body experiences and astral projections
that he groups together in this manner, referring to them
as 'temporary releases' and distinguishing them from the
so-called 'permanent releases': permanent release is
death, or, if you prefer, the series of phenomena and the
experiences associated with the event of death and what
follows it; i.e. *post mortem* existence. This distinction
constitutes the starting point for a comparison that
Crookall then proceeds to make in terms that, to me at
least, seem rather appropriate.

What is it that frees itself of the physical body?
Essentially, as Crookall explains, what breaks free is a
subtle body, something that he calls 'psychical body' or
'soul body'. The natural home of this body is the kind of
paradise broadly described in Chapter 4, and whose
pronouncedly anthropomorphic character is explained by
the fact that it is a free mental creation, somewhat similar
to what happens in our dreams: it is through these
images, created in an absolutely spontaneous manner,

that there takes shape what is effectively an experience of liberation from the bonds of matter, a liberation that the subject may achieve either in definitive form (by passing away) or in temporary form (by an astral projection, which is here to be understood in the wider sense that also includes the near-death experiences).

At this point it will be helpful to make clear, as Crookall does, that the psychical body is separated from the physical one by a subtle intermediate body, the 'etheric body', 'vital body' or 'vehicle of vitality, sometimes also known as the 'veil body'. Anticipating a line of thought that will be further pursued in Chapter 8, one may here say that, while the natural environment of the psychic body is the anthropomorphic 'paradise' of a mental nature that we have already begun to glimpse, the natural environment of the 'vital body', or 'vehicle of vitality', is a condition that must be defined as clearly inferior. It is the condition that, seeking to express it by a name, the ancient Greeks call *Hades*, the Jews *Sheol*, the Tibetans *Bardo*, and the Indians *Kamaloka*.[189]

In this condition one has the feeling of being enveloped by fog, in a mental landscape that is rather dark, shadowy and squalid, well in keeping with the essentially unhappy frame of mind of the subject, who feels himself to be enmeshed in a low condition, in a state not easily shaken off. A state of non-realization, if you like. A condition of solitude. The subject feels as if he were enclosed within himself, a prisoner of himself. He could possibly free himself if he desired this in a decided manner, if he changed his personal attitude: and yet, even though he desires to break free, he does not yet succeed in willing it sufficiently.

What I have just tried to define is a rather typical way of being of the Hades condition, even though this condition is far more complex and is made up of a wide range of extremely variegated forms. We shall leave this matter for further examination in Chapter 7, where we shall review the various categories of spirits who find themselves in Hades for a certain period of time, short or long as the case may be. Here it will be sufficient to say that one does not go to Hades on account of a condemnation pronounced by a judge issuing sentences from on high, in some extrinsic manner; rather, one goes there by the action — automatic, as it were — of a law of cause and effect: it does not matter whether by one's own 'fault' or by simple effect of circumstances, the subject at this point has put himself in a certain state where, with his soul that has just freed itself of the physical body, he is determined to enter into the Hades condition.

This phenomenon can also be defined in terms of the simple relationship between the psychical body and the vital body. Entry into the Hades condition is brought about quite simply by the fact that the psychical body, though having freed itself, remains enveloped in a layer that is denser than its own vital body or vehicle of vitality. The causes responsible for this phenomenon can be defined as morally negative; but they could be any type of incident or event that causes the subject at that particular moment to project himself outside his physical body, in such a way as to leave his psychical body shrouded in a denser layer of the corresponding vital body.

It may be best to let Crookall continue in his own words. In *The Study and Practice of Astral Projections* he makes a distinction between *natural* and *enforced* out-of-the-body experiences: as far as the former are concerned, he reports cases of subjects who came close to death, who were gravely ill or exhausted, but also some involving people in the best of health; among the latter he makes a further sub-division, distinguishing between cases caused by anesthetics, suffocation, falls or hypnosis. Crookall's conclusion is that 'in those *temporary* exteriorizations which occur *naturally* only a little of the vehicle of vitality, or "body-veil", goes out with the Psychical, or Soul, Body'. On the other hand, 'in those *temporary* exteriorizations which are *enforced*, much of the "body-veil" is ejected from the body and it more or less effectively enshrouds the Psychical or Soul Body.' It is for this reason that subjects who are expelled from their physical bodies by violent action or by artificial means, generally '*either* remain in earth *or* enter "Hades" ... conditions.'[190]

It is possible to remain in the Hades condition for the entire duration of the astral projection if the psychical body continues to be encapsulated by the vital body. But if it succeeds in breaking free, albeit only partially, the subject may (though always for a limited period of time) enter or at least come to the confines or pay a brief visit, catch a glimpse as it were, of that 'paradise' beyond (so-called simply for want of a better term).

A rather characteristic sensation that may be felt by a subject who projects himself astrally with his physical body enshrouded by a dense layer of the vital body, can be that of seeing all around him 'a foggish light'.[191] This expression, which Crookall uses in connection with one of the cases he has analyzed, can be compared with other testimonies, a case in point being reported by Kenneth Ring.[192] In Ring's case, indeed, the subjects generally recall a sensation somewhat like floating, or travelling suspended in mid-air, through a kind of tunnel or some kind of vast space without any particular shape or size. This environment seemed pitch-black, or very dark, and sometimes even a little less dark or even of a whitish colour. The passages from the testimonies that Ring reproduces verbatim give the impression that this type of experience continued for the entire duration of the astral projection (or near-death experience), or that it lasted for a very long time before the subject eventually attained to an experience of light. One of these subjects, a woman who came close to death in the course of an open-heart operation, stated quite explicitly that, while she was passing through a dark tunnel that seemed to have no end, she kept saying to herself: 'When am I going to see the light? I'm dead, but when am I going to see the light?'. She closed her account by telling the interviewer: 'It seemed there was no light. I never saw the light.'[193]

To establish a parallel with the kind of detachment of

the soul from the psychical body that is no longer temporary but definitive, let us add, still guided by Crookall's conclusions, that something very similar can happen, for example, to a person who dies suddenly and in the flower of his youth. In this case, once again, we have a violent, enforced detachment that, just as in the case of an astral projection caused by an accident or some artificial device, maintains the subject in an earthly condition and so makes him experience Hades conditions. Thus a soul who on passing away 'is yet enshrouded by the "body-veil", or vehicle of vitality, may have difficulty in seeing the "earth-veil" or "Hades condition".' It may well be that he will not even see the spirits who have come to help him, even though at that moment they may be very close at hand. His manner of seeing the new world he has reached will 'tend, at least at first, to be vague, unsatisfactory and dream-like'.[194] Indeed, Crookall draws a very precise parallel between the situation of a subject who suffers an astral projection in a violent and enforced manner, and that of a person who dies suddenly, in the flower of his youth, or in a negative context, where the natural course of things suffers violence or undergoes a forced change.

Having summarized these conclusions reached by Crookall, we can now return to the one atypical case reported by Osis and Haraldsson, where an American housewife had a vision of 'hell' during an astral projection. Let us note, first of all, that the terms in which the experience is reported suggest that it is to be likened to an astral projection in the strict sense rather than to a near-death experience: in fact, the woman did not come close to death, she simply had her vision while undergoing a bladder operation. This means that she must first have been anesthetized, presumably total anesthesia. It was therefore the anesthetic that induced her astral projection. In other words, we here have a case of astral projection caused by artificial means. We are thus back to the type of case considered by Crookall (who concluded that the subject of an astral projection caused by unnatural factors either remains attached to the terrene sphere or enters, albeit for a limited period of time, into Hades conditions). The artificial character of her projection therefore already predisposed this Rhode Island patient to the alternative possibility of projecting herself, if not into a wholly earthly environment, at least into the Hades sphere. The guilt feelings that haunted this woman then did the rest, ensuring that what would otherwise have been a Hades experience, somewhat vague and colourless, would assume the terrifying outlines of a vivid vision of hell painted in all the colours of the patient's religious traditions. Quite apart from the extremely dramatic and disconcerting character of the experience undergone by this woman, one cannot but note at this point that cases of astral projection — and I am here using the term in the wider sense — connected with experience of Hades conditions, must be far more frequent than is suggested by the cases that Osis and Haraldsson report from India and the United States. Crookall, indeed, almost arrives at establishing a rule to the effect that those who are projected in a forced and unnatural manner will either enter Hades for a very limited time, or will remain altogether attached to the earth.

But let us linger for a moment and give more detailed consideration to the point on which Osis and Haraldsson concentrate their attention. Their study is focused on near-death experiences. Even though Crookall tends to liken near-death experiences to astral projections, there would yet seem to come to the fore a factor that very clearly differentiates near-death experiences (at least those to be understood as such in the strict sense) from out-of-the-body experiences or astral projections. True pre-death experiences are those in which the subject, either instantaneously or very rapidly, finds himself thrown into the 'paradise' sphere that lies beyond Hades. Hades is therefore crossed in a few fleeting moments: this rapid passage of Hades finds its symbolic expression in the experience of crossing the famous tunnel, the dark approach that leads into Paradise with all its light. It corresponds to the emerging of the psychical body from the 'veil' constituted by the 'vehicle of vitality'.[195]

It may well be that the aforementioned 'law' (if we may call it such) suggested by Crookall is applicable to astral projections in the strict sense, rather than to near-death experiences. The character of astral projections seems more prone to being conditioned by external factors (Crookall speaks of anesthetics, suffocations, falls and hypnosis), while the observations of Osis and Haraldsson suggest that near-death experiences cannot be so conditioned. This difference may be due to the fact that near-death experiences go well beyond the pure and simple astral projections. Quite independently of any external causes acting in an accidental, artificial or even violent manner, once the typical mechanism of a near-death experience has been triggered in a given subject, this experience, as Osis and Haraldsson keep on under-scoring, can no longer be conditioned by such external factors. This pre-death experience, once it has begun, once the subject has set his foot on the road, as it were, runs its course in a manner in conformity with its nature. Pre-and near-death experience appear to be a small foretaste of what the true and full death of the subject is going to be like. The Hades experience, on the other hand, is an 'en route' experience, an experience of near-death, of incomplete death, of death that has not yet attained its natural goal. For this reason, a pre-death experience, precisely because it constitutes a foretaste of the experience of true and full death (i.e. of the goal to be attained) is necessarily different from a Hades experience, which is an experience of incomplete death, of having turned back from half-way along the road.

It would seem that dreams are on the boundary of astral projections, and that certain dreams can be defined as incomplete astral experiences.[196] Here the psychical body would seem to emerge from the physical body, though it remains well enshrouded in the famous 'veil': hence the impression of fogginess, of vagueness, of indistinct shapes, that dreams normally leave with us.

As an aide-mémoire or schematic image, think of a ladder where the lowest rung constitutes the soul (or psychical body) perfectly integrated in the vital body and the physical body. The second rung would be when the soul emerges from the physical body, though it still remains shrouded in the veil of the vital body. The coming forth of the soul 'dressed' or 'wrapped' in this manner, could be very fragmentary, in which case one would have no more than a normal dream. A less incomplete emergence of the soul, though still wrapped in the vital veil, would give rise to the type of astral projection that is caused by artificial means, and that leads the subject to go through a Hades experience, feeling himself surrounded by fog, etc. (in keeping with Crookall's definition). When the soul succeeds in detaching itself from the body in a definitive manner (on the occasion of death), though even then remaining for some time wrapped in the usual veil, one would arrive at a *post mortem* experience of the Hades type (in line with the other definition given us by the same author). Complete emergence of the soul, either already devoid (or almost) of the veil or succeeding to break free of it (or almost) as it passes on its way, would give rise to a typical pre-death experience with its glimpse of the anthropomorphic 'paradise' of mental creation to which we have already dedicated considerable attention, quoting a large variety of examples. A definitive detachment of the unveiled or almost unveiled soul from the vehicle of vitality, or even of a soul that succeeds in freeing itself of the veil after the detachment has taken place, would lead to permanent entry of the deceased into the previously glimpsed 'paradise' condition.

No matter what causes may have produced it, a near-death experience is always a foretaste of the ultimate goal. It is like the experience a mountaineer may have when, raising his head and looking upwards, there appears the top of the mountain unencumbered by clouds. He sees the top, his eyes behold the goal, even though this does not mean that he is about to attain it.

Perhaps there is still a long way to go, the remaining climb may even be difficult and painful. Let us imagine a man who is still enmeshed, and deeply so, in a manner of being that keeps him low down; and let us imagine that this man, thanks to the convergence of circumstances and factors of a fortuitous nature, succeeds for a moment in having an ecstatic vision of the ultimate goal of perfection that awaits him at the end of his road of evolution. It is a moment of exaltation and ecstasis, a moment when a man feels himself taken up and swept on high. But it is a flight that he cannot sustain for very long, it is just a brief flight that will inevitably be followed by a drop back into his usual manner of being, a condition from which he will be able to raise himself only little by little, step by step. It may be that our subject may have a pre-death experience of a truly transcendental nature, and yet, upon real death, will have to spend a long time in the Hades condition before he will eventually succeed in making a permanent entry into a 'paradise' condition.

Perhaps an example drawn from religious experience will make this a little clearer. Ecstasis by itself does not make a saint. Rather, true saints will distrust those who seek ecstasis for its own sake: they will exhort them to progress in the love of God, in dedication, in virtue, in the spirit of sacrifice, in sanctity understood as an offering to God of the whole of one's being and of every action and instant of one's life. An ecstatic condition, albeit even a permanent one, will then come of its own accord as the result of effective progress on the road to sanctity, of sanctity pursued as such and for its own sake. It is sometimes said that God grants a few moments of ecstasis to the soul at the very moment when it sets out on this road: it is a kind of spiritual 'sweetening' that God grants as a reward, but also and above all as an encouragement to face the subsequent trials with courage and tenacity, for they could be very hard indeed. But the ecstasis will be followed by the 'dark nights', by the moments of aridity, the temptations, the wilderness of the soul, the moments of loneliness and the 'God, why has thou forsaken me?'; the moments when, hammered in the forge, the soul will really become purified and tempered, eventually to be transformed into the pure vehicle of the divine presence, into 'man of God', into 'angel' who announces God and truly manifests him. [197]

Just as ecstasis does not make a saint, so the mere fact that a human subject has a near-death experience in transcendental terms does not imply, by itself, that the man in question will go 'straight to paradise' on dying. It could well be that at the moment of having the experience, he succeeded in briefly freeing himself from the wrapping of carnality that usually encumbers him and clouds his vision. The veil, however, is destined to fall back on him, to enshroud him and to become of even greater encumbrance as soon as he returns to his customary mode of being; this mode is the only one that really counts in determining his immediate *post mortem* destination, the initial phase of his ultraterrene existence.

If this conclusion were not valid, there is yet another hypothesis to formulate and put forward: it could be that all the subjects who have a near-death experience of a transcendental nature do so because the transparency that is revealed to them at that moment, far from deriving from purely accidental causes, really corresponds to a transparency that characterizes their normal and stable way of being. In other words, all such people are 'pure souls' and, as such, infallibly destined to reach paradise; that is to say, to gain access to that happy sphere immediately after death, and to do so in an authentic and direct manner. But where does that leave the souls who are destined to pass a more or less long waiting period in Hades (a condition that makes its appearance in a wide range of different religions and the reality of which is attested, as we shall subsequently see in Chapter 7, by a very large number of mediumistic communications)? Would one have to conclude that every time one of these souls passes through a near-death condition, the experience that is associated with it is either not consciously lived or is immediately forgotten? If so, we would be face-to-face with the provident cunning of Nature, which — given the inevitability of death — has no wish to discourage anybody and, if anything, encourages creatures in such a way as to predispose them to face the moment of death with serene abandon.

In sharp contrast with this suggestion, however, we could return to our erstwhile hypothesis, though completing it with a further assumption that would place these experiences or interior events into a different temporal order. Why, indeed, should we not assume that a soul, either at the moment of death or immediately after, can have such visions of paradise (or at least analogously gratifying experiences of liberation)? And then, at a later stage, pass through the Hades experience that is its destiny until such time as it achieves its purification? A hypothesis of this kind is supported by, among others, the following excerpts from communications received personally by me, and which, taken in their overall context, seem fairly credible (though I cannot guarantee their authenticity in any way).

An entity presenting itself as 'Don Guglielmo', a deceased Catholic priest, says:

> 'As soon as the body dies and the soul is set free, the experience is wonderful, but afterwards you have to purify yourself ... [In purgatory] you feel all alone ... there is a terrifying silence [and] it all seems as if it would never end.'

Another soul, a deceased school teacher, declared that he went through an experience of the kind we have here designated by the name of Hades. He attributed this to having been a 'materialist' throughout his life. Here is how he summarized his *post mortem* experiences up to that moment:

> 'As soon as I died, I saw beautiful landscapes and heard enchanting music, but then I found myself in a silent and desolate place that was full of smoke.'

Lastly he said that he had been 'fast asleep', immersed

in a 'long slumber' from which he had awoken only a
little while ago, though without having as yet recovered
his memory, nor even his name.

No matter what might be the answer to this problem,
which is certainly not an easy one to solve, the striking
concordance of these near-death experiences strongly
suggests that our destiny is not annihilation but that we
can look forward to a survival that could be unlimited,
the attainment of a condition of full and happy spiritual
life. As regards the modalities of this condition, and
whether it represents our ultimate destination or will
eventually be left behind to pass on to something that
awaits us beyond, even further along the scale of possibilities — all these remain open questions and represent
great problems. How can we face up to them? How can
we seek to solve them? We could do this in an abstract
manner, entrusting our search to purely rational considerations, be they apriorist, interferential or exigeant,
considerations of the type already referred to in Chapter
2; but there also remains open to us the other possibility,
namely to keep on using the phenomenological method
that we have employed up to this point and which
seemingly has not been wholly devoid of results, though I
do not want to deceive myself unduly on this score.

Let us therefore concentrate our attention on the
phenomenon and the manner in which it presents itself.
Let us consider the experiences and the testimonies that
we can gather. Let us continue resolutely along this road
of analyzing experiences, this time focusing our attention
not on the testimony of men who still live in our midst,
but rather on that of the deceased, who come to testify —
once again with suggestive and no less impressive
concordance — through mediums; at least those of them
that can reasonably be considered among the more
reliable.

Chapter 6
The Crisis of Death

Analyzing the essential characteristics of out-of-the-body and near-death experiences, we have been able to note many respects in which they resemble each other, many features they have in common. As we now extend our analysis, we shall be able to note similar coincidences, just as specific and numerous, between these experiences and those of the crisis of death and the new life that awaits us after death. Indeed, as David Lorimer puts it, if 'near-death experiences are an extension of OBEs', it is equally true that 'reports of the death experience include the features noted under NDEs', even though 'this time there is no return to the physical body.'[198]

Who, then, can provide us with testimony of these death experiences? Certainly not 'living' men still incarnate in this earthly dimension. Projectors have told of their experiences out of the body, just as resuscitated patients, and even the sick and dying (while still alive), have testified about their experiences up to the point at which they themselves arrived. But the experience of death, no matter how many affinities it may have with astral projections and near-death experiences, no matter how close a relationship of analogy and continuity may link it to such experiences without any real solution of continuity, is and remains a further experience that no 'live' person in this world can recount. We have therefore to turn to the 'dead', or rather, to the deceased, those who have passed on, always provided that it is possible to establish some kind of a communication with them.

Can we deny *a priori* that such a possibility exists? If nothing else, survival is at least a hypothesis — and one that the facts we have analyzed so far cannot but enhance. If the deceased therefore survive in some dimension or other, no matter how different it may be from our own, what could possibly authorize us to deny any and all possibility of communicating with them before we have examined, with all due attention, the presumed messages they send us?

When coming face-to-face with any new phenomenon, one can in the last resort adopt only one of two basic attitudes. Firstly, one can classify it, collocate it, label it. Indeed, this is a very common and widespread habit: sometimes one does it to deny the phenomenon or to reduce its import; sometimes one seeks to affirm its existence in a particularly positive manner, granting it a maximum of space and importance. But there is also the exact opposite attitude, that of showing oneself wholly open and receptive, suspending as far as possible any judgements and prejudices one is tempted to formulate before having had sufficient time to appreciate the phenomenon in all its manifestations. This is the attitude of availability, of readiness to listen and perceive. It is a phenomenological attitude. An important school of thought, a branch of philosophy that has flourished since the beginnings of our century, adopts this method, which is simply that of going out to meet things as they reveal themselves, to see phenomena as they present themselves: this school of philosophy is therefore known as phenomenology.

As far as mediumistic communications are concerned, there already exists an extensive literature. These communications claim to offer us messages coming from 'beyond'. There are people who acknowledge this claim and accept it in exactly the terms in which it is offered: they are the so-called spiritists, people who give these messages a spiritist interpretation, attributing them to the 'spirits' of the deceased, to 'entities' that manifest themselves, so it is held, through the vehicle of the 'medium'. There are also people who, though admitting the good faith of the mediums and others attending these séances, consider the messages themselves as the product of an elaboration that essentially takes place in the unconscious of the medium, with the additional possibility of contributions from the psychisms of other people in attendance, though generally without their being aware of this. It could be that in the medium there form what psychologists are wont to call 'secondary personalities'. But it could also be that such secondary personalities are formed with the contribution of psychic energies unconsciously poured out by each of those present, energies that would thus come to constitute an autonomous and independent thought form, with its own life and a limited initiative of its own; in other words, they would come to constitute a kind of fictitious personality. This second hypothesis, which is clearly in contrast with the spiritist view, is traditionally known as the 'animist hypothesis'.

It does not necessarily follow that all the paranormal phenomena of a spiritual trend have to be interpreted exclusively on the basis of either of these two hypotheses. Certain phenomena that at first sight appear to be spiritist in nature, expressing themselves in terms of communications, responses, messages, etc., clearly reveal themselves to be of unconscious origin as soon as they are studied just a little more carefully: it soon becomes apparent that it is really the medium who is talking, expressing his or her repressed desires, frustrated aspirations, and so on; i.e. his own personal psychic problems. But the fact that some, or perhaps many, of these phenomena appear to be of an animist nature does not imply that the animist interpretation must be applied to all the possible phenomena. Indeed, there are other phenomena that strongly suggest a spiritist interpretation such that the attempt to explain and interpret them entirely on an animist basis would do no more than provide an 'explanation' so forced, contorted and improbable as to make the spiritist explanation seem simple common sense, and a welcome relief from the mental meanders and immense toil involved in the animist approach.

The conclusion cannot but be as follows: the extent of the paranormal phenomena suggesting a spiritist interpretation is so consistent and complex, that exclusion of all possibility of explaining them on this basis is too arbitrary an act. The best and most prudent thing to do is simply to suspend and postpone any definitive judgement.

The known facts suggest the survival of disincarnate souls in a dimension different from our own, although they can in some way return here to manifest themselves to us, to communicate with us. Let us now see to what extent this survivalist and spiritist interpretation is supported by the facts. If we want to test the validity of this interpretation, we can assume it as a working hypothesis. In other words, we shall consider the phenomena *as if* the spiritist hypothesis were true and then see what happens. From this moment onwards, therefore, I shall talk about the more credible mediumistic messages as if they really came from disincarnate souls: let it be clearly understood, however, that I do so by way of hypothesis, trying to see what emerges as we proceed along this road, and also testing whether the overall picture is consistent with itself and the totality of the phenomena considered or, alternatively, contradicted either internally or by the facts. Lastly, even if I felt able at a certain point to draw a positive conclusion, this would not necessarily commit the reader, who remains free to judge for himself, to draw his own conclusions.

Having thus decided to proceed on the assumption that the deceased really do survive and can in some way communicate with us, I am left wondering in what terms I should refer to them. I prefer not to call them 'dead', for in the perspective that is beginning to unfold in front of us they are as alive as we and, in certain respects at least, far more alive. We could rather refer to them as the 'passed on' or the 'deceased', this in the sense that they have left our world, that they no longer have a function, a task, an earthly mission to perform. As to ourselves, still in this terrene dimension, it would be quite inappropriate if — in the perspective we are about to consider — we were to designate ourselves purely and simply as the 'living': we are not the only living, if anything we are those who 'live incarnate', we are the living whose soul or psyche is still incarnate in a physical body. Subject to this clarification and for want of a better term, we shall nevertheless refer to ourselves as the 'live' or the 'living' in this conventional sense.

I suggest the first reference to be made in coming to grips with the theme of the crisis of death is to a book by Ernesto Bozzano entitled *The Crisis of Death as Described by Communicating Deceased*.[199] Getting to grips with a new argument is somewhat like entering water. One can do it little by little, starting from the beach or bank, first testing the water with our toes to make sure that it is not too cold for comfort, and then immersing first the entire foot, the ankle, the knees, and so on, advancing slowly toward the deep until the water reaches right up to one's neck. But there is another way of getting into the water: one can simply dive in. This may take a little courage, but once done, one is in the water and can swim at ease. Readers will recall that in the previous chapter we came to grips with the theme of *near-death experiences* by considering the general characterization given by Raymond Moody. Before that, we had done something very similar in connection with *out-of-the-body experiences* by direct, though necessarily summary, reference to the results of the well-known survey made by Celia Green. In facing up to our third theme, the *crisis of death*, it would be as well to repeat this approach and dive right into the topic by referring directly (once again in summary fashion) to the overall characterization of this experience that Bozzano gives in a well-known passage from his book listing twelve *fundamental features*.

Bozzano, who in his day was probably the greatest

living expert on paranormal phenomenology, felt justified in making the following affirmation at the end of his book:

> 'The mediumistic messages in which the spirits of the deceased describe the various phases through which they passed in the crisis of death, and the manner in which they entered into the spiritual environment, match each other so closely ... that one cannot find a single case which is at variance with the affirmations of other communicating spirits.'[200]

It is quite true, of course, that here, as always, one has the exceptions that prove the rule. These exceptions can occur in one of two forms: they can either modify, abbreviate or eliminate some experiences, or they can give rise to other and unusual experiences. Basing ourselves on what has been said so far, we shall for the moment accept Bozzano's conclusions as a working hypothesis, though not without checking them more thoroughly at a later stage. After describing the crisis of death in terms in which each communicating spirit claims to have experienced it, Bozzano notes that they all concord in the following features, affirming:

> '1. That all of them eventually found themselves in human form in the spiritual world.
>
> 2. That for some time, or even for a long period of time, they did not realize they were dead.
>
> 3. That during the pre-death crisis, or a little after, they passed through the trial of summarily recalling all the events of their existence ("panoramic vision" or "epilogue of death").
>
> 4. That in the spiritual world they were welcomed by the spirits of their relatives or friends.
>
> 5. That nearly all of them passed through a more or less lengthy phase of reparatory sleep.
>
> 6. That they eventually found themselves in a radiant and marvellous spiritual environment (in the case of morally normal deceased), or in a shadowy and oppressive environment (in the case of morally depraved deceased).
>
> 7. That they had found the spiritual environment to be a

new world that was objective, substantial and real, a spiritualized version of the earthly environment.

8. That they had learnt that this was due to the fact that thought was a creative force in the spiritual world and thus enabled a spirit living in the "astral place" to reproduce around himself the environment of his memories.

9. That it had not taken them long to learn that thought transmission was the language of spirits, even though newly arrived spirits delude themselves that they converse by means of words.

10. That they had found that the faculty of spiritual vision enabled them to perceive objects simultaneously on all sides, just as they could see inside them and through them.

11. That they had discovered that spirits could instantaneously take themselves from one place to another — even when they were very far apart — by virtue of an act of will; nevertheless, they could walk in the spiritual environment or float a short distance above the ground.

12. That they had learned that the spirits of the deceased will fatally and automatically gravitate to the spiritual sphere to which they belong, this by virtue of the "law of affinity".'[201]

In quoting Bozzano's conclusions word for word, I intend formulating a series of theses that I hope will not shock my readers unduly, but nevertheless stimulate their curiosity: they are theses that I must now try, if not to 'demonstrate', at least to develop further, explain, argue, support with facts in one way or another, and within the limits to which this can be done in a brief overall treatment of this type. As with the out-of-the-body and near-death experiences, I shall now pass on to dealing with experiences of the crisis of death in detail, point by point. In doing so, however, I shall not follow the order in which Bozzano lists the basic features, but rather adopt a 'logical' order that seems more appropriate in facilitating the general unfolding of the facts.

I have already had occasion to mention the existence of a very extensive mediumistic literature, referring to this even in the Introduction to this book, and the time has now come to illustrate matters by specific quotations from various texts that form part of this literature. I propose to do so by reviewing, above all, books that provide testimony of specific experiences, or at least purport to give such testimony. I shall be far more sparing in quoting what one might call more doctrinal volumes, limiting myself to such passages as either relate experiences that one presumes to have been really lived, or which review such experiences in a more or less direct and straightforward manner. The fact that I make no mention of the works of Emanuel Swedenborg and Allen Kardec is justified not because I consider them to be irrelevant, for this is far from being the case, but rather because I prefer to draw my material generally from books less committed from a theoretical and speculative point of view, thus limiting myself to mentioning only straightforward testimonies of experiences that seem to be reasonably free of prejudice and not written for the specific purpose of demonstrating some point. Although I can undoubtedly be accused of other omissions, they are justified by similar considerations. I shall make only very few exceptions to this rather rigorous criterion, generally for special reasons that will become evident in each case.

We can now pass on to individual accounts of the crisis of death and what follows it. I have already mentioned the fact that, in a certain sense, the deceased can be defined as 'alive'. In analyzing her new experience, for example, a woman who had only recently passed away remarked that it was indeed a very strange sensation to know oneself to be dead and yet to feel so exuberantly alive.[202] This experience of feeling so extraordinarily alive from the first moment of awaking in the other dimension, is reported in innumerable other testimonies to be found in this type of literature.

In this connection it seems only natural to me to recall the beginning of the well-known book *A Heretic in Heaven*, which its transcendental author, a deceased who identifies himself as 'Daddy' (a 'euphonious sobriquet given him whilst still on earth'), opens with the following words:

'I am dead. Very dead. Dead to time, dead to sense, dead to matter. Dead to all those animal instincts, surgings and cravings which, if the earth man wishes to make a success of his life, he must curb and control. Dead to all those cramping, confining limitations which characterize terrestrial life. But alive — wonderfully alive — in the life that really matters.'[203]

Another book, *The Other Side God's Door*, quotes the words that a deceased, known on earth as Tom Barry, uses to announce himself:

'Tom Barry is not the Tom Barry you used to know. He is many times more alive and hopeful, and full of promise of things he never dreamed of on earth.'[204]

When we look at the existence of the newly deceased once he has overcome the crisis of death and fully passed into the other dimension, we shall see little by little that this sense of being more alive than ever before is accompanied by an extraordinary sense of mental lucidity and of liberation of the mind from the bonds of matter, so much so that the mind can forge its individuality and even the external environment — within certain limits — by mere virtue of acts of thought.

Here is how the entity 'Felicia Scatcherd' described her decease, which occurred in very favourable circumstances:

'I got very tired and so drowsy, I slipped off in the morning into a light sleep, I think — then I saw strange lights, curious glowing threads, and I felt myself floating and my brain seemed so clear — and I said to myself "I am quite well; I knew I should recover". I soon began to realise what that recovery meant! I felt so free mentally, I longed to write things and to meet people, and to talk to them and tell them I felt as if I were twenty again ... I got rather sleepy again — the threads still held me and made me sleepy ... I was not actually asleep; it was just as if I was comfortably drowsy, and old, happy memories came before me ...'[205]

One may here note that what is going on is a process by

which the soul breaks free of the body. This process is gradual and continuous, but not devoid of phases of turning back: when these take place, the subject has the impression of becoming drowsy. Then the psyche takes another step forward, moving in the direction of ever greater detachment: to the extent to which it succeeds in breaking free, the subject increasingly identifies himself with nothing but his soul and becomes possessed also by a sense of great mental vivacity and clarity, eventually passing through the experience of panoramic vision of his entire life spent on earth.

'All the lovely scenes of the past that you have forgotten, scenes in your earth life, will pass before you like a panoramic vision and bring it all back again,' is the way an entity puts it in Arthur Findlay's *The Way of Life*.[206] And not only the beautiful memories, because this vision — which, as we have seen, can occur also in a near-death experience — makes it possible for the subject to assess how he spent his past existence on earth: 'I could see everything I'd ever done wrong at once', recalls a British soldier killed by shell splinters during the First World War.[207]

Let me note here, that in this particular case the panoramic vision of the subject's past life assumed very markedly the character of an examination of conscience, and that this examination of conscience took place before a 'being of light'. In this case the being is Jesus Christ, the soldier having two successive visions of him. He first saw the crucified Jesus. A few moments after this first vision had dissolved, the young man again saw Jesus, this time coming towards him in a blaze of light. It was at this point that our soldier felt himself driven to ask forgiveness for his past shortcomings that had been brought home to him in the instant of the panoramic vision with which we are here concerned. The spirit guide presiding over these mediumistic communications asserts that 'many soldiers see visions of the Christ' at the moment of death.[208] Quite apart from the personal considerations with which the guide seeks to explain the fact (which are opinions and therefore fallible, as he himself admits), we here have an attestation of a phenomenon that if not universal is at least very common, and corroborates what we have already noted in Chapter 4 about the appearance of the 'being of light' in near-death experiences.

Paul Beard, in his book *Living On*, notes that 'many accounts describe a meeting with the Christ, some of them at very early stages in discarnate life.'[209] This could really be Christ, as the author immediately goes on to say, but also a very elevated Being who appears with the features of the Christ or is mistaken for him.

Basing myself on the results of my own researches regarding this aspect, I would be inclined to go no further than to take this 'being of light' as a 'guide'. It could possibly be a soul of a higher level, this greater elevation expressing itself also in visual form and giving rise to the greater brightness with which other souls perceive its image. This guide seemingly has the mission of welcoming the newly deceased and instructing them, thus helping them to accept their new state and to put themselves into the spiritual condition that will enable them to progress therein.

That such a 'being of light' or 'guide' can be mistaken for Christ can be readily deduced from an example that I take from Neville Randall's *Life After Death*: immediately after his decease, a certain Mr Higgins found himself by the edge of a river, though with no idea of where the river might be, and saw a young man in a long habit coming towards him; he first took him to be a monk, but then thought that it could also be Jesus, since he bore a marked resemblance to the traditional iconographic representations of the divine personage; very quickly, however, he realized that it was neither Jesus nor a monk, but a spiritual guide who had been assigned the task of receiving him in the beyond, comforting him and giving him the first instructions so badly needed by his disconcerted and bewildered spirit.[210]

Similar versions of 'beings of light' in long habits,

taken to be Christ, are also found in certain near-death phenomena as described by Paola Giovetti,[211] who also reports the relevant testimonies. While this annotation really forms part of the subject matter considered in Chapter 4, it here confirms the fact that a being of light, though no more than a simple guide, can be perceived as a very high spiritual figure — or even the highest — of the tradition to which the newly deceased belongs. Now, each tradition can have its corresponding beyond (or, if you prefer, its corresponding slice or section of the beyond), and the guides of this beyond cannot but be in a very close relationship with the highest of the sacred figures of the given tradition.[212]

But let us rather give another individual example that will bring us back to the panoramic vision theme, quoting the case of a soldier who died of typhus in a military hospital during the American Civil War. Remarking that dying was a little like falling asleep, 'Jim Nolan' went on to say that just a moment prior to the fatal crisis his mind had become extremely active: 'I thought of every incident and circumstance of my life. I could see and hear all that ever transpired with which I was associated. I recalled jokes, fun and frolic, and enjoyed them as I did when first I heard them around the camp-fire.'[213] This last remark shows that the panoramic vision cannot really be defined as a memory, but rather represents a re-enactment of one's past life, which is relived in a very intense fashion, in some way projected into the present, felt for a moment as re-happening in the present.

This feeling of being more alive than ever that comes with the lethal crisis and immediate post-mortem period, is associated also with a feeling of still being the same person. The 'I' is not dissolved, nor is the personality annihilated: 'I am the same old Rudy you knew before, only now I am a Rudy heightened in perceptive faculty. And I seem to feel emotions more keenly too.'[214]

The entity 'Julia Ames' explains this in an even more specific fashion:

'When the soul leaves the body it remains exactly the same as when it was in the body; the soul, which is the only real self, and which uses the mind and the body as its instruments, no longer has the use or the need of the body. But it retains the mind, the knowledge, the experience, the habits of thought, the inclinations; they remain exactly as they were. Only it often happens that the gradual decay of the fleshy envelope to some extent obscures and impairs the real self which is liberated by death.'[215]

The newly deceased realizes that just as he survives, so also do the others, each with his own personality. Indeed, he experiences this almost right away when, either immediately after death or sometimes just before dying, he becomes aware of the presence of dear friends and relatives who died before him and now come forward to meet him, to receive him on the threshold of the new dimension that he has entered or is about to enter.

'Felicia Scatcherd', in the communication from which I have already quoted, tells us that, at the moment of her decease, the soul's detachment from the body was facilitated by the attitude of absolute calm she assumed on the advice of spiritual entities who had come forward to help her:

'I did as I was told — I kept very quiet and then gradually there came a change; the threads disappeared. I was in a kind of cloud that took shape gradually, and I found it was my own shape, just the invisible body, but I learnt from the others I could mould it and make it with my mind.'[216]

In another communication we are told that the ethereal body abandons the physical one in much the same way as a butterfly emerges from its chrysalis; and, as soon as this happens, other spirits come to the help of the newly discarnate spirit. To all intents and purposes, 'it is a new birth'. The soul arriving at the dimension of the beyond is 'like a new born babe in every truth, So bewildered, so utterly at a loss.' So much so, that often the spirit believes he is in a dream. 'Well,' as the communication continues, 'first we have to convince him that he is dead.'²¹⁷ As a general rule — even though such a rule can have many exceptions caused by a wide variety of circumstances — the newly deceased first meets all or some of his dear ones, and they have the task of first receiving the souls who pass over into the spirit world.

How does the newly deceased manage to recognize his dear ones? He does so not only because he feels or perceives their spiritual presence, but also because he sees them in exactly the same way as he did when they were alive in this world. This should not surprise the reader at all, for we saw in Chapters 1 and 3 that assuming a form similar to that of the physical body, a form in some way both visual and perceived by the senses, is a process that already occurs spontaneously in astral projections. Rather, we there saw the process taking place in all its various phases.

Each of the previously deceased friends or relatives who comes to meet the new arrival in the spirit world can therefore make sure of being recognized by presenting himself in exactly the same form he had while on earth; this form can correspond to the one he had at the time of his death, but sometimes the spirit may also seem as if rejuvenated or, if he died while still a child, as if he had grown up in the meantime. While the first manner of presentation is intended to make recognition easy and immediate, the second (rejuvenated) manner represents a visual — and also symbolic — expression of the fact that the deceased in question has become spiritually young again (now that he has freed himself of his old and probably decrepit physical body); or, in cases where death occurred at an early age, that he has 'grown' spiritually, that he has matured in a spiritual sense.

This meeting with one's dear ones is a theme that crops up all the time in experiences of the crisis of death: all the communicating deceased testify that such an encounter takes place sooner or later, generally at a rather early stage and, in some cases, even prior to death. The testimonies that diverge from this pattern are those of the so-called earthbound spirits; i.e. spirits who have not yet succeeded in fully passing over and have therefore remained in the Hades condition, either in solitude or in the company of other entities in a similarly low condition, but in either case cut off, for the moment, from the spiritual level where their dear ones, entities of a higher vibrational level, can render themselves perceivable. But the fact that they remain temporarily invisible for the newly deceased who have remained at a lower spiritual level does not prevent them from helping their dear ones in an unbeknown manner. One of the fundamental laws that seem to regulate existence in the other dimension is, in fact, that entities who have attained a higher level can see and watch those who have remained at a lower stage, while the opposite is impossible.

The newly deceased thus sees his dear ones or other spirits who come to receive him, help him, instruct him, guide him: as a general rule, moreover, he sees them in bodily form, even though these spirits no longer have a physical body. Considering every other person to be associated with a bodily form is a mental habit that operates within us even in our dreams, where we see in bodily form even human persons who do not exist or, at least, do not exist in those particular dream situations. In our dreams, moreover, we also see a great many things of our world in their accustomed empirical forms, even though, strictly speaking, the things we see do not exist or are not as we see them. This helps us to understand two specific aspects: firstly, that the mechanism of our mental habits in some way co-operates to ensure that the deceased will see other deceased in human form, and secondly, that the dying, the moribund, will likewise see in human form the spirits of their friends and relatives who come to welcome them. [218]

One may argue here that a person about to die finds himself in a state of altered consciousness and that his visions can therefore be hallucinatory, that they do not correspond to truth and that his testimony is highly suspect. But objections of this kind can be answered by noting that what the moribund see is often confirmed

The Crisis of Death

from other sources. Quite apart from the observations of Osis and Haraldsson reported and discussed in summary form at the end of the last chapter, which would seem to lend considerable support to the transcendental visions of the dying, there is yet another important consideration to make; that in some cases these visions have also been confirmed by clairvoyants. The clairvoyants in question, being people in good health and therefore of sound mind and body, can be regarded as more credible from this particular point of view: it would therefore be rather significant if they should see the same things as the dying tell us they perceive in the terminal phases of life.

There is certainly no lack of testimony in which such sensitives confirm the visions of the moribund. However, I shall limit myself to a single example as representative of the very large number that could be quoted in support of this contention. Gastone De Boni recalls the case of a nurse, Joy Snell, who, being also a valid medium, had the same visions as the dying patients she was looking after, saw the same deceased persons as appeared to them and was therefore in a position to confirm their testimonies to the full. On one occasion she was nursing a friend who was dying of pneumonia. An hour before he eventually passed away he fixed his eyes high up on the ceiling in front of him and said that he saw his little boy who had died the year before at the age of six. The nurse, who had known the child very well, could not but confirm the exactness of what her dying patient was asserting. Moreover, she was also able to follow the gradual process by which the ethereal body of her friend was breaking free. When completely detached from the physical body, the child took his father by the hand, and together the two astral forms moved away and disappeared. 'Joy Snell tells us,' so De Boni concludes his account, 'that no patient of hers ever died without her seeing by his bedside one or more angelic forms who had come to meet his spirit and guide it to its new dwelling place.'[219]

The newly deceased also discovers that, just like the entities that come to meet him and receive him (and afterwards also all the others he encounters), he too possesses a human form similar to the one he had on earth. This is a form that immediately reveals itself as being of a certain relative consistency, for it is a form that can be defined as being in some way bodily, even though it is no longer physical. It is a bodily form of subtler vibrations, wholly similar to the one that emerges from the physical body in out-of-the-body experiences, and also in near-death experiences when these assume a parasomatic character.

The newly deceased may find himself already in possession of a human form that has thinned and lost in consistency without his becoming aware of it, though in other cases he may follow the entire process by which his subtle bodily form gradually frees itself of the physical body. We have already seen that very often the newly deceased have the impression of reawakening in the new dimension, where they find themselves with an astral body that has already formed completely: this fact suggests that the formation of the astral body and its emergence from the physical body must have taken place while the subject was drowsy and in a state of relative unconsciousness. On other occasions, however, the deceased will follow the emergence process in all its details, a case in point being provided by the narration of 'Felicia Scatcherd' quoted earlier.

In his turn, a young Englishman killed during the fighting in the Transvaal, South Africa, tells us that he was killed almost instantaneously. Compared with the more gradual death process when decease is due to illness or old age, the detachment of the soul in this case seems to have taken place far more rapidly, though it was not unopposed and still called for some kind of effort to be made by the subject:

> 'I seemed to be tied to the physical body and to be making a great effort to get free. It was an ever-thinning cord attached to the head. I had, at first, no perceptible body, but as the separation proceeded, my spirit-form took shape. Finally I succeeded in getting free, and found

myself floating over the country and viewing the fighting.'[220]

Let us now see how this self-same process is followed from outside (i.e. by a clairvoyant present at the time of decease), rather than from within the dying person. Arthur Findlay quotes Hudson Tuttle, a sensitive, who used the following words to describe the death process of a person who had died in his presence:

> 'Slowly the spiritual form [spiritual body] withdrew from the extremities and concentrated in the brain. As it did so, a halo arose from the crown of the head which gradually increased. Soon it became clear and distinct, and I observed that it had the exact resemblance of the form it had left. Higher and higher it arose, until the beautiful spirit stood before us and the dead body reclined below. A slight cord connected the two, which, gradually diminishing, became in a few minutes absorbed and the spirit had forever quitted its earthly temple.'[221]

Testimonies confirming this given by Hudson Tuttle in even more detailed terms are very numerous indeed, but for our immediate purposes we shall limit ourselves to quoting his words by way of example.

What is this 'cord' that is mentioned in the testimonies? It is a fluid filament that continues to connect the soul to the body until it breaks free and projects itself. Keeping the vehicle of vitality united to the body, the astral cord makes it possible for the physical organism to receive the transmission of vital forces that in themselves belong to another level and derive from a thinner level of existence. Indeed, the astral cord is the very thread that the ancient myth would have cut by Fate. When this thread is broken, the physical body no longer receives any inflow of vital forces, so that it keeps living by mere inertia and, from that moment onwards, begins to decompose. Although some deceased do not seem to see the astral cord at all, it is very frequently mentioned, at least in passing; and we find it not only in the testimonies of projectors, but also in mediumistic communications where the deceased recounts the circumstances of his death, and in the observations of clairvoyants who happen to be at the bedside of a dying person. In all these, indeed, the astral cord comes close to being a commonplace.[222]

In our discussion of ecsomatic projections and near-death experiences, we saw how the thin body is normally perceived as dressed. Indeed, preparing a dress for it is something very simple: it needs no more than a mental act (or a series of mental acts, if one really wants to clothe it in the best of fineries), because in this respect, and especially in this purely spiritual dimension, thought is once again capable of directly creating reality. When the process of creating the astral dress (or even the subtle body itself) is a spontaneous one, it takes place through the subject's will: if not always at the level of clear and conscious awareness, there are his mental habits, the habit of thinking of himself in this particular way, with a certain body and with certain clothes, with a particular external appearance. It is a process wholly analogous to the one that takes place, one or more times a day, in our dreams.

Many discarnate spirits therefore feel a strong need of creating for themselves an outward bodily appearance, though others will be perfectly at ease with no such need. The words of 'William Stead', another communicating entity, are very revealing in this respect:

> 'I believe some spirits clothe themselves with a thought-body; but there are others, and I am one of them, who do not think it is necessary. The body has been left behind, why should I formulate one like that I had discarded? If I were to materialise to you I must assume a form in order to be visible. Otherwise there is no need for me to do so.'[223]

This vital nucleus capable of assuming the form of a subtle body never becomes exhausted, not least because it is continuously sustained by the vital energies — if we may call them such — of the environment in which it lives. Consequently, the astral body is 'never weary'.[224]

Nor does it ever fall ill or become affected by any kind of deformity.[225] Rather, it recovers any parts or limbs that the corresponding physical body had lost in the course of its existence, even though the mutilation sometimes becomes so firmly established in the subject's mental habits as to induce him, even after his decease, to keep feeling himself and seeing himself in that erstwhile manner.[226]

The assumption of a body-like form seems to be a need and therefore a matter of fact for the great majority, and indeed for almost all the souls who survive in the spheres that are closest to the earth, which in practice are the very ones with whom we communicate. Here is how one of these entities puts it, very spontaneously and almost ingenuously in Neville Randall's *Life After Death*:

> 'I've been told — I don't know this — but I've been told that the very highly advanced souls — it is not necessary — in fact they don't feel the need to have bodies! Of course that's something I can't understand. But they say that when you become very highly advanced, you cease to have the need for a body, and you cease to exist in shape.'[227]

As a general rule, a deceased 'appears to us of an age and in the clothes in which we can recognize him.'[228] A deceased who died as a child will therefore first present himself in the appearance he had at the time of death; but then, at a later stage, he will probably change to adult form, that is to say, assume the appearance that, spontaneously and symbolically, will best express his attained spiritual maturity.[229]

Souls that have passed over can perform various types of movements and displacements, and these merit special consideration. They include displacements in our own earthly environments whenever spiritual entities come into contact with it, insert themselves in it and realize a presence therein (it does not matter whether it be visible or invisible); displacements from one place or another in our three-dimensional space; displacements in mental environments that can sometimes assume consistency in other dimensions; and displacements that can take place from one such mental environment to another.

A characteristic feature of the manner in which spiritual entities move from one place to another, even when far apart, is that they can do so instantaneously. The movement is performed with the speed of thought, as if thought arrived directly and immediately at the place in question with no need to pass through any intermediate place (i.e. any place that, from the point of view of topography, geography or three-dimensional space, can be defined as 'in between'). As can be seen this manner of moving is closely analogous to the equally immediate and instantaneous displacements we have already noted in out-of-the-body projections and near-death experiences, in either of which the subject can cover enormous distances in exactly the same manner.

Indeed, this is a theme that we find repeated time and time again in mediumistic literature: 'We desire a place, and we are there,' writes 'Judge Hatch' with the hand of Elsa Barker,[230] echoed by 'William Stead' who says: 'We think of a place and we are there.'[231] And it is sufficient to think of a person being in the place in question: 'Think of him; mentally concentrate upon him and you will then see him.'[232] It does not matter whether the distance is great by geographical standards: 'Your brother met your father at once. He tells you that he went to Southport and spoke to your mother. He saw his wife and child in bed, he also saw you and your husband.'[233] Another remark made by 'William Stead' seems to confirm the validity of his statement that has just been quoted:

> 'I was at first amazed at the speed of my movements. I thought myself somewhere and I was there. I did not have to get there. There was no intervening time during which I travelled from place to place. It was immediate — like the old story of the magic carpet.'[234]

This does not mean that there cannot be at least the illusion of a movement in space, an illusion that derives, if for no other reason, from the mental habit of conceiving a voyage from one place to another as a passage through all the places that lie between them. For example, we can catch some allusions to an experience of this kind in the following episode that takes place wholly in the beyond and involves only personages who have already passed over:

> 'Dad asked if I should like to go and see Gran. She lives a long way off. So we went. I hadn't seen her yet. Dad was with me all the time. So Dad said, "Wish we were there". So we did it. We both shot up in the air, and in a second we'd got there.'[235]

This testimony talks of the impression of a movement through space, flash-like, but still a movement. And it seems one must infer that what is involved is really nothing more than an impression derived from a mental habit. What separates one situation in the spirit environment from another is certainly not three-dimensional space. It may sometimes seem such, but this is only an illusion or some form of partial illusion. A partially illusory form, for example, is the one in which a truth can be expressed by a symbol. In our particular case, the factual truth of a movement or displacement (which really occurs) can be expressed through the symbol of a voyage performed through space: through a three-dimensional space that does not in actual fact exist. Why is it that the reality of a non-spatial displacement is expressed or grasped via a space symbol? This surely happens because the subject, though deceased, still preserves the mental habit acquired on earth of conceiving movement solely in terms of displacement through physical or three-dimensional space.

There is another manner of moving, similar to the one that we employ in our earthly condition. Spirits may walk, but they do so in a rather unusual manner, without their feet actually touching the ground: they seem to glide over it as happens in dreams. This, for example, is what we are told by the transcendental author of *Heaven Revised*.[236] And something very similar can be found in

Autobiography of Two Worlds, where we learn that when Topsy, a young slave-girl who had died on an American plantation, was borne away by Sister Francesca, her new spiritual mother, 'they appeared to travel through space by a gliding movement, not touching the ground.'[237]

Both these phenomena take place in ultraterrene environments; that is to say, in mental environments like those of our dreams. Space does not have any objective existence in these environments, it is simply space that is 'thought'. The vision of space that we find in the two experiences just reported is of a symbolic character. The space symbols are the product of psychic activity that is once again conditioned by mental habits acquired during existence on earth.

At this point it may be interesting to dedicate a word or two to the type of movement that enables a deceased to leave his sphere for a short while and manifest himself in a given earthly environment (say, where there is somebody with whom he is anxious to communicate). It is clear that if the deceased limits himself to making himself present in some place on this earth, only he will be able to bear witness to the 'voyage' he has made; but if he also manifests himself, his testimony through the mouth of a medium will be corroborated also by testimony given by some living incarnate individual.

Having established this as a general principle, I should now like to recall a particular passage from the aforementioned *A Heretic In Heaven*, the book dictated by the entity 'Daddy' to the wife of the medium Ernest Peckham. It is therefore quite implicit that this account given by 'Daddy' is borne out by Peckham himself, nothing to the contrary being said either in the preface to the book or, more specifically, in a footnote concerning the episode itself.

Having passed over only recently, 'Daddy' was wondering whether his friend Peckham had heard the news of his demise. In actual fact, Peckham had been very ill at the time, so that the sad news had been kept from him. While he was pondering the problem, 'Daddy' heard the voice of another entity, his spirit guide, who told him: 'Think of him; mentally concentrate upon him and you will then see him.' Following this advice, 'Daddy' immediately had the impression that he was 'falling through space', passing through some very thick fog. (This impression of 'falling' could have been the symbolic translation which brought home to 'Daddy' that he was passing to a plane that in some way could be said to be 'lower', though this must certainly not be understood in the sense of being spatially situated 'below'.) When 'Daddy's fall came to a halt at a place where the fog was clearing, he could see the Peckhams just as if he were looking at them with his physical eyes from only a short distance away: they were taking a leisurely stroll along the waterfront of a seaside resort. 'I called out to him, "Peckham, old chap, I'm dead". He looked around with a startled air, appearing to have heard me. Then the mist enveloped me again for a while, and when it dispersed I found myself once more in my own domain.'[238] Peckham was at the seaside resort to convalesce; at that time he had not yet heard the news of his friend's death, and therefore learnt it in this fashion.

Another episode useful by way of example is the one in which the entity 'Julia Ames' manifests herself to her friend Elena (whom she was wont to call by the more familiar name of 'Hoodie'), still alive in incarnate form. The two women had made a pact that the one who died first was to try and manifest herself to the other. Elena tells us that on two occasions she had woken up with a start and seen her friend seemingly alive and smiling. On both occasions Julia had remained perfectly visible (though silent) for several minutes, but had then become transparent and eventually disappeared, leaving in her place a kind of luminous pillar that likewise disappeared a little later. It had seemed to Elena that Julia wanted to give her a message, or at least say something, but had not succeeded in doing so.[239]

Let us now see how the same incident is reported by the other party, the entity 'Julia'. Her account will give us quite a detailed idea of the kind of problem that arises, so let us give the floor to 'Julia' for her statement:

'It is not an easy thing to manifest, except under very favourable conditions. For my part I have manifested in many ways. The first two were to Hoodie. After that I have manifested myself to Mrs B. at the materialization séance. I have manifested myself to the photographer, and some other cases. But in all it requires an effort, and the effort cannot be maintained beyond a certain point. And in the case of a prolonged manifestation — that is to say from half an hour upwards — it is necessary to obtain the co-operation of many on this side. You will notice that even in materializing séances where the conditions are good, visitors from this side soon take their departure. And in ordinary apparitions the vision is almost momentary. I was held several minutes for Hoodie to see me, but that is rare. Usually we can make the picture visual for a moment or two, then it dissolves away. To make the picture is the easiest and the most common. To make it speak is rarer, and to make it touchable and apparently solid as well as vocal and visible is the hardest of all. And as much force is required to materialize there is seldom enough left to speak with. For the photographing there is less difficulty, for the finer substance can be used to reflect the light rays so as to affect the plate. But unless you have favourable conditions on your side we can do little or nothing on this side.'[240]

The concrete problem that 'Julia' had to face in manifesting herself to her friend Hoodie was that of 'making the picture', because Hoodie was not a clairvoyant. 'Julia' received the following advice from another and more expert entity:

'The secret is simple. But do not despise it for its simplicity. Think earnestly, steadfastly; think the picture, the form, the appearance, of your former self. When that is done, take it with you, and wait for the timely moment when the spiritual senses of the recipient are not clogged or darkened by the whirling vibrations of mundane care. Then you will find that you will be seen.'[241]

And so it was.

In close analogy with what happens in out-of-the-body experiences, a deceased, on manifesting himself in one of our earthly environments, may find at a certain point that the density of his subtle body can vary. Indeed, changes can take place from one moment to the next: thus, there will be one moment when the manifesting deceased passes through physical bodies, while just a moment later this may no longer be possible for him; quite the contrary, solid objects will then cause resistance and thus oblige him either to shift them or to act on them in some other way. A very extensive phenomenology may even enable us to record such telekinetic phenomena,[242] finding some specific rationale in them, or to refer them to the initiative of some special entities who are inspired by particular motives and intentions.

As regards the phenomena and the manner in which they are lived by the entity that provokes them, we have seen the problems with which 'Julia' had to grapple in order to materialize sufficiently for manifestation. Of considerable interest in this connection is *Life Eternal*, a book attributed to the spirit entity of the late William T. Stead, in which the famous English psychic researcher talks about his own attempts at communicating with the men of this world. He examines the various problems associated with trances, direct voices, materializations, automatic writing, psychic photography, telekinetic phenomena, apports and so on, as they are lived and experienced on the other side; i.e. in the dimension in which and from which spirits operate.[243]

Once a certain degree of materialization has been achieved, it becomes possible for the spirit to act on material bodies. It is reasonable to think that a spirit can operate with his own energies rather more effectively if his demise is only of recent date, and his vehicle of vitality (or vital body) therefore still adheres to his discarnate soul. But once this vehicle of vitality has been eliminated, the spirit will find it essential to utilize human psychic energies made available by the presence of a medium at the place of his manifestation.

At this point, therefore, there arise some particularly complex problems regarding the manner in which the spirit can manifest itself in the best possible conditions, and make use of the energies of the medium not only to produce physical phenomena, but also to communicate messages: the spirit will have to do everything possible to make the messages absolutely clear, faithful to the inspiration that dictates them, and also such that the living can recognize the communicating entity beyond all doubt and without equivocation, by a particular manner of expression, by the words in which a message is couched. An entity can sometimes be recognized by its peculiar manner of expression, but sometimes through certain earthly and strictly personal memories that it shows to have preserved, or through other forms of identification it may succeed in supplying.

Although we men of this world are extremely exacting in this connection, sometimes even ultra-sophisticated, we have little or no idea of the difficulties that the deceased must meet and overcome in order to manifest and communicate with us, or of the many problems they have to face and solve. Paul Beard, in his book *Survival of Death*, gives us at least an outline of these problems, and we begin to get some idea of how the life question is lived 'on the other side', sometimes in a very dramatic manner indeed.[244]

These considerations regarding the manner in which a deceased can act on astral matter, or even on physical matter, can now be concluded with a remark of a quite general nature, namely that this action will be all the more effective when the subject succeeds in operating with what Sylvan Muldoon calls the crypto-conscious mind (see Chapter 2). If the action is to be effective, it has to be executed at the level of the unconscious. The subject will therefore do well to entrust its execution, and the manner of execution, to his own subconscious. Above all, he will do well to entrust to his unconscious the task of determining and deciding all the details, even the most minute ones, of the plan of execution for the operation upon which his conscious will is bent.

As far as mediumistic communications are concerned, it is widely and frequently attested that the communicating entity will succeed far better in its intentions when, rather than dictating each individual word of the message, it simply concentrates on the basic ideas and allows the words to come of their own accord; that is to say, allows the words to form spontaneously in the unconscious psyche of the medium, thus left wholly free to operate in its own way.

Indeed, it is in this sense that a communicating spirit (another soldier fallen in the First World War and identified only by the initials K.H.R.D.) observes that he finds it easier to communicate the substance of his thoughts when he leaves the medium free to couch them in his own words. Here is how he puts it: 'Thought I would get that through better if I let him do the talking. You see, I just rolled up the ideas and let him get hold of them, and roll them out in his well-known literary style.'[245] In a somewhat similar context, the entity 'William Stead' expresses himself as follows to the writing medium: 'You are not able to get my exact words. [Therefore] I impress thoughts on your mind.'[246] 'I am here. On your mind I impress ideas and you translate them into words.'[247] It is clear that the medium must keep his mind passive and receptive, free of all disturbing influences, especially those connected with the theme of the communication which could otherwise be altered or disturbed and confused.[248]

And with these remarks about the return of the deceased, come to manifest themselves to us via mediums, I conclude this chapter dedicated to the crisis of their demise. I have sought to characterize this crisis of death in the light of the attestations provided by mediumistic communications, where certain themes and motives recur with a frequency that cannot be casual, a matter of mere chance. Nor is this convergence satisfactorily explained by those who offer the unconscious as an explanation. An animist theory, or pure parapsychology, clearly cannot simply invoke the unconscious mind as a kind of universal stop-gap capable of exorcising all the particularly troublesome phenomena. A real theory of this kind would have to explain why these extremely typical and significant 'revelations' recur with such frequency. Search as one may, however, it would not seem that any such alternative hypothesis capable of explaining all this in some detail has yet been formulated. Indeed, if such an alternative and adequately articulated hypothesis is ever put forward, it will prove to be so artificially complicated and frivolously fanciful as to make one readily prefer the spiritist hypothesis, as not only more in keeping with the known facts, but also as the simpler of the two hypotheses, and the more sensible and plausible explanation.

Chapter 7
Passing Through Hades

When discussing near-death experiences in Chapter 4, we had occasion to note a characteristic feature of these experiences: at a certain moment the subject arrives at a door or a gate, a bridge, a river, a stretch of sea, a hedge, a fence or any other kind of barrier, and beyond this obstacle he sees, waiting for him with outstretched arms and smiling, his own dear ones who have died before him.

Taken as such, one may presume this situation to be true. And yet, no matter how real it may be in its substance, we may be sure that in the eyes of the subject it will assume an appropriately symbolic form. The well-known ability of the psyche to create images, translating into images even a hidden content that is both real and lifelike, is once again at work here. Indeed, the unconscious psyche is a most fertile and fanciful proponent and elaborator of images and symbols. This is a fact of which we become particularly well aware while asleep, when the unconscious is let off the leash and can elaborate its complex dream images at will.

We had already concluded in Chapter 4 that all the known facts suggested that the transcendental visions of the dying should be considered as visions of the ultimate goal where the process of the crisis of death attains its completion. When the subject attains this goal, one can say that he has fully passed over to the other side and has freed himself of all the psychic residues that previously limited him in some way, darkened his mind and kept him chained to his terrestrial existence. One may assume that complete liberation from a certain positive wrapping should enable the subject to see things for what they are, and even though his new vision of them may not be absolutely correct, it should at least be considerably more adequate than any view of reality that he could enjoy or perceive while still enveloped by a psychic layer of such density. It is to the density of the psychic layer in which human beings are shrouded that we must attribute the fact that even profoundly true intuitions end up by emerging into the subject's consciousness in symbolic form; that is to say, in a form so contradictory in its various aspects that we can consider it to be revealing and concealing at one and the same time, to be both indicative and misleading, both true and illusory.

The transcendental visions that often constitute a large part of near-death experiences are such as to give the subject a foretaste, enabling him to catch a glimpse of what is going to be his condition once completely free of his earthly bonds, after he has fully passed over. But this does not mean that this goal is going to be reached right away. The soul has rid itself of the physical body, but before it can attain its transcendental destination it has yet to free itself of a second wrapping or shell, the one referred to in Chapter 5 as the 'etheric body', the 'vital body' or the 'vehicle of vitality'. The first of these names derives from theosophical literature, while the third is the one preferred by Crookall.[249] What we are concerned with here is a subtle body that adheres very closely to the physical body; indeed, it is the principle that makes it live, that animates its vegetative life. This vehicle not only organizes the life of the physical body, but, drawing energy from subtler levels of cosmic life, continuously sustains and nourishes the life of the physical body, especially during sleep. It is therefore essential for the survival of the physical body. The vehicle of vitality can also project itself out of the physical body to a greater or lesser extent: the important thing is that, in doing so, it should not snap the filament that is invisible to our physical eyes — though sensitives can sometimes see it in very special conditions — and which we know as the 'astral cord'. Severance of the astral cord is, in fact, equivalent to death of the physical body.

Once physical death has occurred, the vital body has no further function to perform. It is therefore only natural that the separation of the soul from the physical body should be followed by its detachment from the vital body: this is what Crookall calls 'second death' (not to be confused with what other authors mean by this term, which Crookall refers to as the 'third death').[250]

Now, Crookall's 'second death' will be greatly facilitated when the subject is of average moral and spiritual development (an ordinary or normal person), and when death occurs naturally as a result of old age. When physical death takes place in such a wholly natural and normal situation, the subject falls into a kind of sleep that may also be populated by dreams. It is at this point that the soul becomes detached from the vehicle of vitality, a process which may require no more than a few moments, but may also take hours, days and even months.[251] In normal circumstances, however, the process will last for about three days (although this duration of earthly time will, of course, be lived subjectively). Crookall cites various relevant testimonies, all in agreement with each other, drawn not only from mediumistic communications and descriptions provided by clairvoyants,[252] but also a wide variety of spiritual and religious traditions.[253]

The process that leads to the soul (which Crookall also calls the 'Soul Body' or 'psychic body') becoming detached from the vital body (or 'vehicle of vitality' in the terminology preferred by Crookall), is described in a similar manner by other testimonies quoted by the same author. These descriptions of the 'second death' process are provided both by spirits who lived the experience in the first person, and by other spirits who happened to be present and were therefore able to observe what was happening to other entities who had only just passed over into the new condition.[254] On several occasions the emergence of the soul from the vehicle of vitality is compared to a butterfly coming out of its chrysalis. [2 5 5]

The vehicle of vitality, though indispensable for transmitting life to the physical body for as long as the latter continues to function, becomes a mere impediment after physical death has occurred. The operation of separation, which takes place easily and rapidly when it follows a 'normal' and 'natural' demise, becomes longer, more difficult and less straightforward when a subject has died in conditions that can be defined as negative: this is particularly true when the subject dies suddenly as the result of some accidental cause (killed in war, for example), losing his life in the full flower of youth; [2 5 6] it is true also of men who are excessively sensual. [2 5 7] Difficulty may also be experienced by men who in life were mainly egoistical, or malignant and evil, inclined to act for the purpose of hurting their fellows. [2 5 8] An excessive attachment to the earth — being enmeshed in one of the many and varied passions that make us 'too human' — will create a mental state within us that leaves us wholly unprepared for death and resistant to it. The subtle body of our vitality is also the veil of our passions, and in such circumstances it proves to be far more dense and cumbersome: to break free of it therefore becomes difficult and, in certain limiting cases, extremely difficult. Although our soul abandons the physical body, it may remain enmeshed by a dense veil of vitality, which in such cases is almost physical and markedly carnal, preventing it from perceiving the spiritual realities of the new dimension and binding it to the earthly dimension.

A negative situation of this type can continue for a long time. Crookall, contrasting it with the condition of those who die in a natural and normal manner, abandoning themselves into the arms of death in a naturally spontaneous fashion, summarizes its characteristics in the following five points:

1. While natural death is usually followed by a kind of 'sleep', a person who dies in an unnatural and forced

manner remains awake, or will wake up almost at once, and thus does not enjoy the benefit of this restoring sleep.

2. The frame of mind of those who die in a natural manner can be expressed by such words as 'peace', 'freedom', 'security', 'happiness', etc., while those who die suddenly and unnaturally remain 'bewildered' and 'confused', at least at the beginning.

3. In the case of natural death the environment experienced by the subject is described as 'beautiful', 'clear', 'light' and 'brilliant', but in the case of sudden death (in the beginning, at least) it is defined as 'misty', 'foggy' and even 'watery'.

4. The presence of the 'astral cord' is often perceived in the former type of experience and only very rarely in the latter.

5. Persons who die a natural death often become aware of the presence of discarnate relatives and friends who come to meet them, not only immediately after their demise but sometimes just before; those who die an unnatural death never have this death-bed experience and have to wait a long time for the joy of such encounters. [259]

The diversity of the two destinations that await the soul immediately after physical death has here been sketched in a rather schematic fashion; in actual fact, these are two extreme situations separated by a wide and varied range of intermediate cases.

Although the results of Crookall's comparative analysis are undoubtedly valued, I think it will be helpful to make some further distinction. There are so many souls who remain half-way along the road, and remain there for a time that is sometimes very long from both an objective and a subjective point of view. They are in the condition that has been described as 'dark', 'foggy' or 'watery', but which is also woeful, squalid and without doubt negative; communications regarding these conditions, as also books and other treatments, for the most part refer to this state by the name of 'Hades'.

This condition is mentioned in many different traditions, under many different names: though the Greeks call it 'Hades', it has its counterpart in the 'Amenti' of the ancient Egyptians, the 'Sheol' of the Hebrews, the 'Kamaloka' of the Hindus, and the 'Bardo' of the Tibetans. If what has here been said about this condition corresponds to a substantial truth, the various peoples and traditions must have derived their idea of 'Hades' both by clairvoyance (or other forms of intuitive perception) and by mediumistic communications, the latter characterizing this transient (though sometimes very long) condition of 'quarantine' by speaking for the most part of 'mist' or 'fog', but also of something 'dark' and 'dim', of 'shadowy forms', 'grey lands', 'grey vapour', 'a white mist', or just 'smoke'.[260]

This 'intermediate world', this 'borderland', this 'world of a half-way state', this 'place where the worlds meet' — just some of the names given to this condition in other communications reported and discussed by Crookall[261] — is also referred to as a passage through water. Before his assassination, Abraham Lincoln dreamt three times that he was in a boat on a rushing river that overwhelmed him. Others who have passed through a near-death experience speak of crossing a wide river or a stretch of water, or of being immersed in deep water, though glimpsing bright beaches beyond it (as we saw in Chapter 4). Mediumistic communications likewise speak of crossing water and of restoring sleep (which generally corresponds to a passage through Hades perceived as relatively easy and quick) from which one awakes 'so terribly wet'.[262]

Experiences of this kind underlie the many myths that regularly insist on the event of death being connected with a crossing of water. The ancient Egyptians believed, for example, that the newly deceased had to cross the sea before they arrived at their destination. The Sumerians were likewise convinced that the sea had to be crossed in order to enter Sheol. 'Deep are the waters of death', as a goddess says to Gilgamesh. Many passages of the Old Testament show that the Jews at one time had a very similar vision.[263] And let us not forget the waters of the Acheron and the Lethe, commonplaces of classical Greek mythology.

In more physiological terms — but we are here talking of a more occult, subtle, astral physiology — we can attribute this prolonged Hades condition in which the subject remains to the fact that his soul is still enveloped by the famous veil sticking to it and from which it cannot escape. Why is it that the butterfly cannot emerge from its chrysalis? The reasons, already briefly outlined, can be divided into two kinds. Firstly, there are the more accidental and extrinsic reasons, as in the case where death comes suddenly and unexpectedly to put an end to a young and flowering physical existence, the typical 'enforced death' in Crookall's terminology. In these cases enforced death is always caused by an external accident, a trauma that leaves the subject shocked, overwhelmed, confused; but it is only reasonable to expect that he will tend to recover his equilibrium quite quickly.

This recovery, however, will be far slower and more difficult when the soul remains enmeshed in the vehicle of vitality as a result of more intrinsic causes, the second of our two kinds of reason: the subject's inadequate spiritual development or his excessive attachment to the earth, for example, but also his passions, his evil nature, his egoism and egocentrism, the fact that he may be obsessed by some fixed idea that absorbs all his attention, to the point where — entirely by his own fault — he becomes a prisoner of that idea. In these cases death is enforced only in the sense that it finds the subject reluctant. But reluctant to do what? Reluctant to accept that death is our true and ultimate condition, the condition that constitutes our point of arrival, a condition one cannot adapt to unless one freely renounces egoism and attachment to the earth, as also the various other harmful aspects of our carnal nature mentioned above.

But what about suicides, then? It is quite true that one

can also kill oneself for very lofty and noble reasons, but here I propose to consider rather the more normal case of suicide, as an act of cowardice and supreme egoism: even though death is voluntary in these cases, the death for which one opts has nothing whatever to do with the death that is our point of arrival, the ultimate goal, the optimal condition that we all pursue. In a death that has attained its perfect fulfilment one has freed oneself of all egoism, so much so that this ultimate state has within it something that is clearly in contrast with the profoundly egoistical spirit that underlies the normal case of suicide and its motivations. I do not, of course, want to judge individual cases — far from it; but, considering the question only in its general terms, I would say that it is perfectly reasonable to expect that a certain type of suicide is inevitably destined to attain death not as the ultimate goal, as a perfective fulfilment, but as an incomplete death, a kind of death that has remained halfway along the road.

Leaving aside the more superficial and temporary effects of the accidental causes that occasion death, as also those deriving from the person's age at the time of death, one can say — taking the longer view — that the first destination of a newly deceased is determined by his human qualities. The immediate destiny of a soul is thus determined by its degree of development, by the evolution it has already achieved. But — all too frequently — it is also true that a degeneration rather than an evolution may be involved. The condition of our psyche is determined, first and foremost, by our thoughts; above all, by the thoughts we repeat and stress, for such thoughts tend to create a thought-shell or habit in the truest sense of the term.

Thoughts can prove to be of various qualities, of different levels. Lofty thoughts, especially when they are repeated and have become a habit and a way of being, will elevate the soul, just as mediocre thoughts will lower the tone of one's spiritual life and turn the soul into a mediocrity. Negative thoughts push the soul back to a lower level and, in extreme cases, may even drive it into a ruinous abyss.

There is one respect in which there is an enormous and fundamental difference between our present existence wholly immersed in matter, and the purely spiritual and mental existence in the beyond. Even though our thoughts, our mental state, the interior attitude with which we face up to the various situations and external events, count a great deal in our life on earth, they are not everything. Our actual condition is also exterior, material, physical. The possession of exterior means, especially wealth and material resources, can help us a great deal, for it can give us at least the illusion that everything is fine and that there is nothing we lack. And thus our intimate and true poverty remains masked, hidden from ourselves. We see ourselves surrounded by an abundance of material things and technical aids, we make use of all this, we believe ourselves to be strong and simply do not think that the advantages are wholly ephemeral: some day we shall leave the things we *have*, and be left only with what we *are*. Sooner or later, however, there comes the moment of truth, the moment of death, when we are deprived of our physical body. And once detached from this physical body of ours, which disintegrates and dissolves, we are left only with our spirituality, with our psychic nature; in other words, there remains only our interior life, which is made up wholly and exclusively of our thoughts.

One can therefore readily understand that, from that moment onwards, our life, the condition of our existence, will be determined by our thoughts, especially our customary thoughts, and by the thought habits acquired in the course of our earthly life. If our thought habits are such as to bind us to the earth in a manner different from our nature as spiritual beings, we are even now enmeshed in a condition that after our physical death will reveal itself to be a Hades condition.

The Hades condition can be defined as a negative mental state, a condition of suffering, of dissatisfaction.

Even though it can also procure us pleasures, these pleasures are always precarious and illusory, ultimately generating suffering because they are degrading for the soul: this suffering finds its full expression in the very act in which the soul becomes aware of the real situation in which it has become enmeshed.

A thought that I take from the book entitled *Thy Kingdom Come* seems to penetrate particularly close to the core of the problem we are here considering:

> 'Beyond death we enter into ourselves. According to the Christian faith we go either to heaven or to hell. How true! Heaven we construct and hell transmute — within.'[264]

As regards hell in particular, it is above all our own conscience that creates it, though this is not an easy concept to grasp and accept. The entity 'Marmaduke', for example, explains it in the following terms:

> 'I have no doubt that the ancient idea of hell was an attempt to show that there will be punishment for sin. Men could not then have grasped the idea of conscience making the hell, and so the material and realistic hell was invented to meet the case.'[265]

To now use the words of Ernesto Bozzano, this confirms that 'the only thing that counts in our incarnate existence is the works we perform, together with our intimate and unexpressed aspirations.'[266] Another factor that combines with these and forms a synthesis with them is the 'Law of Affinity', which inevitably causes all of us 'to gravitate towards our likes'.[267]

Depending on the particular state of his soul, each newly deceased will thus come to find himself in a mental environment that he may perceive in different ways: it may be happy and bright, or dim, dark and sad. In the latter case the newly deceased may find himself in this desolate environment either alone or in the company of other like spirits, spirits of his own level of evolution. It is a mental environment similar to the environments in which we find ourselves when we dream: this dream environment is constructed by our mind, and the same may be said of the mental environment in which the deceased perceives himself to be, for it is a mental 'place' rather than a physical one.

The stay in this condition (a spiritual state rather than a place) may be of short duration but can also be very long: sometimes the negative condition may correspond to a frame of mind that is overcome with relative ease, but in other cases the subject may find himself enmeshed in this condition in much the same manner of an obsession or vice, or any form of psychic deviation. Just as in our dreams our frame of mind is expressed in images of persons, things and places that are similar to images we perceive and experience here on earth, something analogous also happens in these *post mortem* experiences: the spiritual condition of the newly deceased finds expression also in the images of the things, persons and beings that animate and populate his mental environment, that animate the place where he finds himself or imagines himself to be.

Speaking through a medium, 'Dr Horace Abraham Ackley' referred to his own demise by recalling that the first ultraterrene environment in which he found himself after death appeared somewhat like a dim and misty landscape. Many people were there, including quite a few whom he had known in life and who had passed over before him, and these extended him a friendly welcome. But Bozzano notes that most communicating deceased speak of arriving immediately in a bright and radiant environment. How, then, can one explain the wholly different character of the first experience of this discarnate spirit? Bozzano attributes it to:

> '[the] circumstance that, as "Ackley" himself tells us, both he and the spirits who came to meet him had neglected to develop the spiritual element within them while they were still alive, and, consequently, an environment of light, by virtue of the law of affinity, was not in keeping with the transitory but obscured condition of their spirits.'[268]

It is rather interesting to compare the above experience with the one attributed to another entity, 'Captain Hinchliffe', an aviator who perished in 1928 when his aircraft crashed into the Atlantic Ocean during an attempt to make the first non-stop overflight from England to the United States. It may be worth our while to quote a passage of some length from his communications to his wife, for it tells us in his own words what he experienced on this occasion and how he himself interprets this:

'If you ask me where I am, what I am and what I see, I have to tell you that in the first instance I found myself in a grey, damp and most disagreeable country that looked to me barren, almost like the wastes of Belgium I used to fly over. Imagine such a country, with here and there groups of three or four badly grown distorted trees visible under a grey fog, and I think you will get an idea as to what I awoke to. *You* know why I should want to get out of such a state — one in which many people dwell for years ... And why? ... Because they are frightened — most often of what is beyond it — but also because they find in this dreariness, people akin to themselves. And further, since this dreary region comprises that belt of astral or lower regions immediately surrounding the Earth's orbit in close contact with the Earth, and where even the vegetation and moisture are nearly of the same texture as their equivalents on Earth, it is particularly easy from such Resort to still see, realise and allow one's imagination to play over those physical happenings on your Plane in which one may formerly have been immersed or conversant with.'[269]

'Captain Hinchliffe' thus gives us a good introduction to this topic of the discarnate spirits who, for some time at least, remain bound to the earth. What we have just learnt from him can be appropriately integrated by a fragment from the communications of 'Rudolph Valentino'. As the entity of this famous actor explains to us, a passage to the other dimension is literally a new birth, and it is therefore a motive of great surprise, an authentic *shock*, an experience for which not all of us are equally prepared. Many newly arrived discarnate souls therefore remain prey to ignorance, fear and resentment. They cannot immediately adjust to the fact that they have been torn away from a material world of which they were excessively enamoured. They thus 'spend all their time haunting their familiar earthly surroundings and become tied, mentally, to the earth.' Such souls 'are in the lower astral plane, out of the world, yet they are still in it through their tenacious clinging to worldly attitudes of thought.'[270]

These earthbound spirits, all of whom were surprised by physical death at a time when they were still fully involved in a dominant passion, in an excessive attachment to the things of this world, reflect this condition in their mental state and for the most part become its prisoners. They continue to cling to the earth, to particular places and persons. In some respects, therefore, their beyond remains very close to our own world and certain of its environments. The law of affinity ensures that these earthbound spirits will flock together, forming groups with their likes, and this tends to throw their passions and vices into even sharper relief. Singly or collectively, they continue to live their experience, almost as if it were a strange dream or a nightmare. They seek satisfaction, they imagine or dream they are doing what they long for, but sooner or later realize that the gratifications their imagination can procure for them are very insipid indeed, now that they lack the physical body and its senses.

At this state these spirits discover another way of venting their possessive obsessions: they try to cling to spirits who are still incarnate; they try to possess them, seeking to relive their former experiences, to obtain second-hand satisfaction in this way. And thus these earthbound spirits come to haunt the earthly places where their vices can be satisfied and sustained, they haunt the places where their various passions are exercised. Through the intermediary of men and women engaged in the same activities, these earthbound spirits thus taste and relive certain sensations to the greatest possible extent; indeed, in their endeavour to do this as intensely as possible, they act as tempting spirits seeking to persuade these living people to behave in a certain manner.

The greedy deceased return to contemplate their treasures or to pursue their interests; there are even cases of their deriving enjoyment from contemplating the gold accumulated on earth by others, by live incarnate men. Here the testimony of 'Judge Hatch' will suffice:

> 'I have seen a miser counting over his gold, have seen the terrible eyes of the spirits which enjoyed the gold through him.'[271]

The entities who dispense spirit teachings to William Stainton Moses say that, as a general rule, the longings of the body do not become extinct even though the deceased has been deprived of the power to satisfy them. They take the example of a drunkard, saying that he:

> 'retains his old thirst, but exaggerated; aggravated by the impossibility of slaking it. It burns within him, the unquenched desire, and urges him to frequent the haunts of his old vices, and to drive wretches like himself to further degradation. In them he lives again his old life, and drinks in satisfaction, grim and devilish, from the excesses which he causes them to commit. And so his vice perpetuates itself, and swells the crop of sin and sorrow.'[272]

The situation could hardly be clarified much better than in the passage just quoted, even though its literary style may be that of bygone days. 'Judge Hatch' relates another astral experience he had after he had been placed in a position from which, though wholly neutral, he could see and contemplate both worlds. He saw a young man enter a saloon bar, lean on the counter, order a glass of whisky, and then send it down in a single gulp. By the side of that young man:

> 'taller than he and bending over him, with its repulsive, bloated, ghastly face pressed close to his, as if to smell his whisky-tainted breath, was one of the most horrible astral beings which I have seen in this world since I came out. The hands of the creature (and I use that word

to suggest its vitality) — the hands of the creature were clutching the young man's form, one long and naked arm was around his shoulders, the other around his hips. It was literally sucking the liquor-soaked life of its victim, absorbing him, using him, in the successful attempt to enjoy vicariously the passion which death had intensified.'[273]

Although these motives are to be found (at least in brief touches) in more or less the entire literature of mediumistic communications, there can be no doubt that the most picturesque examples are given in these letters by 'Judge Hatch'. We cannot say whether and to what extent the author entity has allowed his hand to be guided by a taste for drama and colourful situations, but one can at least say that he seems to have thoroughly grasped the substance and the essence of the question, its hard core of truth.

The characterization that 'Judge Hatch' gives us of spirits obsessed by wrath, violence and hate seems particularly apt. These spirits, so he tells us, love to excite discord even on earth. If a living man feels hate for one of his fellows, or becomes angry with him, or simply says something uncomplimentary about him, he provides an opportunity for one of these negative spirits to intervene by immersing himself in his frame of mind, inebriating himself with it, egging him on and setting him on fire. Most of the time the negative spirit has no particular passion for his victim, he simply uses him temporarily to satisfy a pre-existing passion of his own. But:

'sometimes the impersonal interest in mere strife becomes personal; an angry spirit here may find that by attaching himself to a certain man he is sure to get every day a thrill or thrills of angry excitement, as his victim continually loses his temper and storms and rages. This is one of the most terrible manifestations that can happen to anybody. Carried to its ultimate, it may become obsession, and end in insanity.'[274]

In *Realms of the Living Dead*, a non-medianic book that sets out to review the things that medianic literature tells us about the spiritual domain, the authors quite rightly relate the phenomenon of these obsessive spirits to a famous passage in St Paul's Letter to the Ephesians:

> 'For we wrestle not against flesh and blood, but against principalities, against powers, against the rulers of the darkness of this world, against spiritual wickedness in high places.'[275]

I have just given a few examples here, but following a list proposed by the entity 'Frederic Myers', one could also mention 'human beings of brutal character, murderers, criminals, drug addicts, bullies, unscrupulous financiers who crave only for power, individuals possessed by jealousy or the desire for revenge.'[276] Another such list can be found in the communications of 'Rudolph Valentino': in the lowest plane of the other dimension —

> 'there are also kings and queens, and all sorts of people of the ruling classes, who will not let go of the idea of temporal power. There are countless souls, too, of the humbler classes who are tied by the limited aspect of their thoughts; peasants, who still cannot see more than ten feet before their ploughs; soldiers, who insist upon believing that might is right, in spite of the fact that death has proved it otherwise to them. All who are narrow and pinched in mental outlook, all such, are tied and earthbound.'[277]

Realms of the Living Dead also notes that there are lustful spirits who float around the places where lewdness is practised, and infest the brothels; likewise there are the gluttons and incurable gourmands who congregate in the kitchens of homes, restaurants and hotels, voluptuously breathing in the vapours and the odours of the food being prepared.[278] And it is said, though unproven, that some of the more intelligent gluttons can recreate favourite dishes not only by creating them in thought as illusions, but also and above all by capturing the emanations of their physical components.[279]

The entity 'Myers', albeit in a somewhat more reductive manner, explains how a passionate hunter can procure for himself on the other side some substitute for his former pleasure of killing such large numbers of poor creatures: he can conjure up the illusion of hunting, though his victims are no longer birds, fish and four-legged animals, but simply their corporeal images created by a thought that succeeds in moulding their shape with absolute perfection.[280]

The images created by thought can assume such consistency and vivacity that many of the deceased are rendered prisoners of an obsession, notwithstanding the fact that it is no longer enhanced and supported by the perceptions of objective physical reality that the bodily senses, as it were, impose on us for as long as we live incarnate on this earth. A deceased obsessed by some dominant passion thus loses the sense of reality and lives as in a dream or, perhaps, in a nightmare. Often he does not even know or realize that he is 'dead', that he has passed over into another dimension. Indeed, his passing over can but be considered as still imperfect, incomplete.

One may therefore ask whether the 'hell' of the various religions really exists. There can be no doubt that many mediumistic communications tell us that, in a certain sense, it does exist. Obviously, it is not a place, but rather a negative spiritual state: we ourselves create it with our negative actions and, even before that, by our negative thoughts. It is a condition that we create ourselves as the automatic result of the things we do and, even more so, the things we think that lean in a negative, antisocial and antispiritual direction. As the entity 'Julia Ames' admonishes us:

> 'You do not realize the exceeding sinfulness of sin until you see its results. And on earth they are often hidden. Here they are revealed. You see what you have been doing. And the sight is often appalling. And as those who love have waiting before them the dear ones whom they loved, so those who hated, or injured or neglected, will also find on this side their victims, who need no whip of torment to scourge the sinner, but have only to reveal to him "See thy handiwork. This thou hast made of me".'[281]

These words seem to find an echo in those of a sinner

who eventually found her road to redemption in the other world, though only after a period of atonement that was so long as to seem interminable.[282] This entity exhorts the living not to doubt that hell exists, assuring us that she has suffered all its tortures and horrors. They were the tortures of the implacable remorse she felt after becoming aware, at a certain point, of her faults in all their enormity. Her soul had thus become afflicted by the memories of all those whom she had corrupted or made to suffer, and not least of those whose death she had actually caused. These memories assumed the form of true visions: she heard with endless horror the crying of her baby left to die of hunger and neglect; she was obsessed by the vision of her poor parents weighed down by the tremendous humiliation that had led them both to die of a broken heart; she was continually tormented by the presence of all her victims. These sufferings, made up solely and exclusively of atrocious remorse, eventually gave way to a very long series of other sufferings that seemed to consist of the consequences of the evil she had done; that is to say, of the actions, and even more so the thoughts, that had degraded her soul and reduced it to its low and doleful condition.

Redemption seems to be all the slower when the soul barricades itself behind its proud and arrogant obstinacy, and is thus prevented from becoming converted: the same entity goes on to tell us that the implacable pursuit of her remorse continued to torment her for a seemingly endless number of years, until eventually there came the day when, no longer able to resist this affliction and having reached the very limit of desperation, she turned her thoughts to God for the first time, pleading with Him to grant her either liberation or extinction. At this point she had taken the first truly decisive step: having invoked God, her soul was put in a condition to receive the aid of other souls, who eventually helped her to lift herself out of this abject situation. She was able to find the road to the higher spiritual domains, which are positive and radiant, and where she resolved to repair the evil she had done in life by endeavouring to do good.

Hell therefore exists: but is this an eternal hell? In trying to answer this question I shall have to limit myself to reporting what is to be found in a certain mediumistic literature that, though not actually crystallizing the condition of the damned, leaves them a clear hope of ultimate salvation. Unlike our situation here on earth, in the other dimension there is no division of time. And therefore, as the authors of *Realms of the Living Dead* explain:

> 'the duration of time is marked only by sensation and so long as these sensations [of the damned souls] endure, time stands still and their despair seems endless, for no other moment can be experienced until the old sensations are worked out and exhausted and new sensations can be experienced.'[283]

> 'I am told that some of these souls are so stubborn, so anchored down by the set conviction of their former mode of thinking, that they are actually blinded, and cannot see or realize the possibilities of advancement in the newer world before them. They are unadaptable, obstinate and unprogressive.' ('Rudolph Valentino')[284]

This is a situation that can last for a period of time corresponding to our years, and even our centuries, as we are accustomed to count them, which 'Valentino' goes on to say. And 'Judge Hatch', talking about an infernal creature we have already met (the spirit of the drunkard), tells us that his situation lasts 'for ever', always provided that 'the words "for ever" may be used of that which seems endless.'[285]

A way that leads to the expiation of remorse seems to unfold as soon as the damned soul begins to ask itself the reason for its great suffering: this is a question that will receive its proper answer, and this answer the soul will make its own by living it intimately as it works its way to a profound and burning awareness of the evil it has done, and in which it has persevered.

Remorse can be induced by the sufferings associated with a low condition from which earthbound spirits seem to draw a kind of contentment that ultimately leaves them wholly unsatisfied. Such a dissatisfaction can also be the result of sickening surfeit: it is a kind of satiety that itself generates dissatisfaction as soon as the spirit realizes that it has had its fill of certain kinds of sensations and gratifications that yet leave it void and empty. It is at this point that the spirit begins to perceive, albeit darkly and vaguely, that there is something far better in life, and that the satisfactions pursued up to that point were and still are rather miserable things.

The lowest astral plane, with all its low justifications that never really satisfy and leave a sense of emptiness, 'is a glittering but false paradise, if I may use that expression', as 'Rudolph Valentino' puts it.[286] Another entity explained it to the Reverend Charles Drayton Thomas as follows:

'It is only when the soul becomes dissatisfied with the almost mundane things of these lower spheres that it, almost automatically, raises itself to higher places. The very act of aspiration, of wishing something better for the soul's sake alone, causes one to rise.'[287]

Yet another redeemed sinner, our friend 'Marmaduke', had this to say:

'We should never have corrected your faults while you yourself were unconscious of them, but dissatisfaction with your own work is the beginning of progress, and now you will improve.'[288]

It does not follow that the lower and more negative Hades condition is reserved exclusively for culpable souls, for side by side with these we find souls that can be more readily defined as victims. The entity 'Myers' gives the example:

'of certain young men of careless, animal and, occasionally, vicious life who die violent deaths. These poor fellows are suddenly wrenched from their bodies while still they are in the prime of manhood. They are not, in any sense, capable of grasping, for a while, the difference between earth life and the Afterlife. So they remain in ignorance, and must remain in a kind of coma until the

delicate etheric body has recovered from the shock of a
too rapid severance from the earthly shape.'[289]

A soul may also remain earthbound as a result of the pain
and sorrow that its departure may have caused to
relatives, friends and others who held it dear. The entity
'Mary Hooker Burton' wrote the following through the
hand of a medium, just three days after she had passed
away:

> 'I am so weary, so tired. I long for rest from anxiety. My
> family draws me so near them, that I feel most grateful to
> you for writing that comforting letter. It will enable me to
> go higher.'[290]

A deceased American municipal official puts the matter
very clearly when he tells us that

> 'grief is a great barrier between souls on earth and souls
> in the spirit land ... and it also hinders our progress
> upward, for we are affected by thoughts and not by
> physical conditions as we were on earth.'[291]

The serenity of his dear ones still living incarnate on the
earth sends out luminous vibrations that attract the
deceased like a moth to a ray of light in the night,
explains the same entity, going on to say that grief, on
the other hand, 'radiates dark clouds, and gives the
appearance of a heavy black cloud enveloping our
friends.'[292]

A deceased may also remain earthbound because his
demise occurred at a time when he was beset by grave
concerns and preoccupations, by ideas and problems that
occupied his mind in an excessive, obsessive manner.
These problems may pertain to things that are not in
themselves negative, but only realities that form part of
our life and with which we have to concern ourselves,
though the concern is here carried beyond its proper
limits.

It is inner maturity that leads an earthbound spirit to
become aware of the fact that there are very different
things to think about and to do, that there are very
different perspectives in our existence. It is the deceased's

maturity that will eventually induce his entity to aim at worthier goals, at the realities of the spirit and the pursuit of higher evolutionary objectives. This maturity, which each individual must achieve on his own account, is nevertheless urged and stimulated by 'missionary spirits': these good souls keep watch over wayward, erring souls standing in need of help, waiting only for the proper moment to manifest themselves to the errant souls. In the spiritual world of the other dimension it is not possible to help somebody who does not want to be helped. Help is made effective only by the fact that those who stand in need become aware of this and therefore ask for help, accept it, and collaborate with those who give it.

The entity 'Julia Ames' speaks of a 'Guardian Angel' and a 'Messenger of Love and Mercy' that God sends to all who die. Those who are in the proper condition at the time of passing into the other dimension see this angel, while those who die with a negative disposition are thereby made blind, and will remain blind until such time as they have purified themselves of all dross. [2 9 3]

Help for errant spirits who have remained earthbound may also be given by us the living incarnate: we can do this not only by prayer and good and positive thoughts, but also by the things we can do to enlighten them, thus enabling them to be aware of their true situation. There are many people of good will on this earth, who, after establishing a mediumistic contact with such errant spirits, speak with and help them, first to become aware of their condition of deceased, of souls who have passed to the other side; their ideas may be still rather confused, to the point of believing themselves to be still 'alive' in this world and merely in the throes of a dream or nightmare.

No matter how strange it may seem, the work of psychic rescue, bringing help to errant souls, performed by Americans Dan and Doris Buckley, is certainly quite outstanding in this respect. Doris Heather Buckley tells us about this altogether extraordinary and unprecedented work of charity and spiritual compassion, in her book entitled *Spirit Communication.* [294] The problem is that of contacting entities that are so bewildered as to be particularly in need of counsel. Such entities are first and foremost (in order of the chapters in the book): fallen soldiers and other war victims; entities who act negatively under the compulsion of unsatisfied desires; suicides; deceased who were violent in life; and entities animated by destructive desires. Conversing with each of these entities may make them aware of their situation, inducing them to assume a more positive attitude. The essential thing is that the entity should cease to haunt certain places, or to obsess certain people or attempt to possess them in order to satisfy his own drives and passions through them.

Dr Carl Wickland, for example, was one of the first to form the conviction that the origin of many psychic disturbances, as also of numerous seemingly grave psychic illnesses, was to be sought in possession phenomena. He subjected his patients to shocks of static electricity that had the effect of driving the obsessing entity out of the patient's body and into that of Mrs Wickland, who enjoyed the gift of mediumship. Once the entity had become lodged in Dr Wickland's wife, at that time in a state of trance, he would start a dialogue with it, in most cases eventually succeeding in persuading the errant soul to go away and not to possess or to molest either the patient or any other person. The essence of the problem was that the entity itself was generally in good faith, not knowing itself to be 'dead' and believing itself to be still 'alive'. The explanations given by Dr Wickland thus proved more than useful, for his methods were essential to get the errant spirit to acknowledge his real state. [295]

Once the erring spirit has found its peace, it can abandon itself to what in spiritist literature is generally known as 'restoring sleep'. It is called 'sleep' by analogy only, and must not be thought of as sleep in the normal sense of the term as experienced and understood by incarnate humans. A soldier fallen during the First World

War talked about this aspect in the following terms:

> 'Before [the sleep] there is always a certain amount of the illusion that you are still just the same person that you were in the earth life.'[296]

This is to say that you believe yourself still an incarnate living on this earth. The effect of the restoring sleep is that 'when the spirit comes out of that sleep he knows where he is, as you sometimes wake up in the morning with some knotty problem solved.'[297] The same entity went on to say, talking about its own waking, that it was no longer in any state of uncertainty, that it was no longer suffering from the impression of believing itself to be still in the world and dreaming that had dominated it up to that time: 'After the sleep you know. It no longer feels like a dream.'[298] On the other hand:

> 'earthbound spirits have not yet passed through their sleep-stage; being earthbound means still thinking that you really belong to the earth-life, and that you are in some curious dream.'[299]

'Daddy', an entity we have already met, tells us that as he gradually woke up from his restoring sleep, he too became aware, a little at a time, that he had effectively passed from death in an earthly environment to life in the world of spirits.[300] And the entity of the young soldier whom we have also met provides us with another piece of information to complete our mosaic:

> 'Those who pass over with full knowledge and understanding of the life beyond do not need that sleep at all, unless they come over with their spirits tired by long illness or the worries of life. In practice, almost everyone needs the sleep period for a shorter or longer time. The greater the difficulty of the spirit in adjusting himself to the new conditions, the longer and deeper the sleep period that is necessary.'[301]

On reawakening from its sleep period, therefore, the soul becomes fully aware of its true situation and so adjusts to it. One can thus say that the soul has reached the other dimension in a decided, total and definitive manner.

Alternatively, one can say that its passing over has now been completed, that it is no longer 'undecided between life and death'; it is now truly dead to the dimension of our physical world, and therefore in a position to fully live in its new dimension of the spirit world.

Chapter 8
A Strangely Terrestrial Paradise

Death is often referred to as 'passing away' or 'passing over': this description is by no means improper, for death really is a passage, a change of state, an entry into a new condition. In earthly existence the psychic life of the subject is incarnate in matter, and takes place through the mediation of the physical body and its sense organs. But at the point of arrival, when fully integrated into the spirit world, the subject has only a psychic life.

But there are also some intermediate points, points of passage where the subject, though having abandoned his physical body, remains for some time shrouded in other shells or wrappings, and in a certain sense these can be defined as bodily, though the 'bodiliness' is undoubtedly of a subtler kind. This ensures that the newly deceased, though now deprived of the sense organs which were lost with his physical body, still perceives the material realities as if he had never lost these organs, and he perceives them in the same manner as before. He thus sees as if he still had eyes and hears as if he still had ears: in actual fact, however, he perceives, sees and hears directly with the psyche. His psyche, as it were, still vibrates at the vibratory level of matter, and it is this fact that enables a newly deceased subject to perceive matter in substantially the same way it is perceived with the physical senses.

It is only at a later stage that the subject, having in the meantime freed himself of certain residues and with his psyche in a more highly purified state, is able to perceive the psychic realities of his new dimension at the same time as the psychic realities of our own terrestrial dimension. In parallel with this, however, he will cease to perceive the physical realities, or, at least, he will no longer perceive them in the ordinary and normal manner: at most he will see them as shadows, as phantomlike realities. He could revert to perceiving them as we do, only if he were first to succeed in adapting the vibrations of his psyche to the vibrations of our material world; i.e. by tuning himself to the earth, by putting himself on the wave-length characteristic of our material life.

Having stated this as a general principle, I shall support it with a few testimonies taken from mediumistic literature. The soldier we met in Chapter 6, mortally wounded by shrapnel during the First World War, expressed himself in communicating with his family as follows:

> 'What I couldn't understand was ... only being able to see a shadow of all of you instead of what I knew you were like. But just after I was killed I saw you as you are in your bodies, but after that every time I came you got fainter and fainter. I can only see the part of you that comes up here when you die now.'[302]

The same communicating spirit told his family that immediately after his death he had met his own father and then remained with him at the very place where he had fallen in battle: but by then he had already become so immersed in the new spiritual dimension that he could no longer see or hear his former comrades still bearing the brunt of the battle, though he was clearly aware of what they were thinking. This is how he reports this fact:

> 'I didn't see any of the chaps all this time, nor hear the "Archies" [German shells] ... I could see what the chaps were thinking. They'd all got the pip because I was killed.'[303]

It is interesting to note the explanation that the spiritual guide present at the séance gave to the medium (who was actually the soldier's own sister) of how and why the deceased was able to read the thoughts of his surviving comrades:

'After death thought becomes a means of communication between you and us ... Most thought is transparent to those in the spirit. A kind of thought-picture forms in front of the thinker which can be seen by others.'[304]

The more the soul liberates itself of certain fluids that cling to it despite its separation from the body and frees itself of these residues, the more it enhances and develops its capacities for perceiving the psychic realities, the realities of the spiritual world. Do we therefore have to infer that it eventually loses all capacity for perceiving the physical realities of the world in the same manner that we see them with our physical eyes? This would not seem to be the case, according to many statements made by communicating spirits; in the following words of Arthur Findlay, for example:

'When we have lowered our vibrations down to the physical plane we experience what exists on your earth's surface.'[305]

At the very most, therefore, the spirit faces the problem of having to learn the techniques that enable it to do this.

Though the deceased are able occasionally to perceive the physical realities of this world as if they still had their bodily senses, in their own dimension they are normally concerned exclusively with psychic realities. The realities of the spiritual world are creations of thought, they are all, as it were, materialized thought-realities. The mind grasps all these realities in a direct and immediate manner. Thought can immediately be seen, read, and perceived as such.

In this connection let us listen to the words of an aforementioned British soldier, identified by the initials K.H.R.D., another victim of the First World War:

'First, there is talk and interchange of ideas with others who are in the same stage of development. At first it is just like ordinary speech between people with ordinary bodies and clothes and features; only you have that curious sense, which one often has in earth life, of understanding a great deal more than is said. You have that sense in the first spirit conversations, only you have it very much more strongly; and very soon you begin to feel that the words are only a kind of artificial framework, almost unnecessary to the thought.'[306]

'Captain Hinchliffe' is even more specific:

'After a while we begin to drop our earthly need for speech in the language of our own countries and begin to use thought transference by sending our thoughts, and projecting our thoughts, from mind to mind on waves that are intelligible to each and everyone. And so, bit by bit, the necessity for speech, and the awkwardness of betraying our personalities through these senses, becomes lessened.'[307]

Just as spirits talk to each other by thought transference, by directly reading and seeing each other's thoughts, so also do they call each other by means of thought. It is therefore with thought that the deceased transmit their appeals and make known their needs, continuing to do so until another spirit comes to their aid with appropriate counsel and suggestions.

One newly deceased, who at first found herself completely alone and isolated, turned her thoughts to her dear ones who had preceded her in death, especially to her two children whom she had lost many years before. Talking about the experience, she made it clear that she was completely unaware of having voiced these thoughts aloud. Nevertheless, almost as if somebody had heard her and hastened to comfort her, she suddenly saw before her two very handsome young men: an instantaneous and infallible instinct told her that these were her two boys grown to full manhood.[308]

Equally interesting are the words of 'Rudolph Valentino' to his wife:

'Once in a while, when I am with you or Muzzie, I feel a little anxious over results, and then the voice of H.P.B.

["Helen Petrovna Blavatsky", his spirit guide] calls down
to me from somewhere, "Steady, darling, steady!" Her
voice often sounds close to my ear, even when my eyes
do not see her, nor my senses feel her presence. Where is
she, that she is able to know what I am doing and to
answer my thoughts when she is invisible?'[309]

In just the same way, the deceased receive the thoughts
of those who still live incarnate, especially thoughts that
are directed to them. 'William Stead' put it to the
medium, Mrs Dawson Scott, as follows:

'Your thoughts reach me and you often think of me. I am
glad you do. I like being in touch with you.'[310]

And the deceased soldier who lost his life fighting in the
Transvaal says:

'I was often conscious of a pull from the earth-life, but
when I responded I found at first that I was unable to
communicate with my friends who were anxious to know
of my well-being and continued existence.'[311]

All in all, therefore, it would seem, using once again the
words of 'Rudolph Valentino', that 'one's innermost
thoughts ... are revealed to anyone in the same degree of
development or higher.'[312] And, if 'every mind can be
read', we may well agree with the conclusion reached by
'Marmaduke' that 'all hypocrisy is futile'.[313]

As has already been pointed out, once the deceased
has fully freed himself of certain fluids and residues that
kept him bound to the earth and the manner of perception associated with earthly existence, he begins to see all
earthly beings as no more than shadows and would not
be able to do better than that unless he first succeeds in
lowering his vibrations to the frequency of matter.
Tuning himself to this frequency, however, will no longer
be something natural and spontaneous, but rather the
result of an initiative that calls for a special ability: since
a soul that has fully passed into the other dimension no
longer vibrates at the frequency of matter, returning to it
even for a few brief moments will be possible only by
virtue of a special effort and technique; what has to be

done is in some way equivalent to the special techniques that are needed, for example, to enable a man to immerse himself in the depths of the ocean (i.e. in an element and a dimension certainly not his own).

The authors of *Realms of the Living Dead* further assert that the presence of a certain type of physical medium also makes it possible for the deceased to perceive our physical realities.[314]

It would seem that a deceased will be able to realize the greatest degree of re-descent into the conditions of our incarnate life when he succeeds in manifesting himself by actual incorporation in a medium. An entity known as 'Annie', who in this way manifested herself through the mediumship of her sister, put it as follows:

> 'I am in the Medium's body now, and she, in her astral or spirit body, has been taken away. I can hear and touch you, and everything appears the same as when I was on earth; but I cannot see you because the Medium's eyes are closed.'[315]

Once a deceased has succeeded in becoming once again attuned to our material plane, he is in a position to perceive not only the exterior images of matter (i.e. the images that we men can grasp with our bodily senses), but also many things that remain hidden to us. This is brought home to us, for example, by the entity 'William Stead' in his communications to the medium, Mrs Dawson Scott:

> 'With us, perception of objects is not limited to their exterior. We see through. ... For instance, I see you; I also see through you and into the substance of the earth. If I knew the names of the different strata I could tell you them. Also I can see through the globe. It is no thicker to me than falling rain.'[316]

The following communication was received by the same medium from her deceased husband, the late Dr Horatio Scott:

> 'I awoke in a new world ... I looked about and noticed a certain change in everything ... a different atmosphere. Things did not look the same. Houses had an air of

insubstantiality. The tree by which I stood was shadowy. I tried to touch it and my hand passed through. Yet where the tree was I had a sense of movement as if it consisted of tiny atoms violently astir.'[3 1 7]

There is a fact here that it is very interesting to note: while matter as such (i.e. purely physical and therefore relatively inert matter) is seen as a simple shadow, life is grasped with greater accentuation by the soul, which, given the vibratory tonality it assumes at that moment, is primarily attuned for perceiving thought and the mental realities. Now, as between thought and matter, life would seem to be something intermediate, and the thought-perceiving soul would here seem to be capable also of perceiving life in some way.

Substantial confirmation of this is provided by Crookall, in his book *The Next World — and the Next*, when he asks, 'What do "They" see of us?'. There are descriptions of the visions that the communicating spirits obtain by their own efforts, without the help of living people, although what they see is often imperfect and involves the difficulties that have already been outlined: there are spirits whose view of things is facilitated by the fact that they have either entered into, or are at least in contact with, the aura of a medium; other spirits report that their capacity to see has sometimes been helped when they have been able to enter the aura of a medium or to possess the medium's body, because this enabled them to see things through the physical senses of a human being.[3 1 8]

As far as a deceased is concerned (though only if he has fully passed into the other dimension), the material realities seem to have both the aspect and the consistency of shadows, so that a spiritual form, an entity, simply passes through them. No matter how strange this may seem, the purely mental realities of the other side appear more concrete and solid to the entities who live at that vibratory level. The sense of strangeness that this arouses within us will be somewhat lessened when we bear in mind that somewhat similar experiences recur quite often in our dreams.

As 'Rudolph Valentino' said, once again to his wife:

'Everything seems to be made of one or another kind of thought-force. This thought-substance, it seems, is far more solid and enduring than the stones or metals of the earth-world. This is hard to realize. It does not look at all as one would suppose thought-force ought to look. I always imagined it to be a misty, cloud-like sort of thing, and here it is more solid and colourful than the solid objects of the earth.'[319]

'Doctor Scott' confirms this by saying 'Our bodies are solid, as solid as yours, but different.'[320] And when the Reverend Charles Drayton Thomas asked his late colleague D.D., 'And does it seem to you that you have solid ground beneath your feet?', he received the answer 'Yes, it does — you remember I used to walk about the streets of London as long as I could.' Another question: 'And you find the things around you perfectly solid?' Answer: 'Yes.' Question: 'Didn't that strike you as strange when you woke up?' Answer: 'No, because you are surrounded by the thoughts of these things, the impressions are on you before you have had time to wonder, you sense them before you think of them.'[321]

All the same, the 'solidity' of the purely mental realities of the ultraterrene dimension is a solidity very much of its own kind. Although these realities do indeed appear very solid, they can be seen not only face-on, but also perceived from all sides at once. The entity 'Daddy', for example, speaking of an ultraterrene countryside consisting of a rolling plain not altogether unlike those in many English landscapes, had this to say:

'A remarkable characteristic of the scene was that objects at a distance were not diminished in size by reason of their distance from me, as on earth. The perspective was different. Furthermore, I was able to perceive them all around, and not only the surface exposed to my gaze, as in earth vision. Very peculiar and very wonderful is this enlarged spiritual vision. As you look at an exterior object, you see through it, and into it and all around it; in fact, your spiritual vision enables you to comprehend, in its entirety, that which you are looking at.'[3][2][2]

The spiritual world of the deceased is a mental world created by thought, and the same can be said of the sum total of the thoughts produced by the mental activity of those of us who live incarnate on the earth. The mode of perception enjoyed by entities *passes through* objects of all kinds, quite irrespective of whether these are the material realities of our world, the mental realities that make up their own ultraterrene world or, lastly, our human thoughts.

Speaking about the thoughts of those who still live on this earth, the entity 'William Stead' completes his previously quoted explanation that he can see through things with the following words:

'In the same way I perceive a thought. I see through it to the elements from which it sprang. I see not only where it began in the mind which formulated it, but I can see back along the chain of minds to the ultimate germ. I can then turn and observe its influence, its development, mark its growth in different minds. My perception pierces to what has been, has a full understanding of what is and can launch out into the future.'[3][2][3]

The realities of the spiritual world appear solid and tangible, and yet they can be moulded by thought. This was explained by the entity 'Amicus', a pseudonym of the late Reverend Stockwell, using the following words:

'Everything in this life external to personality is either an unconscious radiation from man's soul or a direct and purposeful exteriorisation of man's imaginings. In your earlier experiences here, you unconsciously throw off from your own subconsciousness your own environment. The appearances all round about you are the direct reflection of your mental, moral and spiritual condition; but after a while, as you progress, you find yourself in a greatly enlarged world, many of the objects in it being the direct results of your own and others' designedly creative acts. You will by self-volition and mental manipulation create from mind stuff objects of utility and beauty, which though intimately connected with yourself, will be exterior to you.'[3][2][4]

If thought is capable of creating all things, one can readily understand that the entities on the other side use thought to create all the things they desire, and all the things that correspond to their deep-rooted mental habits. Thus, love of nature generates landscapes of great beauty with 'plains, mountains, rivers and lakes; trees, flowers and birds',[325] and also with domestic animals and even the wild animals that the deceased used to hunt while still on earth.[326] The desire to see pleasant hills, or gardens full of flowers that one would like to pick or just to have around, will immediately generate all this.[327]

The deceased can satisfy not their needs, for needs do not exist in this dimension, but rather their desire to have a home in keeping with their taste.[328] The houses on the other side can therefore be very similar to those on earth, surrounded by gardens and meadows; there is no need to open the door, for just as soon as one desires to enter, the very act of thinking places one inside the house, with no further effort of imagination.[329] This close resemblance to the earthly realities seems readily explained by the fact that these are the only realities conceivable by spirits who have only recently abandoned the earth.

The spiritual environment in which an entity finds itself (and which to some extent it also created) is an environment that it can have in common with other entities. As one such entity explained to Arthur Findlay:

> '... all in the same plane can see and touch the same things. If we look at a field, it is a field to all who look at it. Everything is the same to those in the same condition of mental development ... We can sit down together and enjoy each other's company as you can on earth ... We can have a long walk in the country, and meet a friend we have not seen for a long time.'[330]

Such an environment can be common to all only if it is created and maintained by a common will; that is to say, by a superior will that all accept. Very significant in this respect is the testimony of the previously mentioned soldier who fell in the First World War:

'Then you find, and it seems very curious and fascinating, that you can change those things by wishing them to change. You can only do it with quite small and unimportant things, but for instance — you can look at a pine needle on the ground where you are sitting, and begin to think of it as a real needle, a steel needle, and then it is an ordinary sewing needle and you can pick it up. You can't change big things; you can't change the whole scene around you. That is because it's not only your scene, it belongs to lots of other spirits, too; but you can change any little thing, when the change won't affect anybody else.'[331]

To find themselves in a beyond that in many respects so closely resembles the earthly world is a source of great surprise and astonishment for the newly arrived. As the entity 'Tomblin' explained to the Reverend Thomas:

'We none of us seem to know quite what we do expect, but we all expect it will not be like earth. I have met others here who tell me the same thing. They were puzzled because it seemed like earth.'[332]

But the greatest astonishment of all is the one that can assail us the 'living' when we come face to face with a representation of the other side that is so unexpectedly anthropomorphic. Ernesto Bozzano recalls the irony and the jokes with which many people reacted to the publication of Sir Oliver Lodge's book *Raymond*, which is a collection of the communications Sir Oliver received from his son, another soldier who perished during the First World War. The passage that aroused the greatest hilarity was the one set in the spiritual domain that the newly deceased had by then attained, where it is said that at a certain moment a soldier feels the desire to smoke a cigar and immediately finds his wish fulfilled. There, too, we evidently have the possibility of giving shape to a cigar, though certainly not by creating it 'out of solid matter, but out of essences, and ethers, and gases'. And thus there was offered to the dead soldier 'what looked like a cigar'. The soldier grabbed it most avidly, 'but when he began to smoke it he didn't think so much of it; he had four altogether, and now he doesn't look at one.' Indeed:

'they don't seem to get the same satisfaction out of it, so gradually it seems to drop from them. But when they first come they do want things. Some want meat, and some strong drink; they call for whisky sodas ... But when they have had one or two, they don't seem to want it so much ...'[3][3][3]

The idea of having extravagant banquets in the other dimension, drinking whisky, smoking Havana cigars and the like may seem very strange, and even ridiculous, to anybody who approaches these ideas without any prior preparation, to anybody who does not appreciate that we can do exactly the same things in our dreams without afterwards feeling any astonishment at all. Just like dreams, the purely spiritual, mental, psychic existence of the deceased in the other dimension is a genuine creation of thought.

Details very similar to those given us by Raymond in the passage just quoted can be found in great abundance in the literature of mediumistic communications, bearing in mind that we are here concerned with mental creations that have the purpose of ensuring a more gradual detachment from the earthly forms to which our human mind is accustomed. Let us just for a moment try to imagine the large number of men and women who die suddenly (in war, or as the result of an accident, a crime, a stroke, etc.), and thus find themselves projected into the new condition from one moment to the next with no warning at all. They could not conceive a life without earthly forms, just as none of us can recall having a dream that was purely abstract and not in some way based on forms borrowed from our existence in this world. The persistence in the new condition of so many human and earthly forms is to ensure an unhurried detachment of the newly deceased from their long-standing and deeply rooted mental habits, which can only be changed by a very slow and gradual process. The entities responsible for the government of the lower spiritual spheres have, therefore, arranged matters in such a way that their mental environments have an aspect and appearance not greatly different from those we are accustomed to seeing on earth.

By and large, this is exactly the comment made by Ernesto Bozzano, who recalls that mental creation processes analogous to those of the other dimension occur also in our own world, though on a far more limited scale, where they are represented by the phenomena of ideoplasty and are recorded in an objective manner by thought photography.[3 3 4]

As far as our own material dimension is concerned, the phenomena of ideoplasty are limited by the density, heaviness and inertia of matter. Even so, ideoplasty performs a marvellous regulatory function with respect to matter, as one can readily see in all the biological phenomena, always provided that one is prepared to admit that these phenomena are animated by an intimate principle and cannot be reduced — other than disproof by reaching an obviously absurd conclusion — to merely mechanical phenomena. Ideoplasty not only regulates but moulds, forges and in a certain sense even creates, as is well brought out by the process of cicatrization (tissue reconstitution) and, in certain animal species, even reconstitution of amputated limbs. Ideoplasty becomes wholly free and unbridled only in psychic life (which always remains in some way independent of our bodiliness), especially in the free processes of psychic elaboration that occur in dreams; i.e. when the individual is no longer subject to the control of the conscious and rational ego with its inhibitions and censorships.[3 3 5]

In his preface to Bozzano's *La crisi della morte* (*The Crisis of Death*) Gastone De Boni set himself this selfsame problem, wondering whether certain anthropomorphic aspects attributed by mediumistic communications to the spiritual world really have to be rejected as absurd. Let me quote him verbatim:

'Having reflected about these problems ever since 1929, I eventually had to conclude that this is not so. If we want to accede more readily to what we are told about spirit existence, we simply have to think about dream life.

When we dream we evidently find ourselves particularly close to the condition in which we must find ourselves after death. In dreams, indeed, the sensorial world is shut out and we live exclusively in an interior world, which is essentially psychic. Let us now imagine that this state, rather than being unconscious, becomes fully conscious (i.e. as it would have to be if we do survive death). This would mean that the objects we dream would become as *real* for us as the material objects we perceive in our world when we are awake. It is not by any means strange, therefore, that we are told from the other side that the deceased live in houses in the proper sense of the term and continue to live a life that seems material. Here one has to make a distinction between material and real. The psychic sciences have already shown that the psychic world is equally real, indeed that it may well be the only true reality. And thus, reasoning logically, the presumed incongruencies of these transcendental revelations simply do not exist.'[3 3 6]

Mediumistic communications are quite insistent in stressing that *post mortem* experiences are not dreams but experiences of reality: 'It is not a dream. Everything is real to us,' say the entities who communicate with Arthur Findlay,[3 3 7] 'we live in a tangible world.'[3 3 8]

At this point I would add that what we living on this earth experience in our dreams often seems far too irrational, fluctuating and ephemeral to permit its being compared with the rationality, the continuity and the consistency of the spiritual world. (I am of course referring essentially to the levels of the spiritual world where the deceased have already left behind the mental Hades condition, which remains very close to the state of a nightmare or certain mental disorders.) Once the deceased has fully passed into the other dimension, he acquires a condition that, in the sense I have just explained, is clearly distinct from that of a dream. This concept seems to be confirmed by another observation made by the entities in touch with Arthur Findlay:

'Nevertheless, though it is largely a mental world, yet it [the other dimension] is not a dream world, as all on the same plane experience the same way of life. Their countryside, its climate, its scenery, its houses and vegetation are the same to all on the same plane, and its people are individuals like those with whom we come into contact each day on earth.'[339]

No matter how much one may liken life after death to a kind of dream, on account of its purely psychic character, it must be borne in mind that this 'dream' is character-ized by incomparably greater rationality, continuity and stability, and, what is more, by a certain objectivity or inter-subjectivity. Even though in certain respects it can be defined as or compared to a dream, the experience of life after death is undoubtedly a dream of its own kind. Furthermore, if we want to consider the *post mortem* experience from the particular point of view of its marked inter-subjectivity, we can liken it to the experience of concurrent dreams, especially reciprocal dreams,[340] and, more generally, to the cases of mutual telepathic action where 'each of the parties might receive a tele-pathic impulse from the other, and so each be at once agent and percipient.'[341]

For the moment I do not want to go further; it is sufficient to have to some extent justified and explained the peculiar anthropomorphic and earth-like character of such a large number of experiences of the other dimen-sion, as brought out by a true multitude of spirit commu-nications, indeed by almost the whole of credible mediumistic literature. Having shown these experiences to derive from the creativity of thought gives us sufficient reason why they may reveal themselves as authentic for those who live them on the planes here considered. But it also provides us with sufficient reason for understanding how, at a later stage, these experiences can be left behind by those who succeed in elevating themselves to higher planes of the afterlife. Having shown that these earth-like forms derive from the creativity of thought explains not only the 'strangely terrestrial paradise', where form is still wholly dominant, but also the higher heavens, where every form becomes comprised and possessed in its selfsame principle, and all slavery to form disappears once and for all.

Chapter 9
Other Modalities of
Spiritual Existence

The spiritual dimension of the other side appears to be a world constituted solely by thought. Thought creates it, directly, without any instrumental mediation; and it is also thought that knows it, experiences it, directly, and without any mediation of bodily senses.

In this purely psychic beyond, therefore, knowledge is essentially telepathic. Each entity knows the other entities by virtue of a direct contact that becomes established between the two souls, a situation in which the first entity reads the thoughts of the second.

The 'things' of this world, its external realities, are — as we have seen — pure creations of thought. The act of thought that brings them into being confers upon them a kind of objective, or at least inter-subjective, reality. The external 'things' of the other dimension also have a character of permanence, although this is relative and limited in time. And since these 'things' are likewise materialized by thought, because they are once again psychic realities, it follows that the knowledge that can be had of them is always in its substance a form of telepathy.

The contact-knowledge, the experimental knowledge that a deceased has of reality, can have as its object not only psychic realities in the proper sense of the term (i.e. other souls) and objectified psychic realities (i.e. the 'things' of the beyond created and materialized solely by thought), but extends also to the material realities of this earth. These latter realities, indeed, can likewise be known by entities in a direct manner, though the form of extra-sensorial perception used for this purpose is no longer to be defined as telepathy, but rather and more properly as *telesthesia*.

This 'remote perception' without the mediation of the bodily senses can also take place in the clairvoyants who live incarnate in this world and who, so it would seem, are at that moment in a state of partial disincarnation. All the more so, therefore, will telesthesia (as with all other forms of extrasensorial perception) operate in the deceased, who have lost their sense organs at the same time as their physical body.

It is true that the deceased, once they have entered the spiritual condition in a full and definitive manner, tend to develop above all a form of telepathic knowledge, because in their new dimension they are concerned exclusively with psychic realities. But it is equally true that the deceased can reacquire their former direct experience of material things by what we shall call *telesthesia*, or clairvoyance in the present, to use the terminology of parapsychology. They will acquire this capacity in direct proportion to their success in attuning themselves to matter. Since matter consists of energy that vibrates at a lower tonality, a deceased will succeed in re-immersing himself in matter, perceiving the things of this world of ours only to the extent to which he can assume this lower vibratory tonality (i.e. to vibrate at a lower frequency). It is this capacity that enables spirits to make themselves present in our earthly environments, and also to manifest themselves through a medium.

Parapsychology has made us familiar not only with clairvoyance in the present, but also with clairvoyance in the past and clairvoyance in the future. As regards the latter, which is also known as precognition or foreknowledge, it seems only natural that a capacity already found in the living incarnate should also be possessed, and to an even greater degree, by the deceased. I say to an even greater degree because the emergence of psychic powers is always associated with a degree of disincarnation of the subject. If certain phenomena due to precognition can occur when the subject finds himself in a state of partial disincarnation, they will surely occur with even greater intensity in the state of total disincarnation that follows physical death. Nevertheless, one must here bear in mind a consideration that is well put by the authors of *Realms of the Living Dead*:

> 'While those in the astral are, as it were, a step above those in the Physical World and can see many events and conditions somewhat before they manifest on earth — just as a person standing on a platform can see over the heads of the crowd and tell them what is approaching — no matter how sincere they may be, they can seldom predict accurately the time of physical manifestation for that which they see.'[3][4][2]

I need not here go into the reasons they adduce in order to explain these inaccuracies, because here I am only interested in stressing and underscoring the fact that mediumistic communications also contain substantially correct predictions.

That the entities of the deceased also possess the capacity of clairvoyance of past events is a possibility that is not only very clearly affirmed in many mediumistic communications, but often also supported by rather concrete detail. The kind of clairvoyance in the past that the deceased have in the other dimension, is quite analogous to the one that can be observed in our midst, where it is known either by the same name or as *psychometry*.

As far as we can tell at present, it would seem that, just like our own psychometrics, the deceased can re-activate their memories of past events, and even reactualize these events by a vivacious and intense representation that often borders on the authentically dramatic.

In this connection the entity 'William Stead' tells us that:

'... "preserved in time" does not mean fossilised. When we look back, what was happening at any given period happens. The page is opened and the events are actual — not like the dull print of a book. The people live and move and have their being — the merchant is in his office, the errand boy running through the streets, the housewife shopping at her door. The picture moves and is a thing in itself. In the same way we can look forward, and again it is an actual period that we see.'[343]

The same entity gives us an even more concrete idea of how the deceased can thus intrude in other epochs:

'A little before I spoke to you I was at a ruined town in North Africa. I looked backward from the ruin through the phases of its existence — a decaying town, a populous town, a village, big walls and trees, a resting place for the nomad. One or two settled families. The first who brought there his wife and children. I saw back to the far-off days before man came, then before the great beasts came, when crawling water covered the soft ground and the air was a thick mist, and farther still into the dimness of cooling fire wherein was no life.'[344]

Indeed, there is no lack of testimony about similar trips into the past. As the entity 'Feda' explained, the imprints of all events are permanently fixed in the ether, and it is these imprints that can be used by people who have the gift of psychic faculties.[345] And consequently they can be used even more readily by the entities of the deceased, given their state of total disincarnation.

When contact is made with a certain locality, it can be seen not only as it actually is, but also as it used to be at various times in the past. Of one and the same place it is therefore possible to have many different representations, each corresponding to a particular epoch of the past, passing from one time plane to another. It is as if one's impressions of events had become stratified, and one therefore has to pinpoint the layer and the precise event that one wishes to conjure up. As 'Judge Hatch' tells us:

'We read one layer instead of another, either by affinity or by will. It is no more strange than that a man may go among the millions of volumes in the British Museum and select the one he wants.'[346]

That 'Judge Hatch' here mentions the importance of the *affinity* factor is yet another confirmation of the insistent manner in which the great law of affinity is mentioned in transcendental revelations, as governing and regulating all experience of life in the spiritual world. It is by virtue of this law that like and like live in the same spiritual environment, that like and like attract each other in creating new relationships; and even when, as here, re-evoking an epoch of the past, one must first put oneself into a state of being spiritually in tune with the period, just as one has to do when desiring to establish true spiritual, mental or psychic contact with another person.

When a memory of the past is momentarily accessible only to somebody who has lived these events in a personal manner, the subjects involved can project their memories outwards in order to inform other entities or, better, to get them to relive these particular facts in a more concrete manner. It is as if they were re-evoking one or more events by projecting what one might call a three-dimensional film.

'Topsy', the aforementioned slave girl from the plantations in the 'Deep South' in the nineteenth century, had been seemingly abandoned by her parents at a very tender age and, quite understandably, felt considerable resentment for them. But she could not remember what had actually happened. First, her father had been violently separated from his wife and baby daughter, leaving Topsy alone and forsaken on the plantation. It was not until Topsy herself died and found her way into the spirit world that she was at last taken care of. In the end there also came the moment of acknowledgement: Topsy first met her father and, seeing his tall and strong figure, wondered how it was that he had not fought to avoid being separated from her and her mother. That was why her father made her see what, using the language of a later age, we might call a kind of film. Topsy was thus able to relive the moment when her father, bound and whipped, had to suffer in impotent desperation while his wife and baby daughter were being taken away.[347]

The Reverend Thomas offers us another example as part of his experience of communicating with the deceased, an example that also involves past situations and events of greater historical importance:

'My informants say that not only are the people of other days approachable, but, under certain circumstances, the cities in which they lived are reproduced. In some instances these have permanent place in the spheres, while others of them, existing only in the minds of their former inhabitants, can be materialized and given a temporary objective form. Then the ancient city stands revealed, with those who occupied it at some given date moving about in the manner of long ago. This reproduction is for purposes of study and education. Thus, the different periods of ancient Egypt, Greece and other lands, now being studied by archeologists on earth, are made available to students in spirit life.'[348]

If, then, not only the events of the past may acquire a more objective existence, but also the manner (variegated as it may be) in which these events are remembered or imagined, there could well arise a very particular problem. Indeed, if the representation of an event that has really happened and that of an imperfectly remembered (or simply imagined) event can be equally realistic, could it not be that somebody would be led astray into thinking that the astral 'film' of an imaginary event, or an event changed by memory, is the re-enactment of an event exactly as it really happened? If that is so, then certain astral 'films' of fanciful Atlantis-like cities, or of historical events presented in the manner of historical fiction or comic strip, could well correspond to at least partly subjective mental creations rather than to authentic memories of real events. We should therefore be on our guard and use reasonable prudence in evaluating the testimonies of souls that merrily rove through history, passing happily from ancient Greece to Atlantis, more or less as happens in a certain passage of a book from which I have nevertheless quoted an observation that appeared to me to be noteworthy.[349] Let us therefore beware of Atlantis-like cities below the sea, of ancient Rome as seen by American film directors, of medieval life set in a nineteenth-century frame. But in uttering this word of warning, I do not in any way want to belittle the great and very substantial interest that attaches to what these transcendental communications affirm in connection with this novel and quite unsuspected manner of studying the past by re-enacting it in the present.

Be it clear, however, that it is always creative thought-activity that exteriorizes the various images making up the three-dimensional film of which we have spoken. The thought-activity that creates such extremely lifelike successions of scenes makes it possible not only to re-activate the past, but also to give life to new and wholly invented stories. Here, even though the characters may speak, there is no need at all for the narrator to use words of his own (a need that, in any case, is rather rare even in our celluloid films).

When the entity 'George Dawson' was asked 'Are words used in the stories you create?', he replied:

> 'We don't use words because our thoughts are visible. When we formulate a story it is in progressive scenes. Instead of reading the story we perceive it. When Miss S. thinks out a scene that scene becomes indelible. She does not think it in words, she sees it rising through her mind, and she gives it the expression necessary for your world; but it does not begin with words. They are added.'[350]

'George Dawson' also spoke about his painting. But the painting in question does not need any canvas, nor does the artist need a palette or the colours that earthly artists squeeze onto it from a myriad of little metal tubes. It is a form of painting brought into being directly by creative acts of thought:

> 'We think [a picture] into being and the thought remains. We don't have walls on which to hang our pictures, but they become part of the general consciousness. I wander for long periods among visions of beauty which other minds have formulated. I formulate my own visions, sometimes as a single picture, sometimes in flashing scenes.'[351]

And again: 'You do not read here, but the story flows before you from its inception to its finish.' What follows is particularly interesting, for 'George' goes on to affirm that the arts on the other side are far more closely integrated and tend to merge:

> 'On earth the arts were entirely distinct and widely different. The cause of this was that their material mediums were different. Here they are almost inter-changeable.'[352]

Are there books in the next world? 'Judge Hatch' claims to have visited a great astral library and to have read a book there.[353] Another deceased, in earthly life a gardener and friend of the Reverend Thomas, speaks of his contentment in at last being able to satisfy his taste for reading, a desire he always had to repress in earthly life on account of the humble condition of his birth which had not permitted him to stay on at school and continue his studies. All in all, however, one gains the impression that in spirit life the possession of books, or the writing or reading of books, is somewhat like eating and drinking, or like speaking in one language rather than another, namely a need that is more psychological than real, something to which the subject may remain attached by virtue of a mental habit, though it does not represent a deep-seated and irresistible need. In the other dimension, indeed, the essential thing would seem to be the presence of thought, which is capable of expressing itself directly as such and can therefore be grasped, received and 'read' directly, without there being any need for mediating words.

Moreover, whether an intuition is so closely connected with its mode of expression that it will no longer be exactly the same when this expression changes but becomes modified in some respect, represents a subtle philosophical problem that I have seen treated elsewhere (in the works of Benedetto Croce, for example),[354] but certainly not in mediumistic communications. From these communications, rather, there seems to emerge the idea that in the beyond, in the other dimension, expression represents something that is wholly accessory and can therefore be changed at will. I do not know whether and to what extent this idea has been philosophically analyzed, but it certainly seems to be a suggestion that recurs in communications from the other side.

In the earthly dimension the situation would seem to be very different. Here words are necessary and have to be exactly reproduced if a given literary work, or a work of philosophy or science, is to be precisely and properly what its author intended it to be. Moreover, whether our earthly dimension is in itself something that is not essential and therefore disposable or whether it, too, is destined to receive a sanction of eternity on the occasion of the Resurrection, represents a great theologico-eschatological problem that it would be premature to try to consider within the context of this chapter.

I shall come back to the matter in the next chapter, where I shall try to formulate a few thoughts that I hope will make sense. However this may be, expression that is wrapped up in words and therefore made up of letters that can be printed on pages or tablets of durable material and thus read or reviewed one by one, would seem to be a type of expression characteristic of our earthly world, but not by any means necessary at other levels of existence. It may continue to be employed, though only occasionally and accidentally (i.e. due to habit or psychological necessity), also in the spirit world, where thought and its expression assume a far more intuitive, global, synthetic and immediate character.

And it is precisely in this way, as 'Dr Horatio Scott' would have it, that 'formulated thought can become permanent. It has form and shape. In a way it lives.'[355] On being asked by the medium how the books we write and publish here on earth are received in the other world 'Dr Scott' replied:

> 'I perceive it [your book] as a series of scenes that have a faint life of their own. Being formulated they do not perish, and their size and glow is in accordance with the

art force which created them. Poor emanations are faint and quickly fade; but art lives. There is a great deal of it here.'[3 5 6]

'George' underscored the same concept. On being asked the question, 'When art is not first rate what happens to it?', he replied:

'I always think of it as a falling star — it glitters for a second and then vanishes. The hope of the artist here is that his work shall have permanency.'[3 5 7]

And here is the answer that 'George' gave when the same medium asked him 'Do you get our books?':

'The art you produce appears here in the shape of bubbles — I do not mean actual bubbles, but a rounded shape containing all of the work that is of value. These containers are not filmy or breakable, they are clear.'[3 5 8]

Note, however, that in the other dimension the intuitive, immediate and global character of the creations brought into being by thought does not by any means imply that there is inaccuracy or lack of attention to detail. It does not imply that entities in the spirit world cannot analyze, observe, individual things, or dedicate their attention and creative activity to minute detail. All the available testimonies tell us that a personal object, even when it is of simple shape and small size, can be created by simply thinking it in a spontaneous manner. It would be reasonable to think that many of the details that characterize such objects emerge by virtue of memories that survive, remain and operate unconsciously. But when the reality to be created by thought is to have a more complex structure, it will need to be 'finished' by a series of thought acts that are more analytical, pay greater attention to detail, and are more accurate in giving specific form to many individual features.

Even the 'finishing' of the entity's own astral body may call for a series of corrections, adjustments and improvements. 'Dr Scott', for example, forged his own astral body by a series of conscious thought acts, improving it step by step. Here is how he puts it:

> 'I gave myself the old semblance — that first. Then I
> thought the semblance into clothes, and in the pockets
> had the things I was accustomed to carry there ... It took
> me some time to make my appearance as I wanted it. I
> found myself without bits of my anatomy which I
> supposed I had formulated, but which had escaped my
> attention. I was lop-sided and oddly shaped at first, but
> gradually I rectified my deficiencies and mistakes and
> presently had an appearance with which I, at least, was
> satisfied.'[359]

It is a little difficult to understand here whether the entity
'Dr Scott' would not have obtained better results, and
with less toil, if he had simply allowed his memory to
operate at the unconscious level, relying also on what we
have already called the crypto-conscious mind. Indeed,
other sources suggest that entities can choose between
letting the unconscious work on its own (albeit after
having assigned it a task defined in very global terms)
and fashioning one's semblance by a multiplicity of
conscious acts (and thus following in the footsteps of
what an artisan, a technician, *homo faber* does on this
earth). It is likely that these two methods complement
each other when complex works are involved. Indeed,
some other communications strongly suggest this.

The larger and more complex the work that is to be
fashioned, the more the thought-form that creates it will
have to call for three things if it is to have value and be of
intersubjective use, rather than merely giving rise to a
vague and nebulous representation. These are: a very
precise idea, a strong concentration of thought, and a
subsequent commitment that will lead creative thought to
finish the work in all its detail.

'Marmaduke', for example, points out that a thought
used either to communicate or to give shape to things
must not consist of a mere fleeting desire for something
that one would like to have, but rather of a firm concentration of one's thoughts on what one really wants,
constructing it in all its details.[360] Thus, a simple

thought-act will be sufficient to enable an entity to have a long gown of extremely simple cut and shape, but a more fanciful and complex dress will require creative thought to dwell on each individual feature of the garment to be produced. A similar procedure has to be followed if a landscape picture is to be obtained by thought creation: if something more than a confused and decidedly inadequate representation is to be obtained, the creating entity must first have a very clear conception of the ultimate result.[361]

Similarly, as an 'astral architect' explained to Desmond Shaw, a house, a garden or similar works can be brought into being by first imagining the whole in its broad pattern and then gradually forging the details:

> '... much as an impressionist artist with a pencil, first lightly sketches the outline, and then fills in and makes more plain, until the completed picture is before him.'[362]

Bearing in mind that in the other dimension these things are created solely and exclusively to satisfy psychological needs, a long series of concordant testimonies suggests that the construction of complex realities is normally entrusted to specialists. 'Rudolph Valentino', for example, cites landscape gardeners among these specialist artists in the spirit world, and what he has in mind are undoubtedly English-type gardens or parks, which seek to imitate the natural countryside; his 'gardeners' must therefore be understood in the much wider sense of landscape constructors.[363] On another occasion 'Valentino' affirmed that 'houses are built by spirits who have learned how to mould this thought-force',[364] an assertion that is closely in line with what we are told by numerous other entities.[365]

Whatever forms part of the landscape patrimony that the entities of the deceased have in common is safeguarded as such, in the sense that individual entities can only create or destroy objects and realities of limited size and extent, i.e. those that can be created or destroyed without causing detriment to others or to the community. It therefore follows that, even though thought-forms on an individual scale may change all the time, those of greater importance and common usefulness are far more permanent: the creation or destruction of these more substantial thought-forms is decided by the entities that preside over community, and carried out by specialists who know how to do the job; that is to say, by spirits whose particular capacity or vocation best fits them for the task in hand.

Let me quote a passage from Bozzano, who — after noting that transcendental communications seem to agree as regards this matter — puts it as follows:

> 'The configuration of the "astral" countryside is made up of two types of thought objectivations that differ widely and substantially from each other: one of these would seem to be permanent and unchangeable, representing the objectivation of the thought and will of very highly placed spirit entities who bear responsibility for governing the lower spiritual spheres, while the other would seem to be transitory and extremely changeable, being made up of the objectivations of the thought and will of individual disincarnate entities, each of whom can create his own immediate surroundings.'[366]

Are the spiritual spheres really governed by authorities? Surely, nothing prevents us from conceiving an essentially moral authority being exercised for the common good by the wisest, the most illumined, the spiritually most evolved. In this connection, indeed, a rather convincing indication is provided by a large number of different sources — so numerous and frequent as to make the idea seem almost commonplace — that the authority in question is neither coercive nor repressive, but rather a guide in the moral sense. In the spirit world there are neither governors nor officials, but only guides, 'spiritual guides'. There is no need for an authority that imposes its laws by force. 'Amicus' notes:

> 'The coercive and restraining power operating [here] is the law of consequences. A child on earth, when it finds by experience that fire burns, shuns it in future, and so

when the so-called wicked here find to their chagrin — as they invariably do — that evil perpetrated on another results in an immediate increase of their own pains and penalties, they naturally refrain from such practices in future.'

Each entity punishes himself, for such is the retributive justice that is brought into being by this law of cause and effect. The entities that are 'youngest' in their new condition obviously stand in need of someone to promote and supervise their education, of someone who will guide them with wisdom and a firm hand. This work of counselling, teaching and guardianship 'is to many fine souls a self-imposed task and a labour of love.'³ ⁶ ⁷

For the moment, however, let us do no more than note the provident presence of an essential minimum of organization, that operates in a manner in keeping with the essentially spiritual character of even community life in the other dimension. On the other hand, even though the Spirit may be one, it yet gives rise to many different charisms: and it is reasonable to suppose that this variety of gifts and corresponding commitments must have its counterpart in a division of labour that seeks the good of each and all.

Chapter 10
The Ultimate Destination

After a detailed and painstaking review of all aspects of the 'spiritist' view of reality, I have become profoundly convinced that it is fully compatible with even the most orthodox interpretation of the Christian religion. Indeed, the whole of the Bible abounds in episodes that have a substantial parapsychological aspect in keeping with spiritist models of the type here reviewed. The view that spiritism (or 'spiritualism' as it has become fashionable to say) offers us of life after death may undoubtedly bewilder an orthodox Christian in certain respects; but when one really looks into it, there remains nothing that conflicts with the essence of the biblico-Christian revelation. Rather, it only provides further confirmation of this revelation in terms of actual experience.[368] But let us once again approach the matter step by step.

At this point in our review one may observe, firstly, that our attempt to characterize the other side and its modes of existence has brought to light a paradise that is almost too earthly, mundane and anthropomorphic. One may therefore wonder whether it corresponds to the true paradise, or whether it does not rather represent a condition that has to be overcome before one can attain to the only state that could really be considered paradise in the full sense of the term. Spirit communications agree, for the most part, in stressing the imperfect and transitory character of this *Summerland*, as it is often called by Anglo-Saxon spiritists and by the entities with whom they are in contact: this land, so incredibly bright as to seem flooded by summer sunshine, yet reveals itself as extremely earthly and bound to the forms of bodily existence. The communications suggest various patterns and maps of the higher conditions of life after life. There is insistent mention of a further 'death' that seems to consist of the shedding of yet another psychic shell, the one that up to this point enables a soul to live at the level of Summerland by assuming a kind of bodily form that is yet subtle and extremely mouldable. Beyond and above Summerland, however, it is said to be possible to continue individual existence, albeit emancipated from all conditioning effects of form, and in a manner that becomes ever more purified and spiritualized.

At this point, however, one may well ask whether the bodily connection must become wholly forgotten and lost, or whether the spirit, once it has freed itself of the slavery of matter, once it has affirmed its dominion and supremacy over matter, could not continue to assume — or return to assuming — a material dimension as a further dimension in which its life becomes completed. Let us for a moment reflect on the fact that the bodily dimension is the dimension of objectifying scientific knowledge, of technology, of art inasmuch as it is expressed by material means, and also of literature inasmuch as it is expressed by words in the various languages. All this constitutes such a wealth that it becomes rather difficult to say whether the simple fact of forgetting these things, leaving them behind one as it were, constitutes real progress. One may presume that there yet exists some way of assuming all this, though always within the limits compatible with a spirituality of a higher level or even a spirituality that has attained the utmost level, the supreme summit of its possibilities.

It seems to me that the biblical and Christian idea of resurrection well expresses this idea of the need for recovering even the bodily dimension that is lost on the occasion of death, before man can fully realize himself. In this sense, indeed, Christianity speaks of a bodiliness that will have lost all its imperfections and all its limitations,

The Ultimate Destination

assuming the connotations of a glorious bodiliness, perfect vehicle of the loftiest spirituality.

As far as biblico-Christian spirituality is concerned, this constitutes so basic a tenet as to orientate it in a direction that is very different from, for example, Hindu spirituality (notwithstanding the many and considerable analogies that still remain). One might presume that entities deriving from a biblico-Christian tradition that has remained unaffected by influences of disincarnate spiritualism of different origin (gnosticism, catharism, etc.) would be rather clearly orientated in this direction.

And yet it remains a fact that the great mass of mediumistic communications does not come to us from entities that can be defined as 'orthodox'. Both the metaphysics and the theology expressed in these communications frequently reveal theosophic influences (to use this term in its widest sense). The Christianity that so many of these communications propose can in fact be defined — always using the term in its widest sense — as a theosophic, reincarnationist, Indianized Christianity, a Christianity that, judging by what appears to be communicated, seems essentially to say the same things as the oriental religions; a Christianity that would have to be rediscovered in its substance by despoiling it of the dogmas that have become stratified over the simplicity of the original teaching, drawing a veil over this simplicity and misinterpreting it.

The kind of Christianity proposed by so many of these communications does pay an excessive tribute to a disincarnate spiritualism of an Indian type, a spiritualism that conceives the progress of the spirit only in the sense of a gradual disincarnation. Obviously, a teaching orientated in this manner cannot but indicate the goal of all evolution as being constituted by the attainment of a wholly undifferentiated spirit state, a state devoid of all concrete cultural content, and devoid also of all multiplicity and separation. In a consciousness of this kind, indeed, all individual existence would disappear.

Nevertheless, there are many communications in

which individuality is defined as something permanent, even though it becomes modified as it progresses and evolves. As representative of all of these, let me here quote the strong and decided statement made by the entity 'Julia Ames' in connection with the effective condition of the soul in the spiritual dimension:

> 'No, I tell you no. Individuality is not eliminated, but rather accentuated in its essence, and harmonized in its accidents.'[369]

In actual fact, each entity not only remains perfectly identified[370] for centuries, and even for millennias, but is destined to preserve its own individuality for ever, because — even though it ultimately merges with God, even though it ultimately becomes one with God — it continues to be itself, clearly distinct from all others.[371]

As far as the soul is concerned, merging with God and becoming one with Him means acquiring consciousness, knowledge and awareness of all things. The entity 'Frederic Myers' is particularly insistent on this aspect.[372] 'Marmaduke', too, conceives the progress of individuality as a growing comprehension of the plan of the universe and of the very mysteries in which its future is shrouded.[373]

Even though the soul ultimately tends towards all this, it remains very far removed from it while here on earth. Even the passing into the other world does not of itself make it omniscient:

> 'Those people who think of their departed friends as being all-wise, how disappointed they would be if they could know that life on this side is only an extension of the life on earth!'

So warns 'Judge Hatch'.[374] Or, as the entity 'Dr Horatio Scott' says, the deceased 'are very much the same as they were with you. A low intelligence does not become a high intelligence by losing its body.'[375] Furthermore, 'we know no more about God than you do.'[376]

The communicating entities dwell greatly on the limited nature of each individual experience, as also on the limited capacity of each entity for perceiving reality;[377] which would seem to go a long way towards explaining why each entity has its own point of view and its own specific opinion on so many different things.[378]

Rather, one can say that the deceased is still shrouded in the opinions he held while he lived on earth, due to the fact that in the other dimension thought is directly creative, so that each deceased will see his own opinions (no matter what they might be, no matter how true or false they might be) transformed into subjective experiences. He will now see realized whatever he limited himself to believing while still on earth. He was therefore prepared for seeing what he now sees, and the more strongly he held and stressed a given opinion or belief while he lived on earth, the better he will have prepared himself for seeing what he now sees.

In this connection, a consideration made by 'Judge Hatch' seems to be particularly significant:

> 'Now, remember that in this form of matter where I am men are living principally a subjective life, as men on earth live principally an objective life. These people here, being in the subjective, reason from the premises already given during their objective or earth existence.'[379]

> '[And for this reason] the holders of different opinions are often hot in their arguments. Coming here with the same beliefs they had on earth, and being able to visualise their ideals and actually to experience the things they are expecting, two men who hold opposite creeds forcibly are each more intolerant than ever before.'[380]

In conformity with the opinions, convictions and beliefs they professed while still on earth, each deceased will find his own particular paradise on the other side. 'Rudolph Valentino', for example, was told the following by the entity 'H.P.B.' (Helen Petrovna Blavatsky):

> 'If you and your artist friends find happiness and contentment here, then you are in the heaven for artists. But remember ... that the farmers find also a heaven for farmers; the red Indians, a Happy Hunting Ground; and the Buddhists, their Nirvana.'[381]

An individual paradise is a collective, intersubjective reality, even though it may be limited to those who have good reason for thinking themselves entitled to enter it and become part of it. As 'Judge Hatch' explains:

> 'The aggregation of souls is objective: that is, the souls exist in time and space; the heaven which they enjoy is subjective, though they may all see the same thing at the same time, as, for instance, the vision of Him whom they adore as the Redeemer.'[382]

In fact, 'Judge Hatch' visited some spiritual environments where the souls live in a special religious tension. He defines these environments as 'Christian heavens'. Since souls flock together on account of affinity, 'Judge Hatch' gained access to these ultraterrene environments only because he managed to become spiritually attuned. 'Perhaps I could not have gone so easily at any other time,' he explains, 'for my heart was full of love for all men and my mind was full of the Christ *idea*.'[383]

I have no difficulty in supposing that the religious spirits (i.e. the spirits of those who on earth live their particular religion in each and every moment) will gain access, possibly immediately after their demise, to their particular heaven — the Hindu to a Hindu heaven, the Muslim to an Islamic heaven, and so on. But it is a fact that most authors of mediumistic communications testify that they arrived at a place which could be defined as a 'secular' or 'lay' heaven rather than a 'confessional' one. Indeed, recalling her awakening on the other side, 'Julia' notes as follows:

> 'The chief surprise that I found was in fact that we were all so much the same. We did not seem to have become angels or saints.'[384]

We can pair this statement with another, rather similar, made by 'Captain Hinchliffe':

> 'Actually I feel no different. Nothing angelic, nothing ethereal, nothing one would think of as being connected with Heaven or the Hereafter. My actual experience is that I am as real in this life as I have been to you, and

that all growth towards that great Happiness and that
great Heaven they talk of, must be a slower process than
most people believe.'[385]

This manner in which the hereafter is perceived by the
newly deceased seems at first to belie the traditional faith:
if nothing else, it seems to belie the traditional manner of
conceiving life after death.[386] But one must beware of
rushing to over-hasty conclusions, for it seems to me that
really thorough and detailed acquaintance with the
literature of mediumistic communications leads one to
confirm the traditional religious view, at least as regards
its permanently valid core.

Let us consider, for example, the *Letters from Julia*.
As William Stead put it in the preface to this book (and
the William Stead in question was at that time still alive
on this earth):

> 'Protestants and Catholics and Greek Orthodox have
> assured me that Julia has expressed the faith which they
> hold. Mrs Besant told me that Julia must have been
> employed by one of the Masters to teach me the truths of
> Theosophy which I would not receive through any other
> channel. A Sikh professor assured me that with the
> exception of two immaterial points of detail, Julia's
> Letters might be translated and circulated as an exact
> statement of the Sikh faith. The distinguished editor of
> the *Hindoo Spiritual Magazine* expressed his surprise
> that a Western writer should have been able to set forth
> so lucidly the essential truth of the Hindoo religion.'[387]

Similarly, referring to the book *The Progression of
Marmaduke*, Judge Edmonds said in 1853:

> 'that he was struck by the beauty — and at times
> sublimity — of the spiritual communications, and by the
> uniformly elevated tone of morals which they taught ...
> Not a sentiment is to be found that would be unaccept-
> able to the most pure and humble Christian.'[388]

It is quite true that the immediate 'paradise' of very many
newly deceased people does not have the strictly 'religious' character that ought to correspond to the expectations of most orthodox Christians; but this can be
explained by the fact that many newly deceased are not

prepared for attaining to a spiritual condition capable of being defined in such precise terms. 'Captain Hinchliffe', as we have seen, supposes that evolution towards this readiness must be much slower than is generally thought. This much greater gradualness, as the same entity goes on to explain, is because 'the soul or ego is such a delicate structure, that no quick change *can* take place without shocking that soul and, for a moment, putting the whole thing into a disorganized state.'[389]

In other words, each deceased finds the heaven for which he has been prepared, though this does not exclude the possibility of further evolution in a more strictly religious sense, a possibility that is generally either indicated or, at least, hinted at.

But we can readily admit that even at this stage there must be spiritual spheres that come rather close to the Christian idea of heaven, especially in view of the many people who are undoubtedly prepared for finding such a heaven or paradise: a veritable multitude, especially in former times, though the host still exists today, even in the context of our present-day civilization.

Each deceased therefore has his own heaven, always provided that he has a heaven and does not find himself in a condition better described as inferno or purgatory. Each deceased has his own heaven, just as he has his own particular religious views (or otherwise), his own *Weltanschauung* or view of the world, his own conception of life.

Even in this first beyond, the deceased can already perceive and recognize certain things as a result of achieving a certain maturity. Many spirits quickly arrive at an appreciation and understanding of certain realities. One may also expect that, given the greater collective maturity that prevails there, a larger number of them will attain to this comprehension and experience and, indeed, proceed ever further along this road.

This is further confirmed by numerous intuitions to be found in the literature of mediumistic communications, intuitions valid from both the general religious point of view and the more specifically Christian, including the Catholic viewpoint.

Here we shall have to limit ourselves to just a few examples. In *Spirit Teachings*, a book written by entities who made their communications to William Stainton Moses, I see the recognition of the value that could be attributed in the past (though there is no need to mention the particular epoch) to a certain manner of living in adoration of God and seeing all things as cooperating to this end:

> 'Art, literature, and science laboured for religion: and so far from worship absorbing the work of life, it was rather that every act of common life was raised to the dignity of an act of worship.'[390]

This idea is then specified even more clearly in the next passage:

> 'To live in the presence of Deity — to see His image all around, to consecrate every act to His service, to keep mind, spirit, body, pure as He is pure, consecrated to Him, and to Him alone — this is to lead the godlike life.'[391]

In *Letters from Julia* one finds a beautiful definition of the faith that is as original as it is profound, especially in the contrast it creates by defining its very opposite:

> 'Well, so far as you disbelieve, so far you lose your power to be the conductor [the term is here specifically intended in the electrical sense] of the love of God to man.'[392]

Here we have the lived definition of what really seems to take place at the level of the occult, the level of the invisible, when there is a live faith: because the faith, above all else, is truly a trusting abandonment or surrender — entrusting oneself to God, putting oneself into the hands of God to become an instrument of divine initiative. Here, above all, man attains true success, the kind of success that corresponds to his real and ultimate good. And that is precisely the concept that seems to me to be very clearly and happily expressed by Julia when she concludes that:

> 'the secret of all power to help man is for you to be just
> the passive instrument in God's hands to teach, to show,
> to prove what He says.'[393]

The faith also proves to be very effective at the actual
moment of passing over, as would seem to be borne out
by something that 'Judge Hatch' tells us on the basis of
his own experience. He observes that, even though it may
be limited in its explicit import, nevertheless brings with
it a wealth of further implications:

> 'The surest way to escape that painful period of
> transition is to go into the hereafter with a full faith in
> immortality, a full faith in the power of the soul to create
> its own conditions.'[394]

Equally based on experience — and, I would say, on a
form of clairvoyance in the truest sense of the term (or
spiritual vision, if you prefer) — is constituted by the
following affirmation regarding the effective power of
prayer:

> 'Prayer or spiritual aspiration invokes forces which
> dissolve evil thought forms as the sunlight dissolves
> fog.'[395]

I have taken this quotation from *The Realms of the
Living Dead*, where one can even find a recognition of the
efficacy of prayers for the dead, as also of the baptism on
behalf of the dead to which St Paul refers.[396]

In fact, as Crookall points out, the request for prayers
occurs very frequently in mediumistic communications:
'Pray for me!' is very common, and one also finds 'Teach
me to pray!'.[397] The reason for this is that, even though
prayer has very great efficacy for souls, these find
themselves in great difficulty when they seek to acquire
new habits they did not have while on earth, the habit of
prayer being a case in point. The braking weight of the
body makes it far easier for us here on earth to interrupt
our activities, to rebalance them, to change our attitudes,
to opt for new interests. But the other dimension is a

condition in which, rather than creating new interests, one continues, develops and underscores those interests already formed on earth. For this reason it is sometimes said, and rightly so, that in this earthly life we mainly and essentially sow the seeds, while in our existence in the hereafter we shall primarily and essentially gather what we have sown here on earth.

For the soul, so Crookall tells us, the body represents a kind of shooting position from which it can take its aim. Once the shot has been fired, the bullet keeps going in the direction that has been freely chosen for it in the act of aiming, a direction that cannot be changed. This example, which I here formulate simply by enlarging the simile suggested by Crookall, may seem a little too rigid and it surely expresses and refers to a limit situation: but it seems rather obvious that things do *tend* to be just like that. And that is the reason why, for example, a dead criminal turned to the Seer of Prevorst (a woman who lived about midway through the nineteenth century) and confessed himself unable to get down to prayer, to dedicate himself to prayer, so that the good Frau Hauffe began to teach him as she would have done with a small child.[398]

Irrespective of whether one prays for these souls or teaches them to pray, in prayer (which is so beneficial for them) once again the initiative lies with us. This does not disallow that disincarnate souls could manifest themselves on earth and in our midst to take initiatives that aim at our conversion: but as a general rule these are souls who succeeded in sanctifying themselves here on earth or, at least, oriented their road of sanctity in a decisive manner (if not in concrete terms, at least in aspiration, always provided that the aspiration was intense and incisive and had been harboured for a long time, even though a negative situation prevented it from being realized).

If what we do here on earth, as also the thought that precedes it, is destined to become crystallized in the hereafter into a force that is far more automatic and less easy to control, the practical and reasonable consequence cannot be anything other than this: it is here on earth that we must make the greatest possible effort to orientate ourselves towards the good, to act and behave rightly, to acquire good habits: on the other side, in the hereafter, it could already be too late or, at least, our intentions could prove to be far more difficult to put into practice.[399]

The book *Thy Kingdom Come*, which is attributed to Arthur Conan Doyle (the creator of Sherlock Holmes and an ardent spiritualist), puts forward the conviction, based on first-hand experience, that 'the Roman Catholic Church assuredly possesses knowledge of the waiting planes of purgatory and of the Second Death', and further that 'wisely, she enjoins the faithful to pray for the departed.'[400]

Likewise, Jane Sherwood's *Post-Mortem Journal*, said to contain communications received from the late Lawrence of Arabia, refers to a 'process of purgation' that 'is the justification of the Catholic doctrine of purgatory, although its discipline is mental and emotional instead of physical. Yet emotion for us is really physical, so perhaps red-hot pincers and so on are not so inappropriate as symbols.'[401]

The entity 'Rudolph Valentino' sees a certain analogy between the 'astral plane' and the 'purgatory of the Roman Catholics'.[402] Referring to his own voyages in the other dimension, 'Judge Hatch' also testifies that he made a short trip to purgatory, the very 'purgatory of Roman Catholics'. He then adds that one must not laugh at those who have Masses said on behalf of the deceased and their eternal rest. The souls are sometimes conscious of such a thought. They hear the music and they may even smell the incense that is burnt, though more than anything else they feel the power of the thought that is dedicated to them. Purgatory is real, at least in the sense of being a real experience. If you prefer, one may call it a dream, but dreams can sometimes be terribly real:

'Even those who do not believe in purgatory sometimes wander awhile in sadness, until they have adjusted themselves to the new conditions under which they live. Should one tell them that they were in purgatory, they might deny the existence of such a state; but they would readily admit their discomfort.'[403]

There is another thing that *Thy Kingdom Come* tells us in a very significant manner:

'It would seem the Roman Catholic Church has long possessed the knowledge now given to us, and proves its efficacy by practice. She knows well how to tap the sources of power, and those able to witness by the inner vision, can note how each rite of the Roman ceremonial is designed to attract and build up power. As the service proceeds the power can be seen to gather before the altar, a bluish cloud shot with gold (or sometimes tinged with grey, according to its quality) until finally it is projected by the elevation of the Host, to roll forward over the kneeling worshippers sinking deeply into soul-substance, permeating and holding fast the soul to the faith.'[404]

A profoundly religious and mystic spirit also pervades the dialogue between 'Judge Hatch' and 'the man who found God': that, indeed, is also the title of Letter XX in the book 'Judge Hatch' wrote through the mediumship of Elsa Barker. This entity, not least on account of the convictions professed in life, seems to have an idea of Jesus that is more theosophical than strictly orthodox. Nevertheless, he tells us that 'He is revered in all the heavens.'[405]

These traditional religious beliefs are extensively confirmed by an idea that recurs throughout these transcendental communications, namely that the hereafter is a spiritual condition that we prepare during our life on this earth. With our actions, and with our thoughts even before that, we keep on modelling our soul: as soon as we abandon the physical body, together with all the things that today contribute to our comfort, our wellbeing and our power in the material and exterior sense, as soon as we have lost the exterior supports that mask our true condition and hide it from ourselves, we automatically enter into a condition that corresponds exactly to the pure and simple state of our spirit. As Arthur Findlay notes:

> 'our thoughts and actions ... here on earth are building for us our place in the hereafter. How many of us realise that thoughts are lasting things, that they pass on with us through death and will be our companions, to influence us in an even greater degree than now. When separated from the physical body they assume shape and form more potent for good or evil than when clothed by the earthly body.'[406]

That the soul, having become deprived of the body on the occasion of physical death, should enter into the exact condition that corresponds to its state at the time is nothing but an automatic step; it does not represent the execution of a sentence pronounced by some authority operating externally to it. It is thus the soul that creates its own state — and of its own accord — by the quality it decides to confer upon its customary thoughts; and it is therefore clear that each one of us, by himself and at each and every moment, prepares what is going to be his future ultraterrene condition.

The ultraterrene condition into which a soul will thus place itself can be defined as either positive or negative, though one need do no more than consider the extreme complexity of an individual soul and the state in which it can find itself to realize that this distinction is excessively simplistic. If, further, souls group together according to affinity, and if to each group there corresponds a common collective condition, a common mental environment, one would have to deduce that the great variety of individual conditions would have to have its counterpart in an equally extreme variety of spiritual environments: the other dimension would thus have to be structured into a variegated and complex myriad of spiritual environments, each different from the other and covering a vast range that from the lowest of infernal conditions gradually ascends to the most sublime condition of paradise.

The two-fold distinction of hell and paradise, as also
the triple distinction of paradise, purgatory and hell,
would thus seem to do no more than suggest an endless
variety of mainly intermediate situations. It may be that
the dramatic (though always a little theatrical) nature of
an apocalyptic vision involving a drastic and clear-cut
separation of the wicked from the good, constitutes a
highly suggestive element; but, if only one pursues the
thought a little further, where is the person who can be
said to be wholly good or wholly wicked?

'Marmaduke', in turn, tells us that the greater part of
the people who pass over, rather than being either wholly
white (good) or wholly black (evil), seem to be grey and to
cover the entire range of possible shades. There are few
angels and even fewer devils, and one rather finds a great
and amorphous mass of mediocrities. Indeed, this may
well be the real drama:

> '... sin can even be less harmful to the character than a
> careless, senseless life of selfishness and pleasure-
> seeking ...'[407]

And 'Julia' remarks that the simplistic, twin-pole
distinction of heaven and hell, though quite valid as an
abstract principle, is very far removed from concretely
reflecting the real situation: in actual fact, as she puts it:

> 'Heaven shades off into Hell, Hell shades off into Heaven,
> by a million imperceptible gradations.'

Between the two there is no great and fixed gulf, as seems
to be suggested in the parable of Lazarus. This gulf was
probably a figure of speech necessary to bring home to
large numbers of people — by exaggerating the contrasts,
the extremes — the clear difference that exists between
good and evil as such. The borderland that separates
heaven from hell is really crossed by innumerable paths,
along which the dwellers in heaven are perpetually
leading those of us who were spirits in prison, so that we
may redeem ourselves, seeing 'that the joy of Heaven is
indeed emptying Hell'.[408]

Mediumistic communications tell us of many different possibilities, of an extremely varied range. This is undoubtedly true as regards the destination of the soul immediately after its separation from the physical body. As regards the more distant future, however, the communications insist a great deal on the possibilities that each soul has of making further and indefinite progress. It is quite true that, after passing into the other dimension, the soul gathers the fruit of what it sowed throughout the length of its sojourn on earth; but this is very far from meaning that it must become crystallized once and for all in the condition it has entered during earthly life. Indeed, the last of the Seven Principles of spiritualism tells us quite expressly that 'the path of progress is never closed, and that there is no known end to the advancement of the individual'.[409]

The fact that in mediumistic testimonies one does not normally find the heaven-hell schema (or its counterpart, hell-purgatory-heaven) in its traditional rigid application, nor even the crystallization of the damned and the saved in their respective conditions, may at first sight cause considerable perplexity to orthodox Christians: I am well aware of this. Nevertheless, one must try to understand whether these schemas really form part of the substance of the Christian message, and are not, rather, a mere literary form of historical origin that can be shed without difficulty and is even in contrast with the intimate spirit of the message, with everything that is contained in it *in nuce* and able to be culled forth from it. But a detailed treatment of this problem from the theological point of view would require an entire book of its own.

We have already seen that the various testimonies communicated to us from the other dimension tend to confirm what — broadly speaking — appears to be the substance of the teaching hitherto provided by the religions: this teaching is fully confirmed, at least as regards its core of universal and perennial validity. Likewise, many aspects of religious life that could seem strange or outdated (when considered from the viewpoint of a modern and highly secularized mentality), and certainly no longer proposable, received ample and quite unexpected confirmation from these communications. What is more, they receive this confirmation in terms of lived experience and clairvoyant vision; these, too, are truths, they are religious practices justified by a profound intuition, and most effectively channel forces that spring from a Source situated deep within the intimacy of man, beyond man, before him — that is, at the very level of his metaphysical root.

By definition, the deceased are clairvoyants: but they do not always or necessarily have a clear vision of the empirical or phenomenal aspect of things, a vision comparable to the one that we men living on this earth have of these things. On the other hand, they do perceive what one might call the noumenal aspect of things; rather, this is really their natural vision. They sink their eyes into the spiritual dimension that is both the principle and the root of the material dimension. And one can readily understand that, in a dimension that is wholly mental, the spirit, who is the absolute principle of all things, can succeed in making his founding presence felt, that he can make his creative presence felt in a manner that is far more clearly perceived than he can generally convey this presence to the souls who live incarnate on the earth. One can, therefore, just as readily understand that in the spiritual dimension God can be recognized, or rather perceived, far better as the Source of all life, all being, and all good.

In *The Other Side God's Door* we are assured by the entity 'Maud' that it can feel, almost physically, the sense of 'God's breath'. It is somewhat like the sensation a child resting in its mother's arms perceives of her breath. In the other dimension it thus seems to the soul that it is being caressed by the air itself:

> 'And even the air caresses one here! It seems like a sweet breath from a mother's face. To us it is like the breath of God, for we cannot define Him any more clearly here than with you, but we can feel Him without any

doubt.'[410]

Let me remind you that it is not by chance that God is called Spirit: *spiritus* in Latin, *pneuma* in Greek, *ruah* in Hebrew. The common meaning of these words is 'breath', 'puff', 'blow', and even 'wind'. It is the creative breath that brings all reality into being, the breath that also maintains it in being, continuously sustaining and nourishing it so that it might acquire ever greater fullness of being, completeness, perfection. 'We get our light from the source of all light,' was the way an entity put it to Arthur Findlay.[411]

In the other dimension it would also seem that one more readily gets the feeling of being close to the Fount. God 'is with us always', we are told by 'Julia':

> 'This is Heaven — to be with Him. You cannot understand how the consciousness of His presence makes the atmosphere of this world so different from what it is with you ... He is the Source and Giver of all good gifts. All that we know of what is good and sweet and pure and noble and lovable are but faint reflections of the immensity of the glory that is His.'[412]

'Rudolph Valentino', on the other hand, uses somewhat more concrete and empirical terms:

> 'Spirits have shown me how easily this astral body can be vitalized by the currents of vitality. They say these vitalizing currents are the life emanations of God. When the astral body is cut off from this supply, it cries out in pain, which is really a warning for you to try to bring it into contact again with the currents of healing.'[413]

Before a soul becomes clearly and profoundly convinced of this, it will somehow feel it in a manner still vague and indistinct, and yet sufficiently concrete to induce it to pronounce words of gratitude: 'I think God is very merciful and very good,' says a female entity called by Charles Drayton Thomas and identified by 'Mrs D.C.T.', 'I have said so, I should think, several times a day since I have passed over.'[414] The same author, in another of his books, quotes the testimony of another woman, who completed the account she gave of her demise by recalling that both her heart and her mind seemed to overflow with gratitude.[4 1 5]

'William Stead', writing through the mediumship of Mrs Dawson Scott, says:

'Our lives are a manifold expression of the beneficence of God. We are drawn out of our humble beginnings as the flowers are drawn out of the earth; and even as the sum of human happiness is infinitely greater than the sum of human misery, so our happiness on this plane is infinitely greater than what any man feels while he is still in the flesh. Life has developed an increasing power to appreciate and enjoy. On earth joy cast the shadow of suffering, here light — that is, joy — casts no shadow. We are austerely glad of even the developing past, for it was the path to this serener state of being.'[4 1 6]

The praise of God that spontaneously bursts forth from such a condition of spirit, the gratitude felt for God as the giver of all being and all good, leads implicitly to the soul recognizing all this or, at least, perceiving it as an intuition. All this comes from God, we can do nothing by ourselves, at the very most we can collaborate in an initiative that springs from God Himself.

This would also seem to be the meaning of a passage in the book *Thy Kingdom Come*, where the entity 'Arthur Conan Doyle' at a certain point comments on these words of Jesus, 'Truly, I say unto you, whoever does not receive the kingdom of God like a child shall not enter it',[4 1 7] with the following words:

'Except a man be stripped of all pride and egotism — except he realize he is *nothing* without the power of the Almighty Spirit — until a man breaks out from arrogance to the understanding that *"of myself I can do nothing"*, he is dulled to the glories of Heaven. Each must eventually be stripped of all possessions, and stand a naked soul, an infinitesimal *nothing* bathed in a vast abyss of universal knowledge and power. He must go through the Valley of Death — not of the physical body, but of HIMSELF ... Then, and then only, can the Light dawn — for him.'[4 1 8]

As can be seen, in spiritual existence a soul has every chance and possibility of experiencing at first hand that

God is the Spring of all being and all good, that He is really the first Beginning and the Ultimate End of all reality, that He is truly our All. Every chance is given, especially in the hereafter, to experience the full flavour of the love of God.

We shall now see that every chance is also given to live in harmony with this love. In a condition purified of all earthly attachments, as one can readily understand, the classical conflict between the spirit and the flesh no longer makes itself felt.[419] I am, of course, referring here to the lower spheres of the hereafter. From a certain level onwards, however, one may suppose that the flesh, to all intents and purposes, loses its weight. Although the conditions of an existence immersed in matter act as an impediment to the advancement of the spirit, this impediment eventually disappears in a purely spiritual existence.[420]

It is quite true that souls are always the same after they have fully passed over, after they have left behind them even the intermediate Hades condition, but they are no longer subject to the same temptations: they no longer possess things, they no longer compete with each other, there is neither thirst nor hunger, they no longer have a sexual life, and feel no jealousy.[421]

This is made clear by 'Dr Scott', who then goes on to say that in the superior condition of the hereafter all the various things that, in our own world, can induce people to commit crimes have substantially disappeared: there is no longer anything to steal, it is no longer possible to use physical violence. Those who did evil on earth now become aware of its consequences. 'People who on earth were strong for evil remain strong; but evil no longer exists.'[422]

And 'Marmaduke' puts it as follows:

'I want to give you some more impressions of the life here. To commence then: there is no confusion; each one has a place and definite work to do. There is no rivalry, except in a perfectly friendly spirit of comradeship. There is love, deeper, stronger, purer than it can ever be on earth, but no passion ... There is no jealousy. If anyone can do anything better than ourselves we are content, nay glad, to let him take the lead, and we humbly try to follow in his footsteps. You may think that the result must be a lack of emulation and therefore of progress. But no, we all want to improve, but we realize our limitations, and in copying a superior worker or artist, we get a fresh incentive to produce better work ourselves. It is the same in every art and science ...'[423]

'Julia', indeed, can sum it up very succinctly by saying that, compared with life on earth, 'there is more love' in the spirit world.[424]

Again, the author of the book *In the Dawn beyond Death* quotes an entity identified as 'Mrs A.M.', who concludes:

'When you come to this side you find yourself in an atmosphere in which you cannot only endeavour to be Christlike but can, I find, actually be it. That ideal is realized here.'[425]

One may say that the spirit world, the hereafter, is an essentially religious dimension. But can one also say that one there attains what, from a religious point of view, can be defined as a state of perfection? Can one say that one there attains sanctity, beatitude, the state of perfect union with the Divinity — that is to say, a condition in which the human soul no longer has a will that is in any way different from the divine will — and simply becomes a perfect vehicle and means of expression of that will in full and total transparency?

A long series of corroborating testimonies shows that the strangely 'earthly' and anthropomorphic 'paradise' described in Chapters 8 and 9 is not by any means to be considered as the ultimate goal of the spiritual ascent that becomes possible after death. From the point of view of mental advancement (for want of a better term) one immediately notes that, during its sojourn in the Summerland condition, the soul is as a general rule still excessively enslaved by many human and earthly forms, and it does not therefore succeed in conceiving different forms of life. From a more specifically ethical and religious viewpoint, moreover, such an entity would also seem to be subject to yet another limit. Strictly speaking, one would have to say that 'his desires in the astral world, however much they have included love of others, good fellowship and companionship, have also, as he now begins to see with certainty, really largely centred upon himself.' The fact is that the person concerned, 'even when he loved others, much of this was for his own emotional satisfaction.'[426] And hence the need for a further purification, a further advancement and spiritual intensification:

> 'Each must now gradually become as willing to yield up his present values as, in very many cases, he was ready in the end to shed his earthly body on death.'[427]

Here we have yet another 'death', which in many books (including the one from which I have just quoted) is referred to as 'second death', while Crookall (as mentioned at the beginning of Chapter 7) calls it 'third death' because he uses the term 'second death' to designate the abandonment of the vital body, the vehicle of vitality.[428] On the occasion of this further death (be it known as second or third, or any other name) the soul 'sheds all he has valued; his achievements and all the things he has won in the desire world (of which earth, too, is a part) have now to be given up. His gifts no longer exist for him but for the glory of God.'[429]

At this point, therefore, the soul — now despoiled of all its tinsels and egoistical ambitions — can begin to find its true 'self' and thus achieve the unification and full realization that, in some way or other, it had sought from the very beginning.

It is precisely to this ultimate unveiling of the deepest and most profound self that Crookall dedicates one of the final chapters of his book *The Next World — and the Next*. Using his own terminology and numeration, he thus speaks of a 'third death'. The first, to recap, is physical death, i.e. the abandonment of the physical body. The 'second death', as far as Crookall is concerned, is the abandonment of the 'vehicle of vitality' (or 'vital body', the one that in theosophy is known as the 'etheric body'). This second death corresponds to the passage through Hades. Following this second death the soul, now enveloped in the 'astral body' (also known as the 'soul body'), becomes integrated into the spiritual world, more precisely the one that many communications refer to as *Summerland* and which Crookall calls *Paradise*. The 'third death', then, is the one in which the soul eventually sheds even the 'astral body' and, bearing nothing other than the 'spiritual body' enters the condition that Crookall calls *Heaven* rather than *Paradise*. It is there that the soul's individuality acquires 'mystical consciousness' and 'eternal life'.

This third death, once again, takes place during somnolence, sleep or blackout of consciousness.[430] The testimonies reported by Crookall, rather than dwelling on the accidental and dramatic character of this separation from a vehicle that no longer serves any useful purpose, put the accent on a deliberate transition said to take place gradually (there are some who say 'insensibly') as the result of a development process and the expansion of the spirit.[431]

The entity 'William Stead', communicating through the mediumship of Mrs Hyver, makes an incidental, almost by-the-way reference to his third death when he draws the following parallel:

> 'If I still have my astral body, I shall be able to make that body visible to the medium: if I have left my astral body [at the third death], and if I have only my spiritual body, which is in reality my true self, I shall be obliged to construct an image of my old earth body.'[432]

Particular philosophical significance here attaches to a statement made by Lord Dowding, to sum up the teachings in this connection he had received in the course of numerous communications:

'A very important point is that at the Third Death the
"Personality" of that particular incarnation ceases to
exist, and there remains only the "Individuality", which
consists of the Ego with its Aura containing all the good
and none of the evil brought to it by its various bygone
Personalities.'[433]

For reasons already stated,[434] I shall not here try to
discuss the question of reincarnation, but will limit
myself to noting that this subsisting individuality (which
Crookall refers to as 'the greater, higher, inner, deeper,
real or eternal self') seems destined to despoil itself of all
personal characteristics. No less significant seem to me to
be the expressions Lord Dowding uses when he tells us
that the personality 'evaporates' on the occasion of the
third death, that the aura of the Ego is almost reduced to
a kind of 'blank', and that the whole is tantamount to an
existence that approaches close to 'insensibility'.[435]

This concept of the soul despoiling itself of its personality comes very close to oriental models. But I cannot
help wondering how this reduction of self to a pure point
of consciousness, devoid even of any mental content, can
be conciliated with the idea of a state of perfection that
comprises knowledge of all reality, including empirical,
cosmic and historic reality: a perfection that, when all is
said and done, tends, at its limit, to omniscience. What,
indeed, would remain of that blessed vision, so familiar to
Christian theology, where the soul, contemplating God
and immersing itself in the divine Mind, can see, as Dante
put it, 'lovingly bound into a book/All that is spread over
the whole Universe'?[436]

If it is true that any creative work performed by men
calls for a succession of acts spread out in time, one can
perhaps deduce that the attainment of a truly divine
condition by man, always provided that this be possible
at all, would imply the cessation of creative activity as
conceivable both in the earthly condition and in the
Summerland condition. What would remain conceivable
is a cognitive activity, though this would have to be
realized in the unity of a single act. This would be an act

of knowledge that contemplated in an absolutely simultaneous manner, in a single instant, everything that to us incarnate men appears in a time succession as past, present and future. However, if such an act were to be perfect and capable of grasping all realities at their root, it would have to be at one and the same time also a creative act, it would have to constitute a single whole with the creative act that found the existence of all the realities. If we could truly realize within ourselves the God who wants to be 'all in all'[437] and donates himself to us unceasingly, we would have to succeed in making our own the unique and absolute act that enables God to have true knowledge of all things inasmuch as he creates them.

Let us assume that our ultimate destination is, at its limit, this state just outlined, albeit in threadbare and altogether inadequate words. Such a total 'deification' would be made possible by a series of conditions that one could schematically outline as follows.

Firstly, one would need divine grace. Man cannot presume to ascend to God by himself and with his own forces. It would be a desperate 'titanic' attempt, the vain nature of which is well described in the Bible by the myth of Adam and Eve and the original sin that leads to their being driven out of Paradise; also by the episode of the Tower of Babel and the figure of Lucifer, which the prophet Ezekiel sees as personified by the Prince of Tyre.[438]

Divine grace is the divine initiative that calls men to collaborate. One could say that the various forms in which humanism finds concrete expression all aim — always in the limit — at the various aspects of divine perfection (or, as theologians would put it, at the various attributes of God). It should not be assumed that man must not and cannot aim at perfection in its various aspects: the important thing is that he should act in obedience to, and in collaboration with, an initiative that comes from God, for it is only divine force that can sustain human forces that otherwise would prove altogether insufficient and inadequate.

But, if man is to act in absolute obedience to God and as a pure vehicle of divine initiative, it is essential that he should purify himself (or, better, that he be purified by God), thereby ensuring that all egoistical motivations will disappear from within him, that he will belong wholly to God and to God only, that he will live only by Him and for Him. In other words, man must 'sanctify' himself, or rather must be sanctified by Him who alone can bring about such a transformation in man.

This said, we can now return — hopefully with greater clarity of ideas — to our theme of the third death. At this point it may be helpful to refer briefly to another author, Paul Beard, and to the last part of his well-known book *Living On*, mentioned earlier. Beard eventually speaks of the soul that leaves the Summerland condition and ascends through the three Heavens. I cannot and shall not comment on so precise and schematic a division, but I note that the term *Heaven* is identical to the one that Crookall uses to describe the condition to which one gains access through the 'third death'. Beard, too, speaks of this death, though he adopts a different numeration criterion and therefore refers to it as 'second death': a terminological difference of no importance whatsoever for our immediate purposes. I shall once again refrain from taking up the question of reincarnation, which plays a salient part in Beard's thinking, limiting myself to a very summary consideration of what the author tells us about the transformation that takes place in the three Heavens.

Firstly, one there enters, little by little, into a condition of greater freedom from the conditioning effects of earthly forms. An ever purer and loftier spirituality develops and expands with joy. But the moments of joy are accompanied by, and alternate with, moments in which the upper hand is gained by the note of self-sacrifice, an examination of conscience, a systematic attitude of suspicion as regards the crypto-egoistical motivations that underlie even the seemingly most generous action, the foregoing of every personal gratification, the most rigorous self-correction.

In this connection Beard quotes a passage in which the entity 'Arthur Conan Doyle' talks about his own 'second death' (Crookall's 'third death'). It is an experience that the late creator of Sherlock Holmes describes as 'so marvellous and yet so terrible': at this point, one has to renounce all knowledge, power and acquisition, foregoing everything that our personal self would consider its own; one thus has to despoil oneself to the point of becoming an absolute nothing: to Him who has given us all we must now return everything that we have and are.[439]

One can, of course, abandon all this with a single act of total abandon, though this calls for very special courage indeed, the kind of generous moral strength so characteristic of Arthur Conan Doyle. Spirits of a different temperament, however, will tend to proceed more slowly: they will move forward a step at a time, alternating the forsaking of something with periods of illumination capable of comforting them and sustaining them on their way. In other words, we here have an ascetic itinerary that has to be travelled to the end before one can consider to be fully consummated what the mystics refer to as union with God, true spiritual marriage.

This itinerary accommodates both the need for ascetic purification and the traditional idea of 'purgatory'. Purgatory is the purification and cleansing that enables the soul gradually to shed all egoism, even its submerged or disguised forms, so that in the end it can say that it no longer belongs to itself, but solely and totally to God. If at the end of this process a man, paraphrasing the Apostle Paul,[440] can say of himself 'yet not I, but God liveth in me', this does not imply that he has given way to a force that is purely extrinsic, acting from without: if God is our most profound and true self, surrendering to God means surrendering to what we are deep down within ourselves; surrendering to God thus means finding oneself, it means self-realization, true self-realization and no superficial variety thereof. The saint, the man of God, is a man who, foregoing his own empirical 'I' and abandoning himself wholly to God, has realized himself as man at the most profound level of all, at the very root of his being.

What we have so far seen and considered in this discussion could in some way belie the traditional scheme according to which the soul, immediately after death, is destined to go to purgatory; that is to say, is at once transferred to a condition of penance and punishment, to be promoted to a happy, paradisiac condition only after it has succeeded in fully cleansing itself, only after it has fully achieved its own sanctification. But let me point out that what can be contested in the light of this rather rigid schema concerns only some essentially formal aspects: the need for purification, which is the fundamental idea underlying the very concept of purgatory, does not seem to be either ignored here or played down in any way. All that emerges is that the moment of purification, or (and this is really the same thing) of the ascesis, can alternate, and normally does alternate, with moments of joyous expansion of spiritual life.

This surely explains why the immediate *post mortem* period can be a gratifying experience, and also why a near-death experience may be gratifying (as may also an out-of-the-body experience or astral projection, which in some way resembles a near-death experience, comes close to it, prefigures it). The subject gets a feeling of lightness, seems to be freed of the weight of his physical body, his limits, his pains and aches and imperfections: this, of course, does not of itself mean that the subject is purified of all egoism. If a religious concern stimulates him to continue and make further progress in this direction, so that in the end he will be of God and of God alone, he will necessarily have to travel along an ascetic road. His future existence will thus pass through purgatory phases that can at times be very painful indeed.

Our earthly life, too, alternates between moments of joy and sorrow, expansion and renunciation, of abandonment to facile ecstasy when one feels light and almost carried along by angels, and to painful tribulation in the arid and opaque solitude of a spiritual wilderness, when we are deprived of all comfort and seem to be abandoned to our own nothingness. In our earthly existence we thus have an alternation of moments of humanism and of ascesis. The same thing can happen — and, indeed, one can see no reason why it should not happen — in this ultraterrene life of ours, which seems to be stretching forth towards a goal of infinite perfection.

Chapter 11
The Other World
And Our Own

All the religious traditions, back to the most primitive ones, seek to some extent to help the moribund to die a good death, to make sure that, once they have overcome the intermediate Hades condition, their presence will not be a source of infestation but rather a highly positive and beneficial presence as 'deceased', as 'ancestors', as 'holy souls of paradise', and so on. Even the funerary rites themselves have the function of helping the deceased to pass fully to the other side, because only after such full entry into the superior condition of the hereafter can a deceased return into the midst of men and, in his turn, extend his help to them.

It is obvious, however, that those who have passed to the other side will return to us only if they are motivated by a real interest in and for this world of ours. An example or two will help us to come to grips with this idea. 'Marmaduke', for instance, says that the mental faculties of those who have passed to a superior condition are more alert and therefore more anxious to learn new facts and to understand new inventions, so that even 'the lecture-halls are always crowded with eager [invisible] listeners' who have come from the other side.[441] 'Topsy', in turn, tells us that she came back to the earthly dimension on several occasions 'to learn the ways in which the people lived and to understand something of their difficulties and troubles.'[442]

Many entities follow the events and vicissitudes of the

world very carefully, and some among them seek to exert a positive influence on these events, hoping thereby to stimulate men to elevate themselves. 'Marmaduke', for instance, refers to 'impressions sent from here to those who are now guiding the world's destinies.'[443]

'Rudolph Valentino', on meeting 'Luther Burbank' on the other side and engaging him in conversation, asked him whether he would care very much to visit the earth again. 'Burbank' replied that he most decidedly would, that he was interested in his students there and in their continuance of his work. As soon as he learned new wonders of life's laws, he intended projecting the results of his labours into the minds of such workers as would be receptive to his influence. 'I will inspire them with my discoveries,' he concluded, 'and so help the world.'[444] Having reported this, 'Valentino' commented that this was 'one of the reasons why disembodied souls return to the earth: to help humanity learn more readily the lessons that will most advance it spiritually.'[445]

Professor Fitzsimmons, author of the book *Opening the Psychic Door*, relates something that was confided to him by the late 'Dr Charles Morgan':

> 'For some considerable time you have been writing the weekly Health Column in the *Natal Mercury* under the *nom de plume* of "Altruist". It was I who assisted you with those articles, not alone, but with the assistance of two colleagues here — Dr Edmonds and Dr "Bobs".'

This is confirmed by Professor Fitzsimmons, who tells us how he had written those articles or, rather, how they had been written through him:

> 'When writing or rather starting to write, I experienced a curious eager feeling; then with a rush, as it were, the words flowed through my brain and I wrote rapidly and without having to alter or erase a single word. When the article was finished, the point of the pencil stubbed into the paper and broke off.'[446]

Commenting on this episode, Bozzano notes that the consistency of these two versions is further confirmed by the fact that Fitzsimmons subsequently developed the faculty of automatic writing.[4 4 7]

But deceased doctors do not limit themselves to inspiring articles, and often intervene in a more concrete and practical manner. Antony Borgia, scribe of another book of transcendental communications, notes, for example, that the hand of a surgeon is often guided by a deceased colleague, even though the surgeon receiving the help is very far from suspecting this and would laugh if anybody were to suggest it to him.[4 4 8]

A substantial part of Professor Fitzsimmons' book is dedicated to the manifestations of the late Charles Bradlaugh, who was a convinced materialist and atheist. He had been a social reformer and the whole of his work as a politician and member of the British Parliament was dedicated to improving the lot of the disinherited classes. Commenting on these manifestations, Bozzano notes that, fully in harmony with what inspired the reformer while still alive, this entity:

> 'kept on manifesting itself for years and years, concerning itself with long-cherished topics of human redemption and taking an interest in the politics of the country, as also in international affairs.'[4 4 9]

When a soul has truly and fully passed, through the intermediate Hades condition, to the other side the impulse for communicating with our world may be provided, not by an undue attachment to the earth or a mere need for gratifying personal and not always positive aspirations, but by a concern deriving from love. 'Rudolph Valentino' wonders:

> 'Why am I striving to communicate with you? ... Because I love you. And I love the people of the earth. If my new learning, that I am gaining every minute, hour and day, every atom of time, is of profit to you, it may be of profit to others. And so I am making haste to give it to you and to that world.'[4 5 0]

Only those entities who have already acquired a certain level of spiritual development are motivated in this way, and their intervention may thus prove to be of benefit to men. Unfortunately, however, those who are themselves particularly anxious to communicate with us are far too often spirits still immersed in Hades, in a condition of bewilderment. Their communication initiatives are far from being beneficial to living men, especially when the people involved are unprepared and ingenuous. Indeed, entities of a higher level tend to put us on our guard against this kind of communication. 'Judge Hatch' says the following:

'You know, perhaps, that while on earth I investigated spiritualism, as I investigated many things of an occult nature, looking always for the truth that was behind them; but I was convinced then, and I am now more than ever convinced, that, except for the scientific demonstration that *such things can be* — which, of course, has value as a demonstration only — most spirit-hunting is not only a waste of time, but an absolute detriment to those who engage in it.

'This may sound strange coming from a so-called "spirit", one who is actually at this time in communication with the world. If that is so, I cannot help it. If I seem inconsistent, then I seem so; that is all. But I wish to go on record as discouraging irresponsible mediumship.

'If a person sitting for mediumship could be sure that at the other end of the psychic line there was an entity who had something sincere and important to say, and who really could use him or her to say it through, it would be another matter; but this world out here is full of vagrants, even as the earth. As this world is peopled largely from your world, it is inevitable that we have the same kind of beings that you have. They have not changed much in passing through the doors of death. Would you advise any delicate and sensitive woman to sit down in the centre of Hyde Park, and invite the passing crowds to come and speak to her, or touch her, or mingle their magnetism with hers? You shudder. You would shudder more had you seen some of the things which I have seen.

'Then, too, there is another class of beings here, the kind which we used to hear the Theosophists call elementals. Now, there has been a lot of nonsense written about elementals; but take this for a fact: there are units of energy, units of consciousness, which correspond pretty closely to what the Theosophists understand by elementals. These entities are not, as a rule, very highly developed; but as the stage of earth-life is the stage to which they aspire, and as it is the next inevitable stage in their evolution, they are drawn to it powerfully.

'So do not be too sure that the entity which raps on your table or your cupboard is the spirit of your deceased grandfather. It may be merely a blind and very *desirous* entity, an eager consciousness, trying to use you to hasten its own evolution, trying to get into you or through you, so as to enjoy the earth and the coarser vibrations of the earth.

'It may not be able to harm you; but, on the other hand, it may do you a great deal of harm. You had better discourage such attempts to break through the veil which separates you from them; for the veil is thinner than you think, and though you cannot see through it, you can feel through it.'[4 5 1]

The same concept, albeit in a somewhat different form, is expressed by the entities communicating with William Stainton Moses:

'To those who in a frivolous frame of mind place themselves in communion with the spheres; to those who force themselves from low motives in that which is to them only a curious thing; to the vain in their own conceit, the triflers, the untruthful, the worldly, the sensual, the base, the flippant, there is doubtless danger. We never advise any of unbalanced mind to meddle with the mysteries of mediumship. It is direful risk to them. Those only who are protected and guarded round, who act from no inner motive, but in obedience to the impulse of the guardians, who are wise and powerful to protect, should meddle, and they carefully and with earnest prayer.'[4 5 2]

These two quotations, taken from two widely different sources, surely give us a sufficiently clear idea of the difference between the two types of mediumistic communication, two types that seem as different from each other in the spirit that animates them as in the conditions in which they usually take place. Indeed, I believe that one could call the one type of mediumship positive, while the other is decidedly negative. The first type of mediumship, the one that takes place under the control of evolved and beneficent entities, can perform a useful function: it can help men to acquire consciousness of their ultraterrene destination and do this in a manner that, even though not scientific in the strict sense, is at least rationally convincing; it can do it on the basis of a set of experiential data rather than mere hearsay, likewise avoiding doctrines passively received from others, and logical arguments that, in the last resort, are wholly abstract.

The second form of mediumship, on the other hand, appears intrinsically negative and something to be avoided, unless it be practised by specialists for the purpose of study and with all appropriate precautions. Unprepared people who rush in lightly should be discouraged: mediumship should always be taken seriously, never undertaken for sheer curiosity, but rather in a true investigative spirit. We must always be certain that we are dealing with positive entities of a good level: since like and like attract, we too must place ourselves on a good level by acting in a spirit of authentic research. The level of our moral tension must likewise be adequate to the task in hand, because we are here concerned with a form of research that cannot be carried out in an impersonal manner, independently of what we are as human beings. It is only when we create the conditions for being properly receptive that we can achieve good mediumship, the kind of mediumship really worthy of that name.

Communications can take place through various means, and the medium may be either in a deep sleep, or slightly drowsy, or even fully awake: always, however, the medium must be in a receptive frame of mind that will enable the entity to manifest itself through him or her. The entity may write through the medium's hand or it may speak with the medium's voice. At the extreme, there are also manifestations by direct voice or by direct writing, and in such cases one may hear a voice coming from a point situated at some distance from the medium, or see a pen that writes of its own accord. Even though it remains invisible, the hand that writes in this latter case is in some way materialized; in the case of a direct voice, it is the vocal cords through which the entity expresses itself that are materialized in some way, though they remain equally invisible. The words of the message can be dictated, one by one, in a form and language known to the entity, while in other cases the entity can limit itself to conceiving pure thoughts, which will then assume linguistic expression in the psyche of the medium, thereby to be translated into words that form part of the medium's own culture.

Other forms of communication are known, but without going into the details let me say very briefly that an entity can resume contact with the human and earthly environment by lowering the frequency of its own vibrations. Those who live in a higher vibratory tonality have no difficulty in lowering it, always provided that they want to do so, though the reverse is not possible and so we cannot raise our own tonality. Seen from this point of view, both departure from the earth and return to this side are therefore the result of the disincarnate soul tuning in to a particular vibratory level higher for departure and lower for the return, somewhat in the manner in which a wireless set is tuned to receive various stations.[453] Any attempt to influence living men would likewise be carried out with the help of principally the same techniques.

Such tasks of maintaining contact with the earthly level, influencing it in a beneficial manner and following what happens there, are normally entrusted to the entities that prove to be best suited to this kind of work. Moved by love and a genuinely altruistic interest, these entities agree to remain relatively close to earth; but it does not follow that their continued presence in a lower sphere will harm or retard their spiritual advancement: when they eventually pass on to the higher levels their progress thereto will be all the more rapid, indicating that they have lost neither time nor opportunities as a result of their fidelity to the earthly environment. 'Marmaduke', for example, is firmly convinced of this.[454] The entity 'William Stead', in turn, voices the highest appreciation

of the guides who descend to the lower levels in order to
help their less evolved fellows by letting them know what
they themselves have come to realize. 'In fact,' as he puts
it, 'the guides have, perhaps, attained the highest
spiritual perfection.'[455]

The entities who follow these various vocations and
absolve such widely differing functions, can all be defined
as missionary spirits and collaborators of God, for it is in
His name that they toil to further the building of His
kingdom.

The Reverend Thomas, after pointing out that many of
the entities communicating with him were Christian
ministers, men who had spent their lives for others, went
on to say:

> 'Now, in the clearer light of the Beyond, they find
> boundless scope for mind and heart under the more
> immediate and consciously received direction of Our
> Lord and His highly organized systems of activity.'[456]

'Marmaduke' mentions the fact that man's very nature
makes him inclined to collaborate fully in the scheme of
the creation.[457] Even the prayers addressed to God are
for the most part granted and fulfilled not by Him but by
his vicars, who act in His name and have therefore been
granted the appropriate powers.[458]

If we regard the other side as the spiritual dimension
par excellence — the religious dimension, the dimension
of love — it is by no means improbable, in the light of
what we have already seen and considered, that this
self-same spiritual dimension is also the one that takes
the initiative in spiritualizing this earthly world of ours,
and, indeed, the entire universe of matter.

Spiritualizing means purifying, cleansing. The idea of
a purifying flame or fire destined to regenerate the world
from all sin and evil recurs many times in the Bible.[459]
It is not improbable that this fire must ultimately spring
from what is, as we have seen, the supreme sphere of life
already cleansed of carnality, purified from all egoistical
concern. Fire is a symbol and as such stands for a

Life, Death and Consciousness

spiritual factor that acts on each individual, consuming all the things in him that still attract him downwards, to the depths: earthly attachment, negative impulses, sinful habits, spirit of hate and vengeance, sensuality, longing for possessions and power — in short, everything that is capable of weakening his will to elevate himself, and therefore represents a potential impediment to spiritual advancement.

There are two methods of purification for the deceased. Let us first consider the type of purification that takes place in the highest spiritual sphere, where the soul gradually sheds everything that weighs it down and limits it, where little by little the soul becomes dead to every egoism and egocentrism, and to every exalting experience. Here we have a joyous and spontaneous abandonment of something that was once very dear and then, suddenly, lost all flavour as the result of the discovery of something far better and therefore incomparably more attractive. When certain attachments are not excessive, purification takes place in a spirit of joy and gladness.

The drama occurs only when these attachments resist dying, when they absolutely do not want to die even though the new situation makes it essential that they die. In cases of this kind purification can be very painful indeed. Here we have the Hades experience for the souls of the deceased. It is a necessarily painful experience, though it eventually tends to free man by purifying him in the flame of his own remorse.

Can we conceive an experience like this passing through Hades? Can we conceive such an experience of a purifying flame brought from the other side into our own world, so that this earthly dimension should thus become similarly purified? Can we postulate such an initiative to be taken by the other side? Can we assume that Heaven will take such an initiative, so that the name of God may be sanctified, that His kingdom may come, that the will of God be done 'in earth as it is in heaven'? But, surely, this is precisely what is implied by the entire eschatology of the Bible, of the prophets of the Old Testament, of the Gospels, the Letters and the Apocalypse, and all the preachings of Jesus and of the Apostles.

A very brief communication taken from *The Other Side God's Door* is particularly suggestive in this connection:

> 'Burning light, that searches the souls of men, will blast through the spheres, till like metal in the crucible of the universe all fallacies will melt away in the calm — it can't be done yet! But it will!'[460]

Closely connected with the purification of the world is its spiritualization. Matter is an essential dimension, because each creation has to be identified and requires its matter. It is surely not without reason that matter has been defined as the 'principle of individuation'.[461] Divine creation is the joy of calling into being perfectly individuated creatures: the joy of calling into being individuals, once and for all. Divine creativity delights in multiplicity, in plenitude, in details, in the inexhaustible flowering of distinct individuals. The destiny of multiplicity is to remain multiplicity, but assumed in unity, in that perfect unity of the multiple that is divine harmony; it is also the destiny of the individual to remain an individual, but fully united with Him who wants to be all in all; and it is the destiny of matter to remain matter, though turned into a vehicle of the highest spirituality.

Spiritualizing matter, or spiritualizing the world, means unifying it with the spiritual world, bringing about an encounter between the two dimensions, and making the dimension of the deceased converge upon our own earthly dimension: this is universal resurrection. The deceased arise, the men of the earth levitate towards heaven in all their bodiliness, though fully transfigured and with all their humanism fully received into the kingdom of God. 'It is coming — the great connection between the earth sphere and ours' says another entity in *The Other Side God's Door*.[462]

In *Thy Kingdom Come* there is a passage where this is

presented as a specific need of this human world of ours: when man will have advanced to a certain degree of understanding:

> 'He will live no longer in so dense a material world. The very matter or fabric of the world will become so refined, so etherealized that man will enter more or less to the astral condition of life.'[463]

How is all this possible? In general principle, since the difference between the two dimensions can be reduced to a difference in vibratory tonality it should simply be a case of elevating the lower or lowering the higher. As we have seen, it is possible for entities to transfer themselves to the lower levels, to become present there. In any case, as is said elsewhere in *Thy Kingdom Come*:

> 'Were it possible that astral vibration could be lowered, or that of the physical raised, that both could in some way be unified, then the two would merge, and mortal might see and hear, and win to certain knowledge of a Beyond ... An utter impossibility? Do not let us be too sure!'[464]

Such an encounter and merging, such a perfect synthesis would make it possible for matter, for the universe, for individual men to attain the fullness of the spirit, without dissolving either as matter or as individuals, and to do this in the fullness of the Kingdom of God where everything is saved and nothing is lost.

Chapter 12
Final Reflections

The entity responsible for *Life in the World Unseen* (as quoted in the previous chapter) concludes its account of a series of ultraterrene experiences with the following:

> 'To give you a comprehensive account of all that we have seen in the world of spirit would fill many volumes, and therefore I have chosen what I felt would be of most interest and benefit.'[465]

Being neither a projector nor a deceased, nor having had even a near-death experience, I must necessarily limit myself to considering the experiences reported by other people. The literature made up of these testimonies by projectors, resuscitated patients and communicating deceased is simply immense. And much of it, I hasten to add, is highly suspect. I have concentrated on the cases collected by Bozzano, all of which are supported by substantial proof of identity. Following his indications, I have re-examined the original texts of these cases, because it seemed to me that the fact that Bozzano chose them from among many others he had studied and then left aside,[466] already represented a hallmark of relative reliability. I have also referred to cases outside Bozzano's consideration, and several which have occurred since his death.

However, I have never relied wholly on a single text, as if that text bore an absolute guarantee of authenticity. Quotations and references to individual phenomena are of value to me not because I consider that fact to be ascertained beyond all doubt, but because I know it to be exemplary and representative of many others similar to it. Indeed, my knowledge of mediumistic literature, which is fairly thorough though certainly not complete, confirms to me that the facts I quote are normally representative of many other reports. I cannot, of course, multiply my quotations beyond a certain limit, but suffice it to say that the facts for which I have produced testimony are far from uncommon: on the contrary, they are borne out by such recurring testimony that they could be considered commonplace.

Here, of course, we are not in the domain of science but of interpretation and hermeneutics. Further, we are here concerned with existential hermeneutics, with attributing sense and meaning to lived experiences or experiences that have been testified to by those who lived them, and can be unified by the experiences of each one of us. The conclusions to be drawn from all this are undoubtedly of philosophical significance because — beginning with disincarnation experiences, be they temporary or definitive — they tell us a great deal about what could be our destiny as disincarnate souls once we ourselves have passed through physical death. The philosophical certainties we look for are not scientific certainties, but rather existential certainties we can use to orientate our existence. Even though we nowadays tend to make increasing use of science and its particular type of truth and 'objective' certainty, we still make our more fundamental and day-to-day choices on a series of certainties that are ultimately practical, moral or existential. Each passing day we live in an act of faith and concretely demonstrate that we are so living: faith that the floor of our apartment will certainly not collapse below our feet; that our wives will certainly not give us poisoned food; that the people we pass in the street will certainly not attack us; that passing motorcars will certainly not run us down if we are sufficiently careful in crossing from one side of the road to the other.

When I say 'certainly' here I do not mean an absolute certainty (which one cannot have in these things, as experience readily demonstrates); rather I am thinking of a relative or experiential certainty, borne out by the assurance with which I behave and more than sufficient for me to live my everyday life, as also to orient and give sense and purpose to my life.

Though indirect and therefore second-hand, my knowledge of astral projection phenomena and near-death experiences, as also of the more reliable mediumistic communications, is undoubtedly devoid of true scientific proof. Nevertheless, on the existential level — the level of interpretation, hermeneutics and philosophy — this mass of material cannot but be taken into consideration. Taken altogether, considered in all its wealth and consistency, this great volume of facts and testimonies provides both foundation and substance to a line of argument that, on careful examination, adds immense weight in favour of the interpretation suggested by these testimonies.

Survival cannot be 'demonstrated' by any one individual fact, even when it is ascertained with extreme rigour; confirmation is provided rather by the entire complex of facts taken together, so that even if one or more were to be found less verifiable, or as clearly untrue, there would still remain a multitude of facts of the same kind that would be far more difficult to contest *en bloc*. That is why it is so important that all the alleged facts should be typical, merely examples of that which is consistently recurring in so many strictly analogous testimonies.

Among the many typical facts I could have mentioned I have chosen only a small number, thus adopting the criterion formulated in the passage quoted at the beginning of this chapter: I, too, 'have chosen what I felt would be of most interest and benefit'. However, I have done this with a view to the different readership for which this book is intended. Antony Borgia's book would constitute appropriate and interesting reading for convinced spiritists already initiated into this kind of literature. My book, on the other hand, is intended also for people who have not yet considered spiritist matters. If really open-minded, such people have within them every necessary capacity for arriving gradually at the required sensitivity. Only remember to proceed one step at a time, avoiding an excess of food (for thought) on the plate at any one time. I have attempted to do this by limiting the arguments and avoiding an excess of detail regarding the purely spiritual and mental experience that awaits us after death. Indeed, the literature regarding this matter is so rich in anthropomorphic detail in certain areas as to discourage any reader new to the subject, even when he is devoid of any prejudice and inspired by all possible good will.

This problem could be explained as follows:

1. Any after-death experience is an experience of a disincarnate soul and is therefore of a purely mental character.

2. Something similar may be said of our dreams, during which our psyche would seem to be in a similar, though partial, state of disincarnation.

3. In our dreams a latently 'true' content finds expression in a manifestly imaginary and in some way arbitrary 'false' or camouflaged content: but the latter consists exclusively of old images that we have drawn from our earthly experiences — that is to say, of mundane and anthropomorphic images, the only ones we are accustomed to see or even to forge in our imagination (for instance, when we imagine a centaur or a siren, we do it by associating in a new way two old and well-known images of existing reality, a man and a horse or a woman and a fish).

4. When we interpret a dream, we try to discover its contents or 'truth' that may be of interest for psychology, psycho-analysis, anthropology, mantics (precognition of future events), religion and metaphysics. If we want to do this in a systematic manner we have to distinguish the true contents from the imaginary ones formed by the unconscious psyche to constitute the mythical element of the dream.

5. Something very similar can be done in experiences of life after death; given their exclusively mental content, these experiences are once again brought into being partly by a purely mental and unconscious creation, and are associated with an oneiric mental content that must not be taken too literally but demythicized, or rather trans-mythicized. In other words, we must not stop at the letter of the myth or dream-like experience, but rather look through it in order to grasp a truth that is expressed by these symbols and yet is different from and remains beyond them.

6. If we should therefore be disturbed by the seemingly excessive anthropomorphic character of certain accounts of *post mortem* experiences, we could at first reason that there could be a 'latent content' or more profound truth in the accounts we find particularly traumatic, and then learn to recognise the portion of oneiric elements that are associated with these experiences of life after death, just as we do in recognising the portion of imaginary elements in our dreams.

7. If we adopt this attitude now, it will enable us to take into consideration, no matter how absurd they may seem, even the most anthropomorphic accounts of these *post mortem* experiences — unless, of course, they involve obvious psychological or psychopathological nonsense. As we continue to consider and examine the material in question (albeit with due reserve and caution), it may be that, little by little, we shall come to appreciate the material in a more positive manner.

One consideration that could induce us to assume a more open attitude is the one I am about to put forward, albeit in very succinct form. In a mediumistic session a very heavy table was made to levitate by the creation of a psychic lever. This is how 'William Stead' perceived the phenomenon from his own spirit dimension:

'... the medium had to be reinforced by other sitters. She would not have been able to raise the table alone. She did it with the help of others, who with her formed a strong lever which held the table in the air not for a moment only, but for many moments. The medium then projected this strong lever from the solar plexus, in the form of a wide bar with greater strength than a steel bar of the same dimensions, while each sitter contributed a strong thread of ectoplasm.'[467]

Clearly we are here concerned with a very particular manner of producing a levitation: not, as is usually the case, by purely psychic means (by a purely psychic action, a pure act of thought concentration), but rather by concentrating thought on the creation of a physical object, a physical instrument that would be capable of acting in accordance with normal physical laws. This is the general principle said to govern creation in the other world, and also the interaction of all the seemingly mundane or physical realities, and all the forms and modes of anthropomorphic life.

We should begin by asking ourselves the reason for this maintenance of forms that in the purely mental condition of the other dimension should be considered as obsolete and out of place. There may be some intrinsic needs, which we can ignore, limiting our explanation as the mere persistence of mental habits. Even the dreams we have every night are purely mental, and yet we continue in our dreams to have experiences of physical realities and of physical forms of life and activity. It is our mental habits, surely, that lead us to repeat physical or mundane experiences, almost as if it were impossible for us to conceive forms of life different from these customary ones. Something very similar happens in the experience of the other side, which in certain respects is also an oneiric experience, except that the forms created by our thought have greater 'objectivity' because they now encounter the thought-forms of other subjects who, due to affinity, find themselves in the same condition, consequently they all contribute to the creation of a common mental environment.

Final Reflections

If we take as examples the explanations of 'William Stead', there is no reason why we should not assume that one or more entities, by a purely mental act, can create a garden, a wood, a house, furniture, books, a bicycle, a motorcar, a boat, an aeroplane, and so on. All this would simply depend on their tastes, their desires, and also on their ability to forge these realities with their mind. Operations of this kind are probably not very simple at the first attempt and may call for 'mental techniques' to be learnt and perfected. Anybody who has ever tried to learn and apply new mental techniques on our own plane (yoga, for example) is well aware of the difficulties to be faced and overcome. But there could be one difference: on our own plane everything is made more difficult by the resistance of matter, while in the other dimension affairs may be made all too easy by its absence.

As one example let us consider the first creative experiences of 'Philip', a young man who described them in a communication to his mother:

> 'I am beginning to experiment with my own powers, and I have been doing much practice in thought concentration, because one can create an object for oneself if one is strong enough — but it's not easy. One has to attune oneself to certain positive vibrations and concentrate one's will very hard. I tried to create an armchair to sit on, but I did not succeed very well for it got associated with the chair I always used in your room, and I found myself there. Then Grandpapa and I tried together. We manufactured a car — a Rolls Royce. But when we had got it, we didn't quite know what to do with it — motion here is so very different, and much swifter.'[468]

But suppose one wants to repeat the particular sensation felt when moving around in a car and, more particularly, in a Rolls Royce? Translated into earthly terms, this would be somewhat like possessing a fast car and yet preferring to use a bike or go on foot. A cyclist or a pedestrian is not necessarily somebody who cannot afford to go by car: walking and cycling are experiences in their own right, and as such they are valid in themselves, gratifying for what they are. And we have no reason to suppose that a soul passed over to the other side may not desire to experience realistically once more the very particular feeling associated with riding in a fast car, especially if this happened to be one of his passions while still alive.

Let me add (though with all the necessary reserve) that I have personally communicated several times with an entity who in her life on earth seems to have been a dressmaker. Having studied her personality over some time and with relative thoroughness, I convinced myself more and more that I was dealing with an authentic disincarnate entity. I shall refer to her only as 'Livia'. One of the things I asked her was whether in her sphere of existence there were houses, gardens, woods, and the like. 'We create them with spiritual energy,' she replied, and then went on to explain that she, too, had a house that she had constructed 'together with others' (i.e. with the help of other spirits). I then asked her what kind of concrete activities she still liked to engage in, and she answered 'I still do my work as a dressmaker'. I had read a great deal about the various forms of mental creation, about objects and realities instantly created by an act of thought, and immediately raised the quasi-objection 'But surely you don't do it in the same way as before?'. I was wrong. 'With needle and thread,' was her surprising answer. 'But needle and thread exist only in matter,' I went on. 'I create them with my mind.' Yes, indeed: needles, threads, scissors, cloth and everything else that serves for Livia's work is created by her — or by others — with a series of mental acts. Having at her disposal both materials and instruments, our good 'Livia' works the former with the help of the latter, and she does this first and foremost for the very special creative joy of making patterns, cutting and sewing, just as she used to do when she was on earth. And 'Rose', an entity in Neville Randall's recent book *Life After Death*, does exactly the same thing.[4 6 9]

So there is nothing really strange or inconceivable in all this. I have limited myself to just two examples, but the applications are infinite, and thus there emerges the vast and varied anthropomorphic world that many of my readers may well find difficult to accept, though they remain free to interpret it in the dreamlike manner we have already discussed. Always provided, however, that they avoid formulating definitive judgements, definitive exclusions. We have a field here where one never knows, and a great deal of prudence is required, one way or the other. At all times, however, it will be helpful to go by slow stages and degrees.

It was this selfsame criterion of gradualness that suggested the order in which the various topics have been treated in this book. We began with out-of-the-body experiences, also known as astral projections, all thoroughly alive and in good health, especially mental health. In some of them, moreover, these out-of-the-body experiences are frequent, even habitual, and have become the object of serene and careful study.

We then passed on to considering near-death experiences. These already have a more exceptional character, though they may extend to a more profound ambit, may go 'beyond' mere out-of-the-body experiences (which seem to be more closely bound up with the earthly condition). However, the testifiers to these near-death experiences, if they have really 'come back' to live in normal conditions, are once again men and women as 'alive' as we, people who are 'within our reach'. We can question them when and how we like, examine them and then sift their testimony and compare it with others. However, the matter becomes more difficult when we have to deal with communicating entities. These are 'phantomatic' by definition! In any case, they do create great problems. Having decided to proceed by small steps, by degrees, the best thing was to begin with out-of-the-body experiences.

There is a point of particular interest that emerges here. Certain phenomena to which witness is borne in mediumistic communications, phenomena that to us may seem strange and altogether unlikely, are already fully confirmed by the testimony of projectors: this is particularly true as regards the fact that a disincarnate soul (and it does not matter whether the disincarnation is definitive or only temporary) can give itself a true, lifelike, real bodily consistency, a subtle body that can assume the same form as the physical body (or the form the physical body once had), including the clothes. This seems to be the most discreditable fact; it is the starting point for all the anthropomorphisms that seem to weigh down the accounts of *post mortem* experiences and render them so absurdly similar to earthly events — at least in the eyes of those who come into contact with them for the first time, and fail to take into account the reasons and considerations we have tried to clarify.

Let us, however, summarize a number of features that seem to be common to out-of-the-body experiences, near-death experiences, and experiences of life after death:

1. A first common feature is the fact that the subject feels still very much alive, notwithstanding the fact that the centre of the personality has become projected outside the living organism represented by the physical body.

2. At the moment of emergence of the soul from the physical body, it generally feels — in all three types of experience — a great sense of freedom, peace, wellbeing, joy, lucidity, and a sense of full possession of its mental and volitional faculties.

3. When the subject turns his attention to himself, to what has become the true centre of his personality, he yet feels himself to possess a kind of subtle bodiliness that is no longer physical, but nevertheless consistent and concrete.

4. The disincarnate subject becomes aware that his subtle bodiliness spontaneously assumes, or can assume, a form similar to the human one. This form corresponds to the appearance of the abandoned physical body, and may or

may not be completed by items of clothing.

5. The subject discovers that he can give his subtle body any form and clothing he desires.

6. The subject discovers that he can move about at will, either slowly by walking or sliding (let us call it so) over the ground, or more rapidly, to the point of rendering themselves instantly present even in distant places.

7. Wherever he may find himself, the subject can vary the density of his subtle body, which can therefore attain a substantial density and become visible not only to sensitive people but also to the eye of a camera and the eyes of normal people without any special gifts (though the attainment of the higher levels of density may require the presence of a medium, who will provide a part of his or her own psychic energies for this purpose).

8. The disincarnate subject can normally pass through physical objects, walls and even the bodies of people; but by varying the density of his subtle body he can also simulate the resistance of physical bodies, displace them or act on them in some other way.

9. In certain conditions a disincarnate subject can exert a therapeutic influence on the physical body of an incarnate person.

10. In certain conditions a disincarnate subject can assume medianic control of an incarnate subject.

11. A disincarnate subject can perform any of the aforementioned actions far more effectively if he allows his unconscious mechanisms (or crypto-conscious mind) to come into play.

12. Even without the mediation of the senses of his physical body, abandoned temporarily or permanently, a disincarnate subject can directly perceive both physical realities and souls, be they incarnate or disincarnate, together with their thoughts.

Life, Death and Consciousness

13. Making use of their own psychic activities, by simple acts of thought, one or more disincarnate subjects can create psychic realities, even complex ones, that in their own peculiar way have a certain objective existence as also an objective duration.

14. This faculty, which to some extent can also be noted in incarnate subjects, makes it possible for the deceased to create their own mental environment.

As one can readily see from the summary listing of these fourteen points, out-of-the-body experiences, near-death experiences and experiences of life after death accord very specifically in many common features. Further confirmation can be obtained by drawing a parallel with certain well-known phenomena currently being studied by parapsychology. Let me therefore briefly attempt such a parallel.

For various reasons we can ignore the first two points on the above list. On the third point, however, we may note that the subtle body perceived by the subject has its counterpart in the so-called 'ectoplasm'. The ectoplasm can assume form (points 4 and 5 above), possibly complete with clothing, in apparitions, phantasms and materializations.

That materialized human forms can move slowly and walk (point 6) is borne out by a large number of experiences that consist both of spontaneous cases and cases studied in the laboratory (as regards the latter, one may think of the famous experiments that Sir William Crookes performed over a period of several months with the phantasm 'Katie King', produced through the mediumship of Florence Cook).[470] That the form of a certain person, living or dead or having died a moment before, can instantly appear also at a far distant location is something that is borne out by a rather vast and complex phenomenology.

If we now pass on to points 7 and 8 of the above list, we note that the degree of materialization can vary within wide limits: some materialized forms are so thin that only sensitive people or mediums succeed in seeing them, but there are others that remain impressed on a photographic plate (more sensitive than the human eye), and yet others that we can see with our normal eyesight.[471] There are also forms that offer a slight resistance, somewhat like a spider's web, to those who touch them or pass through them (remember the case, in Chapter 3, of Miss Emilie Sagée whose double was crossed by one of her pupils and opposed a very slight resistance of this kind). There are also phantasms that acquire solidity in the proper sense of the term and which can therefore be touched, leaving an impression of coldness somewhat similar to that of touching a dead body. And there are yet others that leave a clear impression of life and warmth, so that one has the feeling of having touched a live person.[472] That many entities can displace objects or produce similar physical effects can be deduced from a careful observation of many phenomena of a telekinetic nature, providing one is prepared to accept them as produced by disincarnate presences. The fact that a physical body (be it of a human being or an animal, a plant or an even more inert object) can decrease its density to the point of being able to cross the walls or doors of carefully closed rooms and thus transfer itself from one place to another, is confirmed by parapsychology through the various apport and asport phenomena, including some that involve living beings and even persons (a case in point being that of Mrs Guppy and the Marquis Centurione Scotto).[473]

Moving on to point 9, one may compare this feature with cases of therapeutic action performed without in any way touching the body of the patient, sometimes even without being present, from a remote distance.

With regard to point 10, one may mention all the phenomena of mediumship that can properly be defined as such.

Point 11 on the list is extensively confirmed by the whole of parapsychology, for it is well known that its phenomena are enormously facilitated when the subject desists from exercising his will at the conscious level, and allows himself to be guided as much as possible by instinct and such other forces as act on the unconscious level.

Point 12, again, has its counterpart in all the phenomena of telepathy and clairvoyance (the latter not only in the present, but also in the past and even the future).

Considering now points 13 and 14, we may note that the fact that human thoughts also have a certain solidity and objective duration can be confirmed on two levels:

a) when a subject projects his thoughts onto a given object (a piece of cardboard, for example) the same subject, or even another, can subsequently perceive by extrasensorial means that the thought has remained attached to that object. [474]

b) when a subject formulating a given thought is capable of conferring a degree of solidity upon it, the thought in question can actually be photographed (remember the cases of Felicia Scatcherd and Ted Serios). [475]

It is not possible, of course, to commence a treatise on parapsychology at this point, and I have therefore limited myself to a passing mention of some phenomena and cases that are extremely well known. So well known, in fact, that one may suppose the reader to be already familiar with them or, if not, that he can obtain all the necessary documentation easily and quickly with just a minimum of application, as one would expect of a person who has made at least some effort to prepare himself, to render himself receptive.

The experiences and accounts brought together in this book have shown an admirable picture of concordance and consistency. Though this may not necessarily be said of any one of these facts if taken by itself, their totality suggests strongly that the soul does indeed survive, a conclusion of great interest in orienting our life.

The book quoted from at the beginning of this chapter goes on to record the following:

'The percentage is low, deplorably low, of people who come into the spirit world with any knowledge at all of their new life and the spirit world in general.'[4 7 6]

When one bears in mind the decisive part played by our life on this earth in creating and shaping the condition of future life, there can no longer be any doubt as to the need for orienting our present existence in a clear and conscious manner towards this future life. But how can this be done if we always do our best not to think about the destiny that awaits us after physical death? Death is something that happens to others, while our own death is systematically ignored, excluded from our field of consciousness, driven underground and buried in our unconscious: 'removed', as psychoanalysts would nowadays put it.

In recent years, however, the theme of death has been making its way back to the centre of attention, as borne out by an ever-increasing number of studies and centres of thanatology (the scientific study of death). People are becoming concerned with the problem of dying well, of knowing how to die.[4 7 7]

But we have not yet succeeded in bringing back into focus the fact that dying well is possible, above all, when one has lived well; thus knowing how to die presupposes first and foremost that one should know how to live. But how can one orient one's life if one does not know what it is leading to? We seem to be on a luxury liner that we seek to equip for maximum comfort and enjoyment, but nobody, not even the captain, knows where the ship is going. What is worse, nobody is even wondering. If only one thinks about it, it would be difficult to conceive a more ridiculous and unreasonable situation. Even if the rich, consistent and concordant phenomenology I have offered in this book were no more than a deception, a great mystification or a trick that our psyche plays on itself, the basic and unavoidable problem would still remain with us.

Notes

1. Cf. E. Bozzano, *I morti ritornano, Per la soluzione del dibattito sui casi d'identificazione spiritica*, Verona, Casa Editrice Europa, 1946; *Animismo o spiritismo? Quale dei due spiega il complesso dei fatti?*, Verona, Editrice *Luce e ombra*, 1967.
2. C. Green, *Out-of-the-Body Experiences*, Oxford, Institute of Psychological Research, 1968.
3. Ibid., p.24.
4. Ibid., p.25.
5. Ibid., pp.26-7.
6. Ibid., p.40.
7. Ibid., pp.28, 56.
8. Ibid., pp.36, 40, 42, 43.
9. Ibid., pp.51.
10. Ibid., pp.51, 52.
11. Ibid., p.48.
12. Ibid., p.52.
13. Ibid., pp.56-9.
14. Ibid., p.64.
15. Ibid.
16. Ibid., p.65.
17. Ibid., p.66.
18. Ibid.
19. Ibid., pp.60-1.
20. Ibid., p.48.
21. Ibid., p.79.
22. Ibid., p.72.
23. Ibid., p.73.
24. Ibid., p.71.
25. Ibid., pp.72-3.
26. Ibid., pp.76-7.
27. Ibid., pp 32-3.
28. Ibid., p.33.
29. Ibid., p.78.
30. Ibid.
31. Ibid.
32. Ibid., p.79.

33. Ibid., p.81.
34. Ibid., pp.81-3.
35. Ibid., pp.85-6.
36. Ibid., pp.86-7.
37. M. Heidegger, *Being and Time*, section 52.
38. I. Kant, *Critique of Practical Reason*, I, II, II,4.
39. I. Kant, *Critique of Pure Reason*, I, II, II, II, III, VII.
40. Plato, *Phaedo*, 70c-72e.
41. Ibid., 72e-78b.
42. Ibid., 78b-81a.
43. Ibid., 105b-d.
44. Plato, *The Republic*, 526e, 127e, 131c, 533d.
45. M. Schlick, 'Positivismus und Realismus' from *Erkenntnis*, 1932-3, III, pp.1-31; 'Meaning and Verification' from *The Philosophical Review*, 1936, XLV, pp.339-69; R. Carnap, 'Überwindung der Metaphysik durch logische Analyse der Sprache' from *Erkenntnis*, 1932, II, pp.219-41; A.J. Ayer, *Language, Truth and Logic*, London, Victor Gollancz Ltd, 1946. For an overall view of this concept see also D. Antiseri, *Dal positivismo alla filosofia analitica*, Rome, Abete, 1966. For a critique, see also F. Liverziani, *Esperienza del sacro e filosofia*, Rome, Liber, 1970, Chapter IV of the first part.
46. St Augustin, *De vera religione*, c.39.
47. S.J. Blackmore, *Beyond the Body*, London, Heinemann, 1982.
48. Ibid., p.5.
49. Ibid.
50. S. Muldoon and H. Carrington, *The Projection of the Astral Body*, London, Rider, 1968, p.45.
51. R.A. Monroe, *Journeys Out Of The Body*, New York, Anchor Press/Doubleday, 1977, p.18.
52. Ibid., p.238.
53. R. Crookall, *The Study and Practice of Astral Projection*, Secaucus, N.J., The Citadel Press, 1960, pp.143-4.
54. C.J. Ducasse, *The Belief in a Life After Death*, Springfield, Ill., Charles C. Thomas, 1961.
55. F. Liverziani, *La reincarnazione e i suoi fenomeni 'chi' o 'cosa' si reincarna*, Rome, Edizioni Mediterranee, 1985. English translation: *Reincarnation and its Phenomena — 'Who' or 'What' Becomes Reincarnated*, London & New York, Regency Press, 1989.
56. C.J. Ducasse, op.cit., p.203.
57. Although it is of no particular importance for the purposes of the present study, one must not fail to mention the fact that astral projections can be either natural (i.e. sponta-neous) or forced and artificial: in this latter case they are

induced by anesthetics, suffocation, falls, hypnosis, etc. For a fuller classification, see R. Crookall, *The Study and Practice of Astral Projection.*

58. R.A. Monroe, op.cit., p.183.
59. S. Blackmore, op.cit., p.50.
60. R.A. Monroe, op.cit., p.184.
61. K. Osis, 'Insiders' Views of the OBE: A Questionnaire Survey' from W.G. Roll, ed., *Research in Parapsychology 1978*, New Jersey & London, Scarecrow Press, 1979, pp.50-2.
62. R.A. Monroe, op.cit., p.140.
63. Cf. D.S. Rogo, 'The Out-Of-Body Experience: Some Personal Views and Reflections' from D.S. Rogo, ed., *Mind Beyond the Body*, New York, Penguin, 1978, pp.349-62.
64. Yram, *Practical Astral Projection* (English translation of *Le médecin de l'âme*), London, Rider, undated, p.92.
65. S.J. Blackmore, op.cit., p.233.
66. E. Bozzano, *Pensiero e volontà forze plasticizzanti e organizzanti*, Verona, Editrice *Luce e Ombra*, 1967, pp.37-92, Chapter III.
67. J. Eisenbud, *The World of Ted Serios, 'Thoughtographic' Studies of an Extraordinary Mind*, New York, William Morrow, 1967.
68. O. Fox, *Astral Projection, A Record of Out-of-the-Body Experiences*, Secaucus, N.J., The Citadel Press, 1962, pp.79-81.
69. S. Muldoon and H. Carrington, *The Phenomena of Astral Projection*, London, Rider, 1984, p.46; more generally, see also the whole of Chapter VI of the first part.
70. B. Walker, *Beyond the Body, The Human Double and the Astral Plane*, Boston, London & Henley, Routledge & Kegan Paul, 1980, p.98. The person guillotined in the dream is Alfred Maury, a French research scientist who lived in the nineteenth century.
71. Ibid. Walker quotes from a book written by H.H. Prive in collaboration with A. Toynbee and others, *Man's Concern with Death*, London, Hodder & Stoughton, 1968, pp.250-6.
72. R. Crookall, *The Study and Practice of Astral Projection*, pp.219-25 in Appendix VIII: 'Thought-Forms'.
73. R.A. Monroe, op.cit., p.183.
74. Ibid., p.167.
75. Ibid.
76. S. Muldoon and H. Carrington, *The Projection of the Astral Body*, p.277.
77. H.B. Greenhouse, *The Astral Journey*, Garden City, N.Y., Doubleday, 1975, p.68.

78. Ibid.
79. S. Muldoon and H. Carrington, *The Projection of the Astral Body*, p.284.
80. Ibid., p.284.
81. R. Crookall, *The Next World — and the Next*, London, The Theosophical Publishing House London Ltd, 1966.
82. H.B. Greenhouse, op.cit., pp.73-4.
83. L. Landau, 'An Unusual Out-of-the-Body Experience' from *Journal of the Society of Psychical Research*, 1963-4, XLII, pp.126-8.
84. H.B. Greenhouse, op.cit., p.94.
85. Ibid.
86. Ibid.
87. A. Aksakow, *Animismus und Spiritismus*, Leipzig, Oswald Mutze, 1890, pp.604-13.
88. H. Hart, 'ESP Projection: Spontaneous Cases and the Experimental Method' from *Journal of the American Society for Psychical Research*, 1954, XLVIII, pp.121-46.
89. S. Muldoon and H. Carrington, *The Projection of the Astral Body*, pp.273-4, and also the preceding paragraph.
90. Cf. V.N. Turvey, *The Beginnings of Seership or Supernormal Mental Activity*, London, Stead's Publishing House, 1911, pp.43-4.
91. R.A. Monroe, op.cit., pp.56-7.
92. Ibid., pp.70-1.
93. H.B. Greenhouse, op.cit., p.58.
94. S. Muldoon and H. Carrington, *The Projection of the Astral Body*, pp.59-60.
95. R. Allegri, *Padre Pio, l'uomo della speranza*, Milan, Mondadori, 1984, pp.116-17 (testimony given to the author by Father Alberto D'Apolito, who was very close to Father Pio for half a century).
96. P. Delfino Sessa, *Padre Pio da Pietrelcina*, Genoa, Demos, 1952, pp.156-8; cf. C. Camilleri, *Padre Pio da Pietrelcina*, Città di Castello, Editrice Soc. Tip, *Leonardo da Vinci*, 1952, pp.98-9.
97. R. Moody, *Life After Life, The Investigation of a Phenomenon — Survival of Bodily Death*, New York, Bantam, 1976, pp.21-3. Mention should also be made of Moody's *Reflections on Life After Life*, London, Corgi, 1978.
98. R. Moody, *Life After Life*, p.24.
99. M.B. Sabom, *Recollections of Death, A Medical Investigation*, New York, Harper & Row, 1982, p.8.
100. R. Moody, op.cit., pp.25-6.
101. M.B. Sabom, op.cit., p.15.
102. R. Moody, op.cit., pp.26-8.
103. Ibid., p.50.

104. Ibid., pp.50-1.
105. M.B. Sabom, op.cit., p.17.
106. Ibid., p.18.
107. R. Moody, op.cit., pp.28-9.
108. M.B. Sabom, op.cit., p.19.
109. R. Moody, op.cit., p.30.
110. Ibid.
111. R. Moody, op.cit., pp.30-4; M.B. Sabom, op.cit., pp.41-4.
112. M.B. Sabom, op.cit., p.73.
113. Ibid., p.74.
114. Ibid., p.27.
115. Ibid., pp.84-6.
116. Ibid., p.21.
117. The account given by Dr Wiltse of his experience is reported by F.W.H. Myers in his article entitled 'On Indications of Continued Terrene Knowledge on the Part of Phantasms of the Dead' from *Proceedings of the Society for Psychical Research*, 1892, VIII, pp.180 *et seq*. The passage here quoted is to be found on pp.181-2.
118. M.B. Sabom, op.cit., p.33.
119. Ibid., pp.33-4.
120. Ibid., p.48.
121. Ibid., p.47.
122. Ibid.
123. Ibid., p.48.
124. Ibid., p.47.
125. Ibid.
126. R. Moody, op.cit., p.52.
127. M.B. Sabom, op.cit., p.47.
128. Ibid., p.49.
129. Ibid., p.48.
130. R. Moody, op.cit., p.58.
131. Ibid., pp.60-1.
132. Ibid., p.61.
133. Ibid.
134. R. Moody, op.cit., pp.64-73; M.B. Sabom, op.cit., p.50.
135. R. Moody, op.cit., pp.73-4.
136. Ibid., p.74.
137. Ibid., p.75.
138. Ibid., pp.75-6.
139. Ibid., p.77.
140. M.B. Sabom, op.cit., p.40.
141. Ibid., p.51.
142. K. Osis and E. Haraldsson, *At the Hour of Death*, New York, Avon Books, 1979, p.162.
143. Ibid.
144. Ibid., pp.162-3.

Notes

145. Ibid., p.163.
146. Ibid., pp.163-4.
147. Ibid., pp.165-6.
148. Ibid., p.164.
149. Ibid., p.165.
150. Ibid., p.176.
151. Ibid.
152. Ibid., p.177.
153. Ibid., p.178.
154. Ibid., p.179-80.
155. Ibid., p.180.
156. Ibid.
157. Ibid., p.181.
158. Ibid., pp.178-9.
159. R. Moody, op.cit., p.79; M.B. Sabom, op.cit., p.26.
160. R. Moody, op.cit., pp.79-80.
161. Ibid., p.83.
162. Ibid., pp.84-8.
163. Ibid., pp.84-5.
164. Ibid., p.89.
165. Ibid., pp.96-7; M.B. Sabom, op.cit., pp.12, 60.
166. M.B. Sabom, op.cit., p.126.
167. Ibid., p.129.
168. Ibid., p.132.
169. Ibid.
170. Ibid.
171. Ibid., p.130.
172. Ibid., pp.151-78.
173. Ibid., pp.182-3.
174. Ibid., p.184.
175. R. Moody, op.cit., p.99.
176. M.B. Sabom, op.cit., p.185.
177. K. Osis and E. Haraldsson, op.cit., p.78.
178. Ibid., pp.79-80.
179. Ibid., p.173.
180. Ibid., p.188.
181. Ibid., pp.86-7.
182. Ibid., p.88.
183. Ibid., p.139.
184. Ibid., p.160.
185. C.R. Lundall, 'Directions in Near-Death Research' in C.R. Lundall, ed., *A Collection of Near-Death Research Readings*, Chicago, Nelson-Hall Publishers, 1982.
186. K. Osis and E. Haraldsson, op.cit., p.167.
187. S. Richards, *The Traveller's Guide to the Astral Plane*, Wellingborough, Northamptonshire, The Aquarian Press, 1983, pp.66-9.

-225-

188. R. Crookall, *What Happens When You Die*, Gerrards Cross, Buckinghamshire, Colin Smythe, 1978.
189. R. Crookall, *The Interpretation of Cosmic and Mystical Experiences*, Cambridge & London, James Clarke & Co., 1969. The tables on page 15 and after page 130 provide particularly clear summaries.
190. R. Crookall, *The Study and Practice of Astral Projection*, p.142.
191. R. Crookall, *What Happens When You Die*, p.12.
192. K. Ring, 'Frequency and Stages of the Prototypic Near-Death Experience' in *A Collection of Near-Death Research Readings*, pp.126-9.
193. Ibid., p.127.
194. R. Crookall, *The Study and Practice of Astral Projection*, p.199.
195. Ibid., for example pp.127, 192-3.
196. Ibid., p.183.
197. See, for example, though most particularly, St John of the Cross, *The Ascent of Mount Carmel*, Book II, Chapters I and XV [XVII].
198. D. Lorimer, *Body, Mind and Death in the Light of Psychic Experience*, London, Routledge & Kegan Paul, 1984, pp.294-5.
199. E. Bozzano, *La crisi della morte nelle descrizioni dei defunti comunicanti*, 2nd edn, Milan, Bocca, 1952 (1st edn, 1930).
200. Ibid., pp.300-1.
201. Ibid., pp.301-2.
202. Ibid., p.76 (quoted from Mrs E.B. Duffy's *Heaven Revised*).
203. *A Heretic in Heaven, Being the Post-Mortem Memoirs and Reflections of 'Daddy'*, London, Hutchinson, undated, p.9.
204. M. Nixon Robertson, *The Other Side God's Door*, New York, Kegan Paul - Trench - Trübner, 1920, p.40.
205. 'Beyond the Gates of Death, Messages from Miss Felicia Scatcherd' from *Light*, 1927, pp.314-15.
206. A. Findlay, *The Way of Life, A Guide to the Etheric World*, London, Psychic Press, 1953, p.94.
207. 'From Over the Border, A Soldier's Account of his Crossing as Given to his Immediate Relatives' from *Light*, 1922, p.595.
208. Ibid., p.596.
209. P. Beard, *Living On, A Study of Altering Consciousness After Death*, London, George Allen & Unwin, 1980, p.140.
210. N. Randall, *Life After Death*, London, Corgi Books, 1980, pp.41-3.
211. P. Giovetti, *Qualcuno è tornato*, Milan, Armenia, 1981, pp.70, 76, 77, 124.

Notes

212. Ibid., p.124 (Professor Emilio Servadio interviewed by Paola Giovetti).
213. N. Wolfe, *Startling Facts in Modern Spiritualism*, Cincinnati, 1874, p.388.
214. N. Rambova, *Rudy, An Intimate Portrait of Rudolph Valentino by his Wife Natacha Rambova*, London, Hutchinson, 1926, p.164.
215. W.T. Stead, *After Death, A Personal Narrative, New and Enlarged Edition of 'Letters from Julia'*, London, Stead's Publishing House, 1921, p.7.
216. 'Beyond the Gates of Death', from *Light*, 1927, p.314.
217. 'From Over the Border', p.595.
218. W. Barrett, *Death-Bed Visions*, Psychic Book Club, London, 1952 (1st edn, Methuen, London, 1926); E. Bozzano, *Le visioni dei morenti*, Milan-Rome, Bocca, 1953 (1st edn, 1947).
219. G. De Boni's preface to Bozzano's *La crisi della morte*, op.cit., pp.14-15.
220. 'Awaking on the Other Side, Received through the Hand of Margaret Vivian' from *Light*, 1937, p.293.
221. A. Findlay, op.cit., p.91.
222. R. Crookall, *Out-of-the-Body Experiences, A Fourth Analysis*, New York, University Books, 1970, pp.144-68.
223. C.A. Dawson Scott, *From Four who are Dead*, London, Arrowsmith, undated, pp.145-6.
224. F. Dismore, *The Progression of Marmaduke*, London, Stead's Publishing House, 1923, p.184; C.A. Dawson Scott, op.cit., p.93.
225. F. Dismore, op.cit., p.119.
226. H.A. and F.H. Curtiss, *Realms of the Living Dead*, Washington, The Curtiss Philosophic Book Co., 1926, pp.76-7.
227. N. Randall, op.cit., p.150.
228. S. Desmond, *Love after Death*, London, Rider, undated, p.81.
229. H.A. and F.H. Curtiss, op.cit., p.92.
230. E. Barker, *Letters from a Living Dead Man*, London, William Rides, 1914, L.38, p.200.
231. C.A. Dawson Scott, op.cit., p.152.
232. *A Heretic in Heaven*, p.54.
233. 'From Over the Border', pp.595-6.
234. C.A. Dawson Scott, op.cit., p.72.
235. 'From Over the Border', p.595.
236. E. Bozzano, *La crisi della morte*, p.77 (quoted from Mrs E.B. Duffy's *Heaven Revised*).
237. N. Swaine, *Autobiography of Two Worlds*, London, Rider, 1934, p.115.

238. *A Heretic in Heaven*, pp.54-5.
239. W.T. Stead, *After Death*, p.xvii (Preface).
240. Ibid., pp.133-4.
241. Ibid., pp.131-2.
242. Cf., for example, E. Bozzano, *La psiche domina la materia, Dei fenomeni di Telecinesia in rapporto con eventi di morte*, Verona, Casa Editrice Europa, 1948.
243. W.T. Stead, *Life Eternal*, London, Wright & Brown, 1933.
244. P. Beard, *Survival of Death*, Norwich, Pilgrims' Book Services, 1966, pp.89-100.
245. 'Other-World Intelligence, Some Messages through a Non-Professional Medium' from *Light*, 1924, p.274.
246. C.A. Dawson Scott, op.cit., p.176.
247. Ibid., p.147.
248. W.T. Stead, *After Death*, p.130.
249. As regards the different states in which the 'vehicle of vitality' can find itself, see, for example, R. Crookall, *Intimations of Immortality*, London, James Clarke, 1965.
250. Cf. R. Crookall, *The Next World — and the Next*, Chapters IV and V.
251. Cf. C.W. Leadbeater, *Text Book of Theosophy*, Adyar, 1912 (quoted from R. Crookall, *The Next World — and the Next*, pp.112-13.
252. R. Crookall, *The Next World — and the Next*, pp.122-4.
253. Ibid., pp.124-6.
254. Ibid., pp.113-18.
255. Ibid., pp.113-15.
256. R. Crookall, *The Supreme Adventure, Analyses of Psychic Communications*, Cambridge, James Clarke, 1961, p.6.
257. Ibid., p.47.
258. R. Crookall, *The Next World — and the Next*, p.39.
259. R. Crookall, *The Supreme Adventure*, p.22.
260. R. Crookall, *What Happens When You Die*, pp.158-9. Cf. S. Richards, op.cit., Chapter V.
261. R. Crookall, *The Next World — and the Next*, p.106.
262. Ibid., p.102.
263. Ibid., pp.96-7. As regards P.L. Paton's interpretation, mention is made of the following Bible passages: Deut. 30.12; 2 Sam. 22.5; Ps. 18.4; Jon. 2.2-5; Rom. 10.7.
264. I. Cooke, 'Thy Kingdom Come ...', *A Presentation of the Whence, Why, and Whither of Man*, London, Wright & Brown, undated, p.291. A different title was given to the book in the third and all subsequent editions, *The Return of Arthur Conan Doyle*, Liss, Hampshire, The White Eagle Publishing Trust.
265. F. Dismore, op.cit., p.49.
266. E. Bozzano, *La crisi della morte*, p.240.

267. Ibid., p.144.
268. Ibid., p.32. The case of 'Dr Ackley' is taken from Mrs De Morgan's *From Matter to Spirit*, London, 1863, p.388.
269. E. Hinchliffe, *The Return of Captain W.G.R. Hinchliffe*, London, The Psychic Press, 1930, p.72.
270. N. Rambova, op.cit., p.197.
271. E. Barker, op.cit., L.43, pp.244-5.
272. W.S. Moses, *Spirit Teachings*, London, Spiritualistic Alliance, 1894, p.24.
273. E. Barker, op.cit., L.36, p.185.
274. Ibid., L.43, p.244.
275. Eph. 6.12.
276. G. Cummins, *Beyond Human Personality, Being a Detailed Description of the Future Life Purporting to be Communicated by the Late F.W.H. Myers*, London, Ivor Nicholson & Watson, 1935, p.200.
277. N. Rambova, op.cit., pp.197-8.
278. H.A. and F.H. Curtiss, op.cit., pp.52-3.
279. Ibid., p.52.
280. G. Cummins, op.cit., p.197.
281. W.T. Stead, *After Death*, p.125.
282. E. Bozzano, *La crisi della morte*, p.289. This is a mediumistic communication taken from *Psychic News*, 1932, No.19.
283. H.A. and F.H. Curtiss, op.cit., p.153.
284. N. Rambova, op.cit., p.197.
285. E. Barker, op.cit., L.36, p.185.
286. N. Rambova, op.cit., pp.203-4.
287. C.D. Thomas, *In the Dawn beyond Death*, London, Lectures Universal, undated, p.104.
288. F. Dismore, op.cit., p.38.
289. G. Cummins, *The Road to Immortality, Being a Description of the After-Life Purporting to be Communicated by the Late F.W.H. Myers*, London, Ivor Nicholson & Watson, 1932, p.88.
290. S.E.L. Taylor, ed., *Fox-Taylor Automatic Writing, 1869-92, Unabridged Record*, Minneapolis, Tribune — Great West Printing Co., 1932, p.319.
291. 'Life on the Other Side, A Homely Description' from *Light*, 1927, p.230.
292. Ibid.
293. Cf. W.T. Stead, *After Death*, pp.27-8.
294. D.H. Buckley, *Spirit Communication*, Los Angeles, Sherbourne Press, for the Millions Series, 1967.
295. C. Wickland, *Thirty Years Among the Dead*, Los Angeles, National Psychological Institute, 1924.
296. 'Other-World Intelligence', p.274.

297. Ibid.
298. Ibid., p.275.
299. Ibid.
300. *A Heretic in Heaven*, p.42.
301. 'Other-World Intelligence', p.274.
302. 'From Over the Border', p.706.
303. Ibid., p.595.
304. Ibid.
305. A. Findlay, op.cit., p.125.
306. 'Other-World Intelligence', p.290.
307. E. Hinchliffe, op.cit., p.80.
308. E. Bozzano, *La crisi della morte*, p.77 (quoted from Mrs E.B. Duffy's *Heaven Revised*).
309. N. Rambova, op.cit., p.157.
310. C.A. Dawson Scott, op.cit., p.47.
311. 'Awaking on the Other Side' from *Light*, 1937, p.293.
312. N. Rambova, op.cit., p.195.
313. F. Dismore, op.cit., p.158.
314. H.A. and F.H. Curtiss, op.cit., p.47.
315. F.W. Fitzsimmons, *Opening the Psychic Door, Thirty Years' Experience*, London, Hutchinson, 1933, p.60.
316. C.A. Dawson Scott, op.cit., p.175.
317. Ibid., p.68.
318. R. Crookall, *The Next World — and the Next*, pp.71-95.
319. N. Rambova, op.cit., p.166.
320. C.A. Dawson Scott, op.cit., p.42.
321. C.D. Thomas, op.cit., p.93.
322. *A Heretic in Heaven*, p.48.
323. C.A. Dawson Scott, op.cit., p.176.
324. Amicus, *The Morrow of Death*, London, A.H. Stockwell, 1922, p.46.
325. N. Rambova, op.cit., p.188; cf. A. Findlay, *The Way of Life*, p.130.
326. H.A. and F.H. Curtiss, op.cit., p.45.
327. M. Nixon Robertson, op.cit., p.105.
328. A. Findlay, op.cit., p.131.
329. N. Swaine, op.cit., p.116.
330. A. Findlay, *On the Edge of the Etheric*, 67th impression, London, Psychic Press, 1977, pp.137-8.
331. 'Other-World Intelligence', p.275.
332. C.D. Thomas, op.cit., pp.72-3.
333. O.J. Lodge, *Raymond or Life and Death, with Examples of the Evidence for Survival of Memory and Affection after Death*, London, Methuen, 1916, pp.197-8.
334. E. Bozzano, *La crisi della morte*, pp.97-101.
335. Cf. E. Bozzano, *Pensiero e volontà forze plasticizzanti e organizzanti*; E. Duchâtel and R. Warcollier, *Les miracles*

Notes

de la volonté, Sa force plastique dans le corps et hors du corps humain, Paris, Hector et Henry Durville, 1914.
336. G. De Boni, Preface to E. Bozzano's *La crisi della morte*, p.16.
337. A. Findlay, *On the Edge of the Etheric*, p.137.
338. Ibid., p.136.
339. A. Findlay, *The Way of Life*, p.135.
340. W.O. Stevens, *The Mystery of Dreams*, New York, Dodd Mead, 1949.
341. E. Gurney, F.W.H. Myers and F. Podmore, *Phantasms of the Living*, London, Trübner & Co., 1886, Vol.II, p.153. Mention should here be made of the definition the authors give of telepathy as 'the ability of one mind to impress or to be impressed by another mind otherwise than through the recognised channels of sense' (Vol.I, p.6). See particularly Chapter VIII of Vol.I and Chapter XVII of Vol.II.
342. H.A. and F.H. Curtiss, op.cit., p.93.
343. C.A. Dawson Scott, op.cit., p.184.
344. Ibid., p.182.
345. E. Bozzano, *La crisi della morte*, p.186 (taken from *Spiritualistic Experiences of a Lawyer*).
346. E. Barker, op.cit., L.32, pp.160-1.
347. N. Swaine, op.cit., p.166.
348. C.D. Thomas, *Life beyond Death with Evidence*, London, Collins, 1928, p.205.
349. E. Bozzano, *La crisi della morte*, p.187 (with reference to *Spiritualistic Experiences of a Lawyer*).
350. C.A. Dawson Scott, op.cit., p.122.
351. Ibid., p.117.
352. Ibid.
353. E. Barker, op.cit., L.14, pp.48-52.
354. Cf. B. Croce, *Estetica*, I, I.
355. C.A. Dawson Scott, op.cit., p.116.
356. Ibid., pp.94-5.
357. Ibid., p.118.
358. Ibid., p.134.
359. Ibid., p.71.
360. F. Dismore, op.cit., p.151.
361. Ibid.
362. S. Desmonds, op.cit., p.152.
363. N. Rambova, op.cit., p.199.
364. Ibid., p.167.
365. E. Bozzano, *La crisi della morte*, pp.252 and 304 (the fourth of the 'secondary details' on which communicating spirits agree).
366. Ibid., p.217.

367. Amicus, op.cit., pp.20-1.
368. Cf. the Revd F.C. Spurr, 'Christianity and Spiritualism' in J. Marchant, ed., *Life after Death according to Christianity and Spiritualism*, London, Cassell & Co., 1925, pp.129-55; and also the Revd G. Maurice Elliott, *Spiritualism in the Old Testament*, London, Psychic Press, 1938. Particularly significant from the Catholic point of view is Father Eugenio Ferrarotti's testimony in Paola Giovetti's *Qualcuno è tornato*, op.cit., pp.127-9; and also Father Pasquale Magni's adhesion, though of a more general nature, in the presentation of L. Sardos Albertini's *Esiste l'aldilà*, Trent, Luigi Reverdito Editore, 1985. Special interest also attaches to the final part of the book by G. Adler, *Es gibt Dinge zwischen Himmel und Erde ...*, Frankfurt am Main, Joseph Knecht, 1974, pp.135-98 (under the title 'Die Kirche vor den Erfahrungen von Parapsychologie und Okkultismus').
369. W.T. Stead, *After Death*, p.42.
370. A. Findlay, *The Way of Life*, pp.222, 229; *On the Edge of the Etheric*, p.135.
371. G. Cummins, *The Road to Immortality*, pp.72, 75; *Beyond Human Personality*, pp.12, 27.
372. G. Cummins, *The Road to Immortality*, pp.34, 74-5; *Beyond Human Personality*, p.27.
373. F. Dismore, op.cit., p.121.
374. E. Barker, op.cit., L.16, p.61.
375. C.A. Dawson Scott, op.cit., p.59.
376. Ibid., p.49.
377. A. Findlay, *The Way of Life*, p.139; G. Cummins, *The Road to Immortality*, p.29; C.A. Dawson Scott, op.cit., pp.37-8, 180.
378. C.A. Dawson Scott, op.cit., pp.52, 38, 180.
379. E. Barker, op.cit., L.22, p.98.
380. Ibid., L.17, p.66.
381. N. Rambova, op.cit., p.200.
382. E. Barker, op.cit., L.44, p.249.
383. Ibid., L.48, p.267.
384. W.T. Stead, *After Death*, p.41.
385. E. Hinchliffe, op.cit., p.71.
386. A. Findlay, *The Way of Life*, pp.207, 209.
387. W.T. Stead, *After Death*, p.xxxv (Preface).
388. F. Dismore, op.cit., Introduction by L. Curnow.
389. E. Hinchliffe, op.cit., pp.71-2.
390. W.S. Moses, op.cit., p.225.
391. Ibid.
392. W.T. Stead, *After Death*, p.17.
393. Ibid.

Notes

394. E. Barker, op.cit., L.48, p.267.
395. H.A. and F.H. Curtiss, op.cit., p.132.
396. Ibid., p.49; 1 Cor. 15.29.
397. R. Crookall, *The Supreme Adventure*, pp.234-5.
398. Ibid., p.234.
399. R. Crookall, *The Supreme Adventure*, Appendix IV, pp.234-41.
400. I. Cooke, op.cit., p.367.
401. J. Sherwood, *Post-Mortem Journal, Communications from T.E. Lawrence*, London, Neville Spearman, 1964, pp.43-4.
402. N. Rambova, op.cit., p.182.
403. E. Barker, op.cit., L.48, p.267.
404. I. Cooke, op.cit., p.367.
405. E. Barker, op.cit., L.48, p.269.
406. A. Findlay, *On the Edge of the Etheric*, p.178.
407. F. Dismore, op.cit., p.182.
408. W.T. Stead, *After Death*, p.127.
409. A. Findlay, *The Way of Life*, p.26.
410. M. Nixon Robertson, op.cit., p.94.
411. A. Findlay, *The Way of Life*, p.128.
412. W.T. Stead, *After Death*. p.5.
413. N. Rambova, op.cit., p.165.
414. C.D. Thomas, *In the Dawn beyond Death*, p.48.
415. C.D. Thomas, *Beyond Life's Sunset* (new and enlarged edn), London, Lectures Universal, undated, p.113.
416. C.A. Dawson Scott, op.cit., p.165.
417. Mk. 10.15; Lk. 18.17.
418. I. Cooke, op.cit., p.97.
419. Rom. 8.5-11, 7.4-6; Gal. 5.16-25.
420. S. Desmonds, op.cit., Chapter XI.
421. C.A. Dawson Scott, op.cit., p.45.
422. Ibid., p.74.
423. F. Dismore, op.cit., p.44.
424. W.T. Stead, *After Death*, p.107.
425. C.D. Thomas, *In the Dawn beyond Death*, p.32.
426. P. Brookesmith, ed., *Life after Death*, London, Orbis, 1984, p.197.
427. Ibid.
428. R. Crookall, *The Next World — and the Next*, pp.127-33.
429. P. Brookesmith, ed., *Life after Death*, p.197.
430. R. Crookall, *The Next World — and the Next*, pp.127, 128, 129, 131, 132.
431. Ibid., pp.129-31.
432. W.T. Stead (via Mme Hyver), *Communications with the Spirit World*, Cricket Press, 1927, p.21 (quoted from R. Crookall's *The Next World — and the Next*, p.130).
433. Lord Dowding, *Lychgate, The Entrance to the Path*,

London, Rider, 1945, pp.18-19.

434. See Chapter 2.

435. Lord Dowding, op.cit., p.19; R. Crookall, *The Next World — and the Next*, p.127.

436. D. Alighieri, *Paradiso*, XXXIII, 86-7.

437. 1 Cor. 15.28.

438. Gen. c.3; ibid. 11.1-9; Ezek. 28.1-19.

439. I. Cooke, op.cit., p.163; see also P. Beard, *Living On*, Chapter IX.

440. '...It is no longer I who live, but Christ who lives in me': Gal. 2.20.

441. F. Dismore, op.cit., p.119.

442. N. Swaine, op.cit., p.148.

443. F. Dismore, op.cit., p.40.

444. N. Rambova, op.cit., p.201.

445. Ibid., p.201-2.

446. F.W. Fitzsimmons, op.cit., p.50.

447. E. Bozzano, *La crisi della morte*, p.233.

448. A. Borgia, *Life in the World Unseen*, London, Odhams Press, 1954, p.159.

449. E. Bozzano, *La crisi della morte*, p.235.

450. N. Rambova, op.cit., p.183.

451. E. Barker, op.cit., L.29, pp.134-7.

452. W.S. Moses, op.cit., pp.241-2.

453. A. Findlay, *On the Edge of the Etheric*, p.134; *The Way of Life*, pp.95, 137.

454. F. Dismore, op.cit., p.122.

455. W.T. Stead, *Life Eternal*, London, Wright & Brown, 1933, p.140.

456. C.D. Thomas, *In the Dawn beyond Death*, p.8.

457. F. Dismore, op.cit., p.74.

458. Ibid., p.76.

459. See, for example, Jer. 6.29-30; Ezek. 22.17-22, 24.9-14; Zeph. 3.8-9; Zach. 13.7-9; Mal. 3.1-3; Matt. 3.10-12; Luke 12.49; 1 Cor. 3.10-15; 2 Pet. 3.

460. M. Nixon Robertson, op.cit., p.133.

461. See Aristotle, *Metaphysics*, XII, 8, 1074a; Avicenna, *Metaphysics*, XI, 1; St Albert Magnus, *Metaphysics*, III, 3,10; St Thomas Aquinas, *De ente et essentia*, 2; *Summa Theologiae*, III, q.77, a.2.

462. M. Nixon Robertson, op.cit., p.125.

463. I. Cooke, op.cit., p.169.

464. Ibid., p.381 (Appendix).

465. A. Borgia, op.cit., p.191.

466. I am referring to Bozzano's classifications preserved at the Bozzano-De Boni Library (maintained by the review *Luce e ombra*). Particularly important for the purposes of the

present study are the cards grouped together under the headings 'Crisis of death', 'Spiritual existence', and 'Spiritual spheres'.

467. W.T. Stead, *Life Eternal*, p.239.
468. A. Gilbert, *Philip in Two Worlds*, London, Psychic Book Club, 1949, p.121.
469. N. Randall, op.cit., p.105.
470. See the letters written by W. Crookes to *The Spiritualist* and published in the issues of 6 February, 3 April and 5 June, 1974.
471. The classic work on apparitions is E. Gurney, F.W.H. Myers and F. Podmore, *Phantasms of the Living*, London, Trübner, 1886 (abridged edn prepared by Mrs Henry Sidgwick, London, Kegan Paul — Trench — Trübner, 1918). As regards more recent studies, mention should be made of G.N.M. Tyrrell, *Apparitions*, London, The Society for Psychical Research, 1973; C. Green and C. McCreery, *Apparitions*, London, Hamish Hamilton, 1975; A. Mackenzie, *Hauntings and Apparitions*, London, William Heinemann, 1982; H. Evans, *Visions, Apparitions, Alien Visitors, A Comparative Study of the Entity Enigma*, Wellingborough, Northamptonshire, The Aquarian Press, 1984. As regards photographs of apparitions, see S. Edmunds, *'Spirit' Photography*, London, The Society for Psychical Research, 1965, which also contains a bibliography that I recommend should be supplemented by E. Imoda, *Fotografie di fantasmi*, Turin, Bocca, 1912, and J. Coates, *Photographing the Invisible*, London, Fowler, and Chicago, The Advanced Thought Publishing Co., 1911.
472. As regards the vast range of materialization phenomena, see E. Duchâtel and R. Warcollier, op.cit., Chapters VIII and IX.
473. Mrs Guppy, a famous English medium and an extremely corpulent woman, dematerialized in her own home in 1871 while she was checking accounts with her maid, and rematerialized in another house some three miles away, where a séance was being held at the time (see 'The Transit of Mrs Guppy, An Account of the Transportation by "Spirit Power" of a Medium for a Distance of Three Miles in 1871' in *Light*, 1918, p.259). The Marquis Carlo Centurione Scotto, on the other hand, suddenly disappeared from a room in which a séance was being held with his mediumship, and he was later found asleep in the stables (see E. Bozzano, 'Prime manifestazioni della "voce diretta" in Italia, Seduta del 29 luglio 1928 nel Castello di Millesimo', in *Luce e ombra*, XXVIII, 1928, pp.393-408,

where Bozzano, after reporting and extensively discussing the phenomenon that had Centurione Scotto as its protagonist, outlines the history of 'person asportation' phenomena).

474. E. Bozzano, *Pensiero e volontà forze plasticizzanti e organizzanti*, pp.19-23. Among others, the author refers to an article by G. Lindsay Johnson published in *Light*, 1926, p.567.

475. As regards Felicia Scatcherd, see E. Bozzano, *Pensiero e volontà forze plasticizzanti e organizzanti*, pp.43 et seq., and, more generally, the whole of Chapter 3. As regards Ted Serios, see J. Eisenbud, op.cit.

476. A. Borgia, op.cit., p.160.

477. E. Kübler-Ross, *On Death and Dying*, New York, Macmillan, 1969; *Questions and Answers on Death and Dying*, New York, Macmillan, 1974; *Living with Death and Dying*, London, Souvenir, 1982; E. Shneidman, *Voices of Death, Personal Documents from People Facing Death*, New York, Bantam Books, 1982.

Bibliography

Dr Filippo Liverziani has published the following books:

L'eclissi del Dio vivente (The Eclipse of the Living God), Pàtron, Bologna, 1969.

Esperienza del sacro e filosofia (Experience of the Sacred and Philosophy), Liber, Rome, 1970.

Dinamismo intellettuale ed esperienza mistica nel pensiero di J. Maréchal (Intellectual Dynamism and Mystical Experience in J. Maréchal's Thought), Liber, Roma, 1974.

La reincarnazione e i suoi fenomeni — 'Chi' o 'cosa' si reincarna (Reincarnation and its Phenomena — 'Who' or 'What' Becomes Reincarnated), Edizioni Mediterranee, Rome, 1985; English translation, Regency Press, London & New York, 1989.

Le esperienze di confine e la vita dopo la morte (Frontier Experiences and Life after Death), Edizioni Mediterranee, Rome, 1986.

Colloqui con l'altra dimensione — Comunicazioni medianiche, esperimenti e problemi (Dialogues with the Other Dimension — Mediumistic Communications, Experiments and Problems), Edizioni Mediterranee, Rome, 1987.

Sette anime dell'antica Roma — Comunicazioni medianiche al vaglio critico (Seven Souls of Ancient Rome — Mediumistic Communications Closely Examined), Luigi Reverdito Editore, Trento, 1989.

Eternità — Analisi di testimonianze medianiche (Eternity — Analysis of Mediumistic Testimonies), Luigi Reverdito Editore, Trento, 1990.

Sopravvivenza e vita eterna — Le ragioni della speranza (Survival and Eternal Life — The Reasons of Hope), Edizioni Mediterranee, Rome, 1990.

Verso l'apocalisse — Dove si compie il destino dell'uomo (Towards the Apocalypse — Where Man's Destiny is Fulfilled), Hermes Edizioni, Rome, 1991.

Dr Liverziani has also published some sixty articles and essays in philosophical magazines and in books by various authors, as well as two sets of lectures on psychic research and religion.

Ecstatic Ritual

Practical Sex Magic

Brandy Williams

FROM ancient temple dwellers to modern urban residents, priests, poets and people of all walks of life have looked to sexuality to aid them in connecting with the Divine.

In a subject previously obscured by foreign terms and deliberate 'blinds' for the uninitiated, ECSTATIC RITUAL offers the reader clear, concise exercises and ritual forms which comprise a full understanding of sacred and magical sexuality. Heterosexual, gay and lesbian workers, in couples or singly, explore a magical system which methodically explains the worship and union of the Divine within each person.

BRANDY WILLIAMS, who has worked as a professional journalist and freelance writer, has written articles and taught workshops on the subject for a number of years. She has been a Priestess and Historian of the Western Mysteries for over 15 ye

8½ x 5½, 160 pp
Full colour cover
Diagrams and line illustrations
1 85327 051 2 Paperback

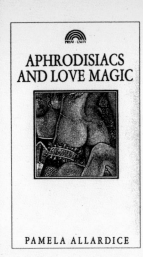

APHRODISIACS
AND LOVE MAGIC

PAMELA ALLARDICE

phrodisiacs
nd Love Magic

e Mystic Lure of
ve Charms

mela Allardice

⌐AKE control of your love life —
with a little practical magic.
mela Allardice looks at traditional
e lore — omens to observe, games
play, potions to prepare and the
st auspicious days for amatory
ngress. In particular, she examines
werful plants, herbs, fruits and
wers which may be enlisted to
p love along. From exotic tropical
e plants to traditional cottage
wers, from symbolic flowers used
bedeck Oriental bridal chambers
herbs employed by French and
lian bridegrooms to fortify
mselves for the night ahead.

is is the first time that such a
rough study has been made of the
y nonsense that makes the world
round. Although few people today

would use potions and divination to
solve the problem of who they are to
marry, many lovers still seek lucky
omens and observe ancient customs,
albeit without being aware of their
significance.

8½ x 5½, 128 pp
Full colour cover
1 85327 031 8 Paperback

PRISM · UNITY

HALLUCINOGENS

CROSS-CULTURAL
PERSPECTIVES

MARLENE DOBKIN DE RIOS

Hallucinogens

Cross-Cultural Perspectives
Marlene Dobkin de Rios

THIS book surveys the uses of mind-altering plants in eleven societies in the Americas, Asia, Africa, Australia, and New Guinea, ranging from the hunter-gatherer level to the complex ancient civilizations of the Aztec, the Maya, the Nazca, the Mochica, and the Inca. Some of the data are derived from the author's research in modern Peru, where plant hallucinogens are used in folk healing. Many other data have been assembled from a variety of scientific and anthropological publications. The lay reader with a general interest in primitive ritual, religion, and healing will find a great deal of information in this concise volume, which is illustrated with drawings of the various plants that can produce altered states of consciousness and with reproductions of ancient Peruvian art that the author sees as drug-related.

Several themes emerge from de Rios's cross-cultural examination of sacred plants. She argues convincingly that plant hallucinogens which have been used from time immemorial, influenced human evolution. She also discusses religious beliefs that may have been influenced by the mind-altering properties of particular plants, and she focuses on the ways hallucinogens have influenced ethical and moral systems

MARLENE DOBKIN DE RIOS is professor of anthropology at California State University.

8½ x 5½, 256 pp
Full colour cover
Line drawings and tables
1 85327 061 X Paperback

PRISM · UNITY

GATEWAY TO
INNER SPACE

SACRED PLANTS, MYSTICISM
AND PSYCHOTHERAPY

Edited by
CHRISTIAN RÄTSCH

ateway
o Inner Space
cred Plants, Mysticism
d Psychotherapy
o. Dr. Christian Rätsch

N recent years there has been
considerable debate about the
ionary experiences induced by
lucinatory plants — often
arded as sacred in shamanic
ieties — and the related use of
chedelics in contemporary
chology.

is fascinating work consists of
ays by many leading researchers
the field of altered states of
sciousness — presented to honour
Albert Hofmann, who first
covered the extraordinary effects
LSD in 1943.

tured here are writings on the
dical use of psychedelics, the
troversial issue of 'molecular
sticism', the relationship of
raments to Gnosis, death and

rebirth themes in shamanism,
comparisons between meditative and
psychedelic experiences and states of
tryptamine consciousness.

Among the many distinguished
contributors to this remarkable
volume are Dr Stanislav Grof,
Terence McKenna, Dr Ralph
Metzner, Professor Hanscarl Leuner,
Dr Claudio Naranjo, Claudia Müller-
Ebeling and Dr Christian Rätsch.

DR CHRISTIAN RÄTSCH is an authority
on sacred plants and the culture of
the ancient Mayans. He has
published extensively in German —
his books include *Chactun — die
Gotter der Maya* and *Bilder aus der
unsichtbaren Welt*.

8½ x 5½, 256 pp
Full colour cover
1 85327 037 7 Paperback

The Celtic Twilight

Myth, Fantasy and Folklore

W.B. Yeats

ALTHOUGH renowned as one of the most famous poets of the 20th century, WILLIAM BUTLER YEATS (1865–1939) was also a devoted exponent of the western mystical and magical traditions. Yeats met with students of the occult in Dublin in the 1880s and was later introduced by his friend Charles Johnson to the Theosophical Society. Yeats subsequently left the Theosophists and in 1890 was initiated as a ceremonial magician of the Golden Dawn — arguably the most influential esoteric order in the western magical tradition — and for a time became its leader.

Yeats exercised a profoundly Celtic influence on his fellow occultists and his love of Irish folklore is reflected in this book, which was first published in 1893. THE CELTIC TWILIGHT brings together many of Yeats' most enchanting and mystical tales — a dazzling array of sorce faeries, ghosts and nature spirits which draw their inspiration fro the visionary heart of Irish folk tradition.

This book is a special tribute to memory of W.B. Yeats and is published fifty years after his de

8½ x 5½, 128 pp
Full colour cover
1 85327 029 6 Paperback

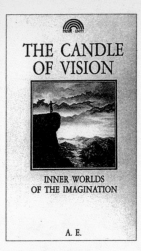

PRISM · UNITY

THE CANDLE OF VISION

INNER WORLDS
OF THE IMAGINATION

A. E.

he Candle
Vision

er Worlds
he Imagination

. (George Russell)
REWORD BY Nevill Drury

IRST published in 1918, this book
is one of the classics of modern
ern mysticism. While it may
that such concepts as 'creative
alisation' and 'imagining our own
ty' are recent innovations of the
an potential movement, they are
found here — in a very lucid
eloquent form.

author was a distinguished
er, artist and poet and believed
each of us can use the creative
ers of the imagination as a
way to other worlds. The
gination can transport us to an
ome, mystical universe and we
sense the vastness of the
ite. This is the true nature of
visionary inspiration.

A.E. was the *nom de plume* of
GEORGE RUSSELL (1867–1935).
Russell was a major literary figure in
the Irish Renaissance and a friend of
W.B. Yeats. Like Yeats, Russell was
strongly influenced by theosophical
mysticism and by the beauty of
Celtic mythology. He was the author
of several works, including *Song and
its Fountains* and *The Avatars*, but
CANDLE OF VISION is widely regarded
as his masterpiece.

8½ x 5½, 112 pp
Full colour cover
1 85327 030 X Paperback

EXPLORING THE
PARANORMAL

PERSPECTIVES ON
BELIEF AND
EXPERIENCE

EDITED BY DR. G.K. ZOLLSCHAN,
DR J.F. SCHUMAKER & DR. G.F. WALSH

Exploring the Paranormal

Perspectives on Belief and Experience

EDITED BY Prof. G.K. Zollschan, Dr J.F. Schumaker and Dr G.F. Walsh

THIS important anthology brings together some of the world's leading authorities in their fields and presents frameworks for understanding paranormal belief and experience. It describes special applications of the scientific method and also features debates between believers and unbelievers in the paranormal. There are chapters on mind-expanding drugs, the near-death experience, mysticism and meditation, an evaluation of the contribution of biology to the study of the paranormal, and an examination of 'miracles'.

Contributors to this far ranging book include such internationally acc-

laimed figures as Charles Tart, Stanley Krippner, Harvey Irwin, Anthony Flew, and John Beloff as well as many other distinguished researchers from the United States Britain and Australia.

The three editors also differ in the views. *ZOLLSCHAN* is a sociologist practising Jewish mystic. Formerl assistant to Sir Karl Popper he h taught in the USA, Canada, Brita and Australia. *SCHUMAKER* is a clini psychologist and is an "absolute believer" in the paranormal. *WAL* is a social scientist and Roman Catholic with an interest in how inter-denominational differences affect belief in the supernatural.

8½ x 5½, 400 pp
Full colour cover
1 85327 026 1 Paperback

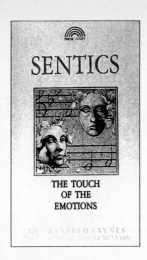

entics

e Touch of the Emotions
: Manfred Clynes

TRODUCTION BY
hudi Menuhin

ENTICS reveals how emotions are
communicated early in life and
music, painting and sculpture. It
a revolutionary, new scientific
cipline which examines the
logical basis of emotion. Its
coverer, *DR MANFRED CLYNES*, is
: inventor of the Sentograph, an
enious device which measures
otional responses through the
gertips. Clynes' research has also
covered genetically programmed
in and nervous system patterns
such basic emotional states as joy,
ger, hate, grief and love. Moreover
has developed the so-called 'Sentic
cles', an exercise technique for the
otions, which anyone can learn
d which can lead to a profound
se of well-being.

The author is one of the most
creative, multidisciplinary minds
working in science today. He holds
advanced degrees in neuroscience,
engineering and music. He is a
university lecturer and has toured
Europe as a concert pianist.

"This breakthrough could only have
been achieved by a musician . . . a
scientist who remains a musician at
heart." Yehudi Menuhin.

8½ x 5½, 284 pp
Full colour cover
1 85327 025 3 Paperback

MODERN
RITUAL MAGIC

THE RISE OF
WESTERN OCCULTISM

FRANCIS KING

Modern Ritual Magic

The Rise of Western Occultism

Francis King

THIS is the inside story of the Hermetic Order of the Golden Dawn and associated occult offshoots — told in its entirety for the first time. The author's researches into the conflict between W.B. Yeats and Aleister Crowley are described in detail, as well as the full story of Yeats' early magical training and practices. Francis King also relates the often difficult relationship between Yeats and the influential Kabbalist, Macgregor Mathers.

However, it is not only the student of the Golden Dawn who will find this book absorbing. King also describes Rudolph Steiner's attempt to take over English occultism and links Bengali Tantricism with the magic of the American Mulatto. All the major figures in modern western magic feature in this book, which since its first publication in 1970, has been rightly regarded as one of the major histories of the western esoteric tradition.

FRANCIS KING is also the author of *Magic: the Western Tradition, Sexual Magic and Perversion* and *The Secret Rituals of the O.T.O.* He co-authored *Techniques of High Magic* with Stephen Skinner.

8½ x 5½, 224pp
Full colour cover
1 85327 032 6

PRIMITIVE
MAGIC

ERNESTO DE MARTINO

rimitive Magic

e Psychic Powers of
amans and Sorcerers

1esto de Martino

HE idea of magic challenges our
basic concepts of reality and the
ural order of things. But for
ve shamans and sorcerers magic
tangible and 'real' as science is
ur modern 'civilisation'. The
tralian Aborigine, for example,
die if pierced by an arrow that
been 'sung' — no matter how
rficial the wound.

astounding book describes
ties where magic is a way of life,
re sorcerers, shamans, diviners
fire walkers form powerful bonds
the psychic realities of Nature.

IITIVE MAGIC is itself an initiation
to the enthralling world of
ent mysteries.

re is no such thing as unreality;
are only various forms of
ty' — Eugene Ionesco

ERNESTO DE MARTINO lives in Rome
and is Professor of the History of
Religions at Cagliari University. He
has a long-standing interest in the
links between parapsychology and
anthropology and is the author of
several works in this field, including
South Italy and Magic and *Death and
Ritual in the Ancient World*.

8½ x 5½, 192 pp
Full colour cover
1 85327 021 0 Paperback

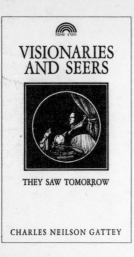

PRISM · UNITY

VISIONARIES AND SEERS

THEY SAW TOMORROW

CHARLES NEILSON GATTEY

Visionaries and Seers

They Saw Tomorrow

Charles Neilson Gattey

8½ x 5½, 288 pp
Full colour cover
1 85327 020 2 Paperback

IN this unique book, Charles Nielson Gattey recounts the stranger-than-fiction life-stories of the most astounding seers and sorcerers of all time. Such well-known characters as Nostradamus and Cheiro are here in all their brilliant and bizarre detail — including the former's visions of the Second World War and a bleak outlook for Britain towards the end of the 20th century and the latter's predictions of Edward VIII's romance and abdication — as well as such lesser-known but equally intriguing figures as Mlle Lenormande, clairvoyante and confidante of the Empress Josephine and Ernst Krafft, alleged by some to have been Hitler's personal astrologer.